225.924 GUN

Paul:
Messenger
and Exile

Paul:
Messenger
and Exile

A Study in the Chronology of His Life and Letters

John J. Gunther

JUDSON PRESS, Valley Forge

PAUL: MESSENGER AND EXILE

Copyright © 1972
Judson Press, Valley Forge, Pa. 19481

International Standard Book No. 0-8170-0504-8
Library of Congress Catalog Card No. 70-181022

Printed in the U.S.A.

Onesiphorus went along the royal road leading to Lystra, and stood there waiting for him, and looked at those who came, according to Titus's description. And he saw Paul coming, a man small in stature, with a balding head and crooked legs, in a good state of body, with joining eyebrows and somewhat hooked nose, full of friendliness; for sometimes he appeared like a man, and sometimes he had the face of an angel.

Acts of Paul and Thecla, chaps. 2–3.

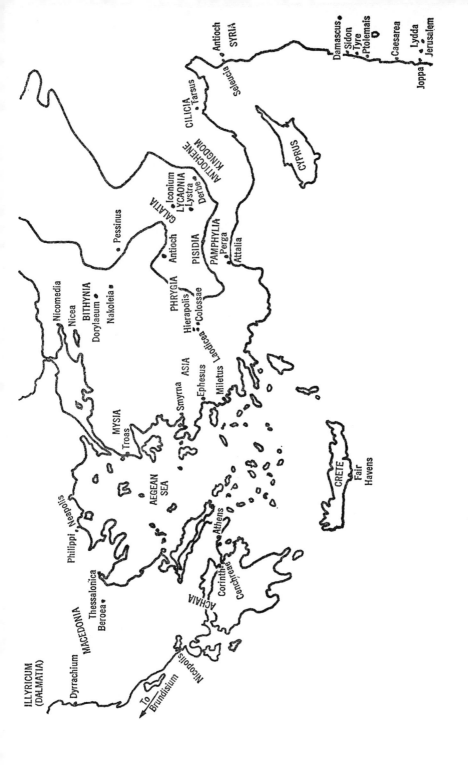

Foreword

This is not a traditional biography or chronology, but rather a combination of features of both. There are several reasons for presenting such a hybrid study. A biography of Paul cannot be convincing unless the chronological framework is successfully defended. For example, if a writer were to locate the place of origin of the Captivity Letters in the wrong city, then information about Paul and his situation obtained therefrom would be misleadingly applied. In short, a biography can be no more accurate or persuasive than its assumed sequence of events. On the other hand, a chronology can be made more meaningful by picturing the environment in which the apostle to the Gentiles experienced dilemmas and made decisions. Such events as the Famine visit and the Acts 15 Jerusalem Council are datable only from a sufficiently reconstructed historical setting. Indeed, a primary test of a chronology is the extent to which it can accommodate and clarify data concerning the life setting.

To detect the precise time and place of writing of each Epistle for its own sake is unimportant. But we do need to ascertain the sequence of the Letters if we are to know Paul's status when writing each. The dating of his Epistles and the events of his life are inseparable problems. They must be resolved in conjunction with each other, for data are reciprocally illuminating (or confusing). For this reason a detailed historical exegesis of Romans 16; 2 Timothy 4:9-22*a*; and Titus 3:12-15 is needed. Chronological questions are associated with not only the background, occasion, and purpose of all Pauline Letters, but also with the unity or integrity of Romans, Philippians, and the Corinthian correspondence. If, as alleged, certain chapters represent different letters, then their historical occasions must be ascertained and fit into the apostle's life. Romans and Ephesians pose other textual questions with chronological overtones: who were the addressees? Can we account for textual discrepancies by positing different "editions" issued at different times?

As the movements of the apostle from one mission field to another provide the cement of a true biography, these, too, must be determined, lest a "Life of Paul" become amorphous or distorted. Geographical and chronological considerations are mutually enlightening; resolutions of questions in each area go together. The definition of "Galatia" influences the dating of Galatians, and vice versa. The travel plans mentioned in Romans, Corinthians, and the Captivity Epistles give valuable clues to Paul's situation.

George Ogg's recent *Chronology of the Life of Paul* has fulfilled the need of coordinating the relevant short studies published since Daniel Plooij's 1918 monograph. Although I have made some references to Ogg's book, there is remarkably little resemblance in subject matter and conclusions between that book and mine.

The opening chapter of this book is devoted to Jesus' timing of his ministry. Because the crucifixion provides a *terminus a quo* for the conversion of Paul, we must reach and justify a decision concerning the date of the crucifixion. Suggestions for the date range from 28 to 33 and strongly influence the dating of Paul's first two Jerusalem visits. Chapters 2, 3, 4, and 6 deal with distinct phases of the apostle's career. Independent chapters are devoted to the historical and geographical settings of the Epistles to the Ephesians and to the Hebrews in order to confirm certain conclusions about Paul's life.

I should like to acknowledge indebtedness to those who very kindly read initial drafts of individual chapters: Francis J. Rossiter (chap. 1), the late S. MacLean Gilmour (chap. 3), F. F. Bruce (chaps. 4 and 7), Henry J. Cadbury (chap. 5), Jack Finegan (chap. 6), and Floyd V. Filson (chaps. 2 to 6). I am also grateful to the readers of Judson Press and to Walter Hatfield, a keen lay student of Scriptures. Their fruitful questions, suggestions, and references have eliminated many deficiencies.

Chronological Table

Year	Events	Paul's Life	Letters
30	Crucifixion		
31	Stephen's martyrdom	Conversion (Sept.)	
33–34		1st Jerusalem visit; return to Tarsus	
42–43 (winter)		From Tarsus to Antioch	
44	Helena's arrival in Jerusalem; death of Herod Agrippa I (late spring); recall of Marsus, legate of Syria	2nd Jerusalem (famine relief) visit (Passover)	
46–47	End of famine	First Missionary Journey	
48– (49)		Antioch dispute; Jerusalem Council	
49		Left Antioch for Asia Minor	
50 (49)	Hebrews expelled from Rome	To Philippi and Corinth	
51			Thessalonians
52 (51)	Gallio as proconsul		
53 (52)		To Ephesus, Jerusalem, and Antioch	
54		Return to Ephesus	Galatians (fall or winter)

Year	Events	Paul's Life	Letters
55			1 Cor. 5:9 letter; 1 Cor. (Oct.)
56		Short trip to Corinth (Mar.-Apr.); left Ephesus for Troas, Macedonia, Illyricum, and Corinth (June)	2 Cor. 10–13 (May); Phil. 3:1b-19 (late summer); 2 Cor. 1–9 (late summer)
57		To Philippi and Jerusalem; imprisonment began	Rom. 1–15 and 16 (late winter)
58			Col.; Eph.; Philem.
59	Festus replaced Felix (June); departures of Timothy (June-July) and Tychicus (July-Aug.)	Appearances before Festus (July) and Agrippa (Aug.); left Caesarea (Sept.); reached Fair Haven, Crete (Oct.)	Tit. 3:12-15 (Apr. –May); Phil. 1–3: 1a, 20–4 (May); 2 Tim. 4:9ff. (Aug.)
60		Reached Rome (Mar.)	
60–61			1 Tim. 1:12-16; 2 Tim. 1:1-10, 12, 15–2:1, 3, 8-10; 4:5
62		To Spain	
62–63			Hebrews
64	Fire in Rome		
64–65		Martyrdom in Rome	

Abbreviations

BJRL — *Bulletin of the John Rylands Library*
CBQ — *Catholic Biblical Quarterly*
DCB — *Dictionary of Christian Biography,* ed. William Smith
    and Henry Wace
DTC — *Dictionnaire de Theologie Catholique*
HTR — *Harvard Theological Review*
IB — *The Interpreter's Bible*
IDB — *The Interpreter's Dictionary of the Bible*
JBL — *Journal of Biblical Literature*
JQR — *Jewish Quarterly Review*
JTS — *Journal of Theological Studies*
NT — *Novum Testamentum*
NTS — *New Testament Studies*
PEQ — *Palestine Exploration Quarterly*
PG — *Patrologiae Graccae* (Migne)
RB — *Revue Biblique*
RQ — *Revue de Qumran*
TLZ — *Theologische Literaturzeitung*
TU — *Texte und Untersuchungen zur Geschichte der altchrist-*
    lichen Literatur, ed. O. von Gebhardt and A. Harnack
ZNTW — *Zeitschrift für die Neutestamentliche Wissenschaft*
ET — English translation

Contents

1
A Chronology of Jesus' Ministry

Since Paul's conversion and subsequent ministry obviously follow the ministry of Jesus, we need first of all to establish the dates of Jesus' ministry. However, like so many of the important events in man's religious history, these dates have not been clearly determined. But the clues are now fitting better into place. August Strobel [1] has argued convincingly that Jesus preached in the Nazareth synagogue (Luke 4:16-30) during the Jubilee Year ("the acceptable year of the Lord") which was proclaimed in some quarters on 1 Tishri, A.D. 26. There was a prophecy in the Qumran document, 11Q Melch, of Melchizedek's return for atonement and vengeance at the end of days, during the last year of the tenth jubilee period. [2] Daniel (9:24 and 26) had foretold: "Seventy weeks [490] of years are decreed concerning your people . . . to atone for iniquity, to bring in everlasting righteousness . . . desolations are decreed." Strobel counts every 49th (Jubilee) year from 464–463 B.C., beginning with the year in which Jewish tradition (e.g., Maimonides, *Hilkhoth Shemittah* x, 2-6) calculated that Artaxerxes I despatched Ezra to rebuild Jerusalem (Ezra 7:7ff.) .

Such an expectation occasioned also the public ministry of John the Baptist. Jesus knew that John was looking for a Messiah who would fulfill the prophecy of Isaiah 61:1-2, KJV, (cf. 58:6) during "the acceptable year of the Lord." Jesus himself had proclaimed in the Nazareth synagogue: "Today this scripture has been fulfilled in your hearing" (Luke 4:21) . "Now when John heard in prison about the deeds of the Christ, he sent

word by his disciples and said to him, 'Are you he who is to
come, or shall we look for another?' " (Matt. 11:2-3; cf. Luke
7:18-19). Jesus' message to John (Matt. 11:4-5; Luke 7:22)
pointed out that he was fulfilling completely the role of the
Messiah who was to appear in a certain Jubilee year (Luke
4:17-19), for good news was being preached to the poor; the blind
were receiving their sight. And, by implication, captives op-
pressed by demons, sins, and death (cf. Matt. 4:16-17; Mark 2:5;
9:1; Luke 7:21; John 11:21-26) were being released by Christ.

Other data agree with the deduction that the ministry of
Jesus began toward the end of A.D. 26, a Jubilee and Sabbatical
year. If the chronological clues concerning his nativity (vari-
ously dated between 8 and 4 B.C.) [3] are taken seriously, and if
he were "about *(hosei)* thirty years of age" when baptized (Luke
3:23), an early baptismal date is indicated. Moreover, the forty-
sixth year of the building of the temple (John 2:20), counting
from 20–19 B.C. (Josephus, *Antiquities,* xv, 11.1.380), was A.D.
26–27, if we count inclusively according to the normal Jewish
method of reckoning. The Fourth Evangelist thus dated Jesus'
first public Passover in 27. It is sometimes held that the reference
is to the *naos,* the inner temple (as distinct from the *hieron,* the
whole temple edifice and precincts), the construction of which
was finished by priests in a year and five months (*Antiq.* xv,
11.6.421). However, for the Evangelist *naos* was the term for
sanctuary; elsewhere he uses *hieron,* by which he means the
public temple area. As Jesus was arguing with the Jews where
animals were sold, "this," *touton* (2:20), could refer only to
the temple outer enclosures begun in 20–19 B.C.

The fifteenth year of Tiberius (Luke 3:1-2) is indeterminate.
If Luke sought to be consistent, he had in mind an early date
"about thirty years" after the nativity events. He could have
used the Jewish calendar of his hypothetical source (s), his native Syrian calendar, or the Julian calendar of Theophilus (Luke
1:3). Also he could have counted Tiberius's regnal years from
his joint rule of the provinces with Augustus. [4] On the other
hand, Luke may have known the date of the crucifixion but not
the length of Jesus' ministry. [5] If its duration were underesti-
mated, he may have mentally postdated the work of John the
Baptist. Whatever Luke's sources or calculations were, "the fifteenth year of Tiberius" is too ambiguous to rely upon.

How long did Jesus manifest himself publicly? The Fourth
Evangelist seems more interested in chronology than was Mark.
As the Synoptic Gospels ignore the holy day trips to Jerusalem,
which best mark the passage of time, they are deficient in chronological clues. The ministry of Jesus was of such length, and
his travels of such complexity, that no attempt was made to re-
construct its total outline at any stage in the transmission of the
Synoptic traditions. [6] His public ministry may have been inter-
rupted by lengthy, but unrecorded, periods of separation from
his disciples (compare John 1:37ff. and Mark 1:16-18) and of
withdrawal with them to isolated places, both for hiding and
instruction. He sought to avoid John's short path to martyrdom and to remain alive long enough to gather and train his
disciples, whose understanding was often slow. There were re-
peated threats to his life. In this context we might understand
Mark's version of the Messianic secret (e.g., 8:29-30) ; indiscreet,
premature public claims to be the Anointed One could have
dangerous political, military overtones. Yet he chose his time
to challenge Jerusalem and when to begin preparing his disciples for the fatal consequences of his challenge. Be that as it
may, we must take into account for a chronology his many
unsuccessful visits to Jerusalem, his long acquaintance with
Philip, his ostensible change in attitude toward work in Samaria,
and his widespread travels.

Three Passovers (John 2:13, 23; 6:4; 11:55ff.) require a passage of more than two years. An additional year would be probable if the well-attested definite article is read before "feast" in
5:1, as only Passover was for both Jews and early Christians "the
festival" par excellence. Jesus' first April was spent in Judea,
and at least one other April in Galilee and around its sea.
George Ogg has written: "The imperfects *diétriben* and *ebáp-
tizen* of John 3:22 suggest a stay in Judaea and an activity in the
dispensing of baptism there of some duration." [7] Sydney Temple [8] has confirmed the sequence of the locations of John's baptizing: at Bethabara during the Palestinian winter (John 1:28)
and at Aenon beginning in the spring (John 3:23). Not until
the latter part of the first spring or in early summer did Jesus
take up his Galilean ministry in earnest. John had already been
imprisoned, and Herod heard of Jesus only after the death of
the Baptist. That Jesus during his first year remained in Judea

until the onset of hot weather might be indicated by his weariness and thirst at Jacob's well (John 4:5-9). The reference to fields white for harvest (John 4:35) is not a chronological clue, which might refer to winter *or* spring, but a proverb used to illustrate a spiritual, eschatological harvest alone. The events mentioned in relation to the Passover of John 6:4 cannot be placed in the early spring of the first year in Judea. A portion of this second or third spring was spent on the east side of the Sea of Galilee, where near the time of Passover he fed the multitude (John 6:4, cf. Mark 6:31-32, 39) sitting on green grass. The Fourth Evangelist's timing is confirmed by the withering of grass in April. Jesus was in Galilee during the late winter or early spring when he asked his followers to "consider the lilies of the field" [scarlet flowers?] [9] and short-lived grass (Matt. 6: 28-30; Luke 12:27-28). The plucking of grain (Mark 2:23) also fits best the spring of a second or third year, before the harvesting of the Galilean grainfields; for Pharisaic spying (cf. John 4:1) and opposition to Jesus' freedom from the Sabbath Law are not traceable to the outset of his ministry. His public work, then, encompassed at least two springs before Passion Week: the first, Passover to June, in Judea; the other(s) between March and harvest time, in Galilee and across its sea.

The relatively greater success of Christ's work in Galilee (Acts 2:7; John 4:43-45) and the centrality of the Galilean ministry in the Synoptic Gospels indicate that he spent more time there than the few months between his baptism and temptation in the fall or winter before his first Passover visit and baptizing activity in Judea (John 3:22–4:4) in the following spring, and the Feast of Tabernacles (John 7:2ff.).

If Jesus was baptized in the closing months of 26, and if his work lasted through at least three Passovers and into at least three springs, then we should look for his crucifixion in 29 or 30. Patristic evidence is divided between 29 (Tertullian, Hippolytus, Lactantius, Augustine, Acts of Pilate) [10] and 30 (Julius Africanus, the first Christian historian). [11] The latter's contemporary, Clement of Alexandria (*Strom.* i, 2.146), knew of "careful investigators" (astronomically competent followers of Basilides) [12] who dated the crucifixion on April 7, 30, or on two other days of the same year. Precise modern lunar calculations of Nisan 14 and 15 fit 30 (April 7) much better than calculations of Nisan

14 fit the previous year (March 18). [13] The presence of green leaves on the cursed fig tree (Mark 11:13) is a more positive and reliable indication of a relatively late date in the spring than the fire on a cold night (Mark 14:54) is an indication of an early part of the season. "The trees, which during the winter months have lost all their leaves, begin putting forth the tender leaf buds about the end of March." [14] If we can trust this detail, then a two and one-half-year ministry ending as early as March 18, 29, is improbable.

A deliberately chosen three and one-half-year career culminating in 30, however, is supported by three clues. Jesus compared his own ministry away from Nazareth to Elijah's three and one-half years in the territory of Sidon (Luke 4:23-25). The cursing of the fig tree (Matt. 21:18-19; Mark 11:12-14), if it were a prophetic acting out of the earlier taught parable of the barren fig tree (Luke 13:6-9), indicates that the Lord had given the Jewish nation (cf. Jer. 8:12-13) almost four years to repent, including an extra year of grace, since the beginning of John's preaching in the Jubilee Year proclaimed on 1 Tishri, 26. But the nation had not produced the necessary fruit of repentance. Would the Baptist, with an eschatological message and alleged Essene associations, have ignored the prophecy of Daniel 9:24ff. in timing his own ministry? Not if he were an apocalypticist (Matt. 3:10-11). And if Jesus also expected his people to observe signs, would he not seek to fulfill the same prophecy? "Seventy weeks of years are decreed . . . to anoint a most holy place . . . And for half of the week he [an anointed one] shall cause sacrifice and offering to cease" (Dan. 9:24, 27). His cleansing of the temple at the beginning of his public three and one-half-year ministry illustrates the words attributed to him in the Ebionite Gospel (ap. Epiphanius, Haer. 30, 6.4-5; cf. Matt. 9:13; 12:7): "I am come to do away with sacrifices, and if you cease not from sacrificing, the wrath of God will not cease from you." At least he opposed the sale of sacrificial animals; commercialism and profiteering by "robbers" made the selling unfit for the house of prayer, and the animals unfit for offerings (John 2: 13-17). Such sacrifices should cease: they were impure and did not please the Lord. No Old Testament prophet had acted so decisively, even when radically downgrading offerings. Here is a third indication that from the outset Jesus planned a ministry

of half of a week of years, three and one-half years, in fulfillment of prophecy.

Why Jesus and John waited so long to begin their public min-
istries is no problem if Isaiah 61:1-2 and Daniel 9:24ff. (cf. 11Q
Melch) favor the years 26–30. Both had these passages in mind.
Their opening message, "The time is fulfilled, and the kingdom
of God is at hand" (Mark 1:15; Matt. 3:2; 4:17), can refer only
to the contemporary fulfillment of a scriptural eschatological
prophecy, such as Daniel 9:25. That Jesus fashioned his ministry to correspond with prophecy is indicated by his triumphal
entry into Jerusalem.

"Tell the daughter of Zion,
  Behold, your king is coming to you,
  humble, and mounted on as ass,
  and on a colt, the foal of an ass" (Matt.: 21:5; Zech. 9:9) . [15]

A crucifixion date of no later than 30 can provide a reasonably
firm foundation for building a Pauline chronology. The conversion of Paul must not be postdated through a false fixing of
the time of the crucifixion in 33. With this background question
examined, we may now proceed to the main task of chronicling
the apostle's missionary and literary career.

2

Paul's Visits
to
Jerusalem

We have the most information about Paul's early years of ministry in relationship to his visits to Jerusalem. If we can determine the dates of these visits, then we can work out the sequence of his activities.

THE APOSTLE'S CHRONOLOGICAL RECKONINGS

The most inherently trustworthy source [1] of a chronology of Paul's earliest Christian years is his own account in Galatians 1-2. In the context of trying to establish the independence of his apostleship and gospel from the leaders in Jerusalem, he recounts his few and brief contacts with them. Under oath he swears that on his first visit he saw only Peter and James, the Lord's brother. Against these very limited contacts he sets Christ's personal revelation to him after he had persecuted the church for what he had learned of its deviations from Judaism and ancestral traditions (1:1, 12-16). This crucial call to be an apostle is Paul's primary point of reference when he mentions visits to Jerusalem three years and fourteen years afterward (1:18; 2:1). How absurd it is for his opponents to claim that the apostles in Jerusalem were the source of his teaching authority and his knowledge of Christ! Just as the mention of fifteen days (1:18) serves to minimize apostolic contact, so the specification of three years and fourteen years underlines just how *long* a time it was after his call to the apostleship that he encountered Jerusalem leaders. If Paul cited numbers with the intent of demonstrating his independence, then both for clarity and emphasis he would refer to "three" and "fourteen" years after his call; for a mention of fourteen years with this meaning is rhetorically more emphatic than would be a reference to "eleven" years (after the first visit). Likewise, "three years" after his *call* is a longer period than the number of years after his subsequent *return* to Damascus from Arabia (1:17-18). This "three-year" period is suspiciously lengthy; it is difficult to envision events in the parallel account (Acts 9:19-26) taking thirty-six months, even when allowance is made for the unmentioned sojourn in Arabia. It was not the lengthy time *between* his visits which most clearly showed his independence, but rather the long periods *after* the revelation to him on the road to Damascus before he went to Jerusalem. Moreover, because his non-visit to Jerusalem (Gal. 1:17) is set in opposition to his visit "after three years" (1:18), the common point of reference and departure must be his call. And, if the "three years" starts from this point, it is more natural to assume likewise for the "fourteen years."

As the ancients usually reckoned inclusively (i.e., part of a year was counted as a full year), the "after fourteen years" could mean any length of time longer than twelve but less than fourteen whole years after his conversion. If Jesus was crucified on April 7, 30, and if he appeared to Paul at the end ("last of all": 1 Cor. 15:8) of his eighteen months (545 or 550 days) in the world after his resurrection (Ascension of Isaiah 9:16),[2] then this final earthly revelation is to be dated not far from September, A.D. 31.[3] Paul's second visit to the Holy City is, accordingly, datable "fourteen" (i.e., $12\frac{1}{4}$–$13\frac{3}{4}$) years after his conversion, namely, between the winter of 43 to 44 and the early months of A.D. 45. As the Jewish New Year begins in September, his Jerusalem visit in all probability occurred the year ending in September, 44 or 45.

Further chronological information may be gained if a suggestion of Theodor von Zahn, *inter alia,*[4] is accepted and fitted into this context. The revelation to which Paul refers in 2 Corinthians 12:1-10 occurred when Barnabas brought him from his native Tarsus[5] to Antioch (Acts 11:25-26). Because Barnabas had been sent from Jerusalem to supervise the conversion of Gentiles (Acts 11:20-24), it may be presumed that he sought

Paul to aid him in this very work. It cannot be assumed, however, that the invitation by Barnabas to Paul to labor among the Gentiles was in itself sufficient to convince Paul concerning the Lord's will. Nor is it certain that from the beginning he was a preacher to the Gentiles. He may have hesitated to accompany Barnabas because his own incipient views on justification (Gal. 2:16ff.) were unpalatable to the Jerusalem church and could have endangered Barnabas's position and work. Paul on other occasions had visions which encouraged him about his future (Acts 18:9-10; 23:11; 27:23ff.) and guided him where to go (16:9-10; 22:17-21; cf. 19:21). The words of the Holy Spirit revealed through the fasting prophets at Antioch led to the mission of Barnabas and Paul to Cyprus and Asia Minor (Acts 13: 1-4). For the momentous step of moving the scene of his labors from his native Tarsus to Antioch as proposed by Barnabas, Paul would hope for, if not need, a sign, revelation, or divine commissioning; thereby he would gain understanding, assurance, and endowment with sufficient power. Paul claimed to have experienced an abundance *(huperbole)* of other comparable revelations (2 Cor. 12:7). The one described in this passage was received by "a man in Christ" (2 Cor. 12:2) who was countering the claims of his opponents and defending his own apostolic authority. Both the power of Christ resting on him and his own hearing of unutterable things were accompanied by a contrasting thorn in the flesh, which kept him from being too elated. The context suggests that the specially recalled vision with its unrepeatable message in some way dealt with the significance of his apostolic power. But he was not permitted to boast about what he learned. Since the thorn in the flesh hampered his work as an apostle, the revelations (as the counterpart of the harassing thorn) must have elated him because they confirmed and interpreted his apostolic dignity. In Acts 9:15-16; 22:21; 26:16-20 the varying accounts of his conversion outside of Damascus indicate that tradition was confused on the question of who revealed to Paul his future mission to the Gentiles. This indicates, perhaps, that Paul's awareness and certainty of his Gentile mission grew by stages in accordance with new revelations (cf. Peter's experience in Acts 10:9-17, 34ff.; 11:5-18) and that development in Paul's understanding of his office and revelations left various marks on the traditions. Knowledge of his

mission was accompanied by the revelation of the sufferings
which awaited him (Acts 9:16; cf. 20-33). It was by revelation
that Paul believed that he learned the price to be paid for his
apostolic dignity. He would suffer not only a thorn in the flesh,
but also henceforth persecutions and abuse (2 Cor. 12:10).

One of Paul's many revelations was received earlier, on his
first Jerusalem visit. In a trance he was told by the risen Lord:
"Make haste and get quickly out of Jerusalem, because they will
not accept your testimony about me. . . . Depart; for I will send
you far away to the Gentiles" (Acts 22:18*b*, 21*b*). His mission
to the Gentiles was to be a substitute for one to the Hebrews
(Acts 9:26ff.). His early persecution of believers (22:19-20)
indirectly required him to transfer his apostleship to distant
Gentiles. The guilt feelings which the apostle experienced for
this persecution of the church (22:19-20; cf. Gal. 1:13; Phil. 3:6;
1 Tim. 1:13) may have been the thorn in the flesh which kept
him from boastful pride. For, in listing Christ's resurrection
appearances (1 Cor. 15:8-10), Paul wrote: "Last of all, as to one
untimely born, he appeared also to me. For I am the least of
the apostles, unfit to be called an apostle, because I persecuted
the church of God. But by the grace of God I am what I am."
As in 2 Corinthians 12:5ff. he states that grace empowered him
for his labors, though he had cause for humility. This cause is
termed "a thorn for the [*te* :dative] flesh, a messenger of Satan"
(2 Cor. 12:7) in one passage, but his persecution of the church
(1 Cor. 15:9) in the other. In Old Testament tradition "thorn"
is a metaphor for punishment for sin, whereas "flesh" for Paul
may symbolize sinful passions at enmity with God. As a punishment of the carnal nature which had impelled Paul into persecution, Satan painfully harassed the apostle with reminders of
the suffering of his victims. As Paul believed that sins make
one weak and feeble (1 Cor. 11:28-30) and that Satan tempts
(1 Cor. 7:5) and inflicts physical punishment (1 Cor. 5:5), it
is possible that he had received a recurrent painful weakness
which he viewed as an additional punishment for his guilt in
persecuting Christians. The contemptible, scornful bodily ail-
ment which led him first to preach to the Galatians (Gal. 4:
13-14) involved debilitating and humiliating attacks (cf. 2 Cor.
12:10) in public. [6] The proposed work in Antioch with Hellenists (Acts 11:26; cf. 9:29) who remembered his persecuting must

have occasioned an acute attack of "the thorn in the flesh." To Paul it was then revealed that he should go, and that persecutions on behalf of Christ awaited him (2 Cor. 12:10).

This identification of the vision of 2 Corinthians 12 with one occasioned by Barnabas's summons to Antioch is plausible chronologically, as well. If 2 Corinthians 10–13 is part of the apostle's severe letter (2 Cor. 2:3-4, 9; 7:8, 12) carried by Titus (12:18; cf. 7:6, 13), who subsequently met him in Macedonia, then it is to be dated shortly before Paul left Ephesus following Pentecost (1 Cor. 16:8), A.D. 56. (See the discussion of the Corinthian correspondence in Chapter 3.) Calculating backward from this time of writing, we can tentatively date his vision. As the ancients calculated by counting parts of years as whole years, the "fourteen" years which had passed since Paul's conversion could have been as little as twelve and one-quarter years. By taking the median figure of thirteen and one-eighth years and subtracting it from the early spring of 56, we find that Paul's vision (2 Cor. 12) occurred approximately in the winter of 42–43. If at this time Paul was induced to return with Barnabas from Tarsus to Antioch, where they spent a "whole year" teaching and meeting with the church (Acts 11:26), then their journey to Jerusalem with relief (11:29-30) is datable in the late winter of 43–44. This date corresponds with the above estimated arrival in Jerusalem sometime in 44. Such a correspondence would identify the *second* visit with the famine relief visit. Paul would not wish to wait too long before ascertaining whether he was "running in vain" in preaching his gospel to Gentiles (Gal. 2:2).

A preparatory step in verifying this correspondence is to compare the accounts of the first visit in Acts 9:26-30 (cf. 26:20) and Galatians 1:18-24. Were it not for their similar settings and times, these narratives would not be obviously identifiable. Different objectives motivated each writer. Whereas Paul claimed that he went to visit (*historeo*, which implies reporting and inquiring) Peter and James privately, Luke relates that Paul tried to join the apostles and was rebuffed because they were afraid of him, so that Barnabas had to defend him to the apostles. Whereas Paul states that at this time the Judean churches did not know him personally, we are told in Acts that while Paul was with the apostles he preached openly in Jerusalem

(9:28), and that when he was endangered, the brethren took him to Caesarea. Luke emphasizes, and Paul overlooks, the positive role of Barnabas: a contrast found in Acts 15:2 and Galatians 2:10*b* and 13 as well. Whereas Luke emphasizes the role of the church in making official decisions, Paul writes chiefly about his personal role and that of Peter and James. This difference appears also in Acts 13:1-3 and 15:2, when compared with Galatians 2:1, 11-14. Consequently, we should not expect too much correspondence in the parallel accounts in Acts and Galatians of the second Jerusalem visit and the trouble at Antioch. Some of the differences of narration can be accounted for as further examples of differences between the parallel accounts of Paul's first visit to Jerusalem.

THE FAMINE VISIT

The events described in Acts 11:27-30 and 12:25 may be identified with those narrated in Galatians 2:1-10. [7] Each constituted Paul's second visit to Jerusalem. If Galatians 2 were a description of Paul's third trip, then by omitting mention of the famine visit, Paul would have left himself open to his opponents' charge (cf. Gal. 1:20) that he deceitfully repressed facts. Paul had to allude candidly to all of his Jerusalem visits in proper sequence before his evangelization of Galatia. Even the elders to whom he delivered the relief (Acts 11:30) were in a position to instruct him authoritatively in the faith of Christ (cf. Gal. 1:16-22). In both Acts 11:27-30 and Galatians 2:1-10 Paul and Barnabas came from Antioch to Jerusalem (cf. Gal. 1:21; 2:11) by virtue of a revelation and declared an eagerness to remember the poor in Jerusalem. Agabus, one of the prophets from Jerusalem, foretold through the Spirit that there would be a worldwide famine. Other inspired oracles later mentioned in Acts (21:4,11) include a prediction of Paul's capture in Jerusalem and an instruction to him not to go there. That a prediction implied an appropriate course of action is apparent also from the response to Agabus's first prophecy: the disciples determined to send relief to the brethren in Judea (Acts 11:29). Whether this idea came from Agabus or another charismatic leader of the church at Antioch, its members doubtless deemed both the idea and the resolution to be as divinely inspired as the prophecy itself of the famine. Now, Paul relates that he went up to Jerusalem "by revelation" (Gal. 2:2), without specifying the recipient or nature of the revelation. From the context we may judge that the commission to go to Jerusalem was inspired as were the desire and intent of Paul to explain his gospel to Peter, James, and John (lest his running be in vain) and to remember the poor. If Paul's eagerness and the journey itself were not the outcome of inspiration, then we are at a loss to specify the content of the revelation. Unfortunately, Paul does not say how many revelations were involved; but all major plans and undertakings of the primitive church were deemed inspired. Paul does say that, while the "pillars" made remembering the poor a moral duty for the Gentiles, it was an unnecessary suggestion or condition; for it was already the intention of the apostles to the Gentiles. Both Jerusalemites and Antiochenes were motivated by the desire to preserve church unity. George S. Duncan comments on the passage:

> The verb he uses [*spoudázo*] signifies not mere eagerness. . . . but active engagement in the prosecution of a task. The tense of the verb is aorist (past), indicating probably that the apostle is looking backward—"they were only asking me to do something which had already occupied my attention." [8]

Paul's use of the singular does not imply that Barnabas did not share in his eagerness, since his "autobiographical" use of the singular is paralleled in verses 2, 3, 6, 7, 8, and 9. Paul was trying to establish his own position for the sake of his readers, and conceivably the matter of the forthcoming collection by Paul's own churches for the Jerusalem saints was in his and his readers' minds. In writing to the Galatians Paul indicates that the obligation to send relief is still valid. Moreover, Paul used the indefinite aorist, *espoúdasa,* because his enthusiasm for bringing relief was both a thing of the past in Antioch and of the present when he was in Jerusalem. Had he used the imperfect tense, he would not have done justice to his continuing ardent prosecution of the responsibility. Nothing could be more emphatic than *autò touto.* It is also noteworthy that the present tense, *mnemoneúomen,* implies a continuity of Paul's present remembrance rather than the addition of a new requirement to be remembered only in the future (cf. v.6: *ouden prosanèthento*).

Paul was describing his second trip from the viewpoint of his authority and relationship to the other apostles, especially in regard to the Gentile mission. This purpose of his writing determined his presentation of facts. Therefore, the relief which he and Barnabas brought was of primary significance, not simply for the special occasion of the prophesied famine, but as the continuing responsibility of Paul's Gentile churches. Luke, on the other hand, due to his special interest in the church's sharing and almsgiving "portrayed the visit of Acts 11:27-30; 12:25 . . . as an act of generosity on the part of the Antioch church," as Charles H. Talbert observes. [9]

Can any information about the time of the famine visit be gained from the reference to the elders *(presbúteroi)* to whom Barnabas and Paul delivered the relief (11:30)? From Acts 6:1-6 we learn that in the primitive church the daily distribution and serving of tables constituted the responsibility, not of the Twelve, but of the disciples chosen specially for the work. Nor does Galatians 2:9-10 hint that James, Cephas, and John handled the relief sent to the poor. Thus the Antiochenes sent aid, not to the apostles, but to the elders for distribution. Acts 21:18ff. relates that when Paul and his companions later brought relief from their churches to Jerusalem, they presented themselves to James and the elders. They were the ones who heard about his ministry among the Gentiles and who suggested what manner of loyalty he should demonstrate to the Torah. The elders were among those who considered and passed judgment on the issues facing the Jerusalem "Council" (Acts 15:6, 23). Since Peter is called an elder in 1 Peter 5:1, one cannot even be sure that "apostle" and "elder" were mutually exclusive terms. Are we to conclude that James was absent from Jerusalem at the time the Antiochene relief was received, because his name is unmentioned? Probably not (Acts 12:17). Luke does not report that Paul and Barnabas did not see any apostles at that time, and before he relates the return to Antioch (12:25), he narrates what befell Peter and James, the son of Zebedee, in Jerusalem. Whether this chronology be wrong or right, Luke believed and implied that Paul was in Jerusalem at the same time as Peter and the two Jameses. And if he implied this, no inference can be drawn from his failure to describe the contact of Paul and Barnabas with Peter and the Lord's brother.

Curiously, there is no reference in Luke's accounts of any of Paul's Jerusalem visits to the private meeting in which Peter, James, and John gave the hand of fellowship to Barnabas and Paul (Gal. 2:6-9). This is a problem wherever one locates the setting of Galatians 2:1-10. Above we suggested that Luke (over-) emphasized the public aspect of Paul's work and his relations with all the apostles and brethren in the church at Jerusalem. Because of Luke's disinterest in the personal relations of the major apostles, he was silent about the event described in Galatians 2:6-9. He chose to minimize differences and to mention only the final decision of the council. In this context he underlined the unity of the leaders on the need to encourage the Gentile mission by making concessions. Moreover, Luke did not view Peter as an apostle to the circumcised alone (Gal. 2: 7-9; cf. Acts 10:1–11:18) or Paul as an apostle dependent upon human sanction (Acts 9:15-16; 22:21; 26:17-19). Luke considered the events described in Acts 15 to be the conclusive ones in bringing the Gentiles into the church. Actually, the significance of the right hand of fellowship should not be overestimated. Kirsopp Lake commented: "So far as Paul tells us, the only result of the private interview was that the Apostles agreed that he was doing good work. . . . He was encouraged to go on preaching to the Gentiles." [10] Nor should one expect the author of Acts to include all the facts. His was a selective task and his sources were not unlimited. He made no reference to the dispute about the uncircumcised Titus (Gal. 2:3-5); indeed, he never mentioned Titus anywhere in Acts. Certainly an argument from silence carries little weight in resolving the chronological problem.

Actually Paul's mission necessarily had a dual purpose, or at least outcome. Jerusalem's reception of the aid was related to the questions of the acceptability to Jerusalem of the apostleship of Barnabas and Paul, the gospel which they preached to the Gentiles, and the question of additional requirements for communion. Thus Titus could have gone up to Jerusalem as a model Gentile convert and as a representative of the Antiochene Christians (cf. 20:4; 21:28-29) who were making the offering. Whatever the occasion and ostensible purpose of the visit to Jerusalem, the question of the status of Barnabas, Paul, and Titus could scarcely have been left unresolved, much less undiscussed.

As Barnabas earlier had been sent from Jerusalem to Antioch when it was learned that Cypriots and Cyrenians were preaching to Greeks there (Acts 11:20-22), so the Jerusalemites must have had a few questions about the terms under which Barnabas and Paul, whom he had fetched as a co-worker, were associating with Gentiles. A decision had to be reached on the continuation of their Gentile mission and on the acceptability of what was being preached to the Gentiles.

In behalf of the Antiochenes Paul and Barnabas could not have been altogether certain whether their first offering would be acceptable. Concerning the later contribution sent by Paul's churches to Jerusalem, Walther Schmithals argues persuasively that Romans 15:30-32 indicates that Paul "is affected by *one* fear. . . . The menace from the Jews is connected with the possible rejection of the contributions: 'Pray that the Jews do not harm me and (therefore) my contributions are welcome to the Christians.'"[11] The good textual witnesses to 15:31 omit a second *hina* between *kaì* and *he diakonía*. Schmithals recognizes that a refusal by the Jerusalem church to accept the contributions would constitute a refusal to receive Paul, and, "if it accepted Paul's contributions, then it was declaring in the eyes of the Jews its solidarity with him. This threatened to destroy the possibility of its own mission"[12] to Israel. Association with Paul was forcing the Jerusalem community to choose between remaining within Judaism or leaving it. Moreover, Paul was accused of teaching the abandonment of the Law (Acts 21: 21, 28).

> It was exactly this accusation on the part of the Jews which the Jewish Christians were bound to fear when they included Paul in their fellowship. They were aware of this at the latest since the persecution of Stephen's community. The fear of this accusation led to the agreement . . . in which Paul relinquished the mission to the Jews. It was also the same fear which lead Peter (*phoboúmenos toùs ek peritomes*) on the urging of James to resume the separate life of the Jewish Christians in Antioch.[13]

James himself and some of his companions were eventually martyred on the charge of breaking the Law (Josephus, *Antiquities* xx, 9.1).

To what extent are these observations relevant for interpreting Paul's second Jerusalem trip? Two factors were present at all times for the apostolic church in Jerusalem: (1) that community could not altogether escape responsibility for the abandonment of the Torah by large segments of Christians with whom they continued fellowship; (2) insofar as they were held responsible, their missionary work in Palestine would be limited and they would be potentially subject to the same fate as the Hellenists. Since these Hellenists were responsible for founding a Gentile-filled church at Antioch (Acts 11:19-25), anyone from this new Christian community would be suspect among those who were unsympathetic to the new sect. Paul, too, must already have been distrusted because of his earlier controversies in Jerusalem and his role as a preacher to the Gentiles. When it was discovered that Titus was uncircumcised (Gal. 2:3-5), suspicions were confirmed. Doubtless Jewish hostility to Paul grew during the period leading up to his final visit to Jerusalem, and this accounts for the fears for his welfare when he delivered his churches' collection. Yet his associated fear that this offering might be unaccepted must have stemmed either from hesitation concerning acceptance of the first one (Acts 11:27ff.) or from the possibility of the repetition of the consequences of its acceptance. This fear existed even though, unlike the first time, the Jerusalem church had already signified its willingness to accept help.

In Galatians 2:4-5 Paul gives a clue to trouble on the earlier "relief mission." The "false brethren secretly brought in, who slipped in to spy out our freedom which we have in Christ," were obviously spies masquerading as believers and seeking to discover the implications of "freedom in Christ." The double reference to stealth excludes their being *bona fide* local Judaizers, and it is doubtful that Paul would call conservative Jerusalem Christians who dissented from his gospel at this early date, "false brethren." Nor would *bona fide* Jerusalem believers have to be spies and intruders in their own church! Paul emphatically stated that they did not belong where they sneaked in. However, it is possible that the extremists in the community secretly let in or brought in troublemaking spies from the Sanhedrin or from Herod. To quote Schmithals again: "There can surely be no doubt that the Christian Church was under official observation, especially after the persecution of Stephen's circle. The Jews had to remain informed about the position of the Christians regarding the Law." [14] What better way could there be than to make Titus a test case? Had not Jesus himself been kept under surveillance and frequently tested? Why should temple and Roman officials ignore a growing sect when they had crucified its founder? The surreptitious outsiders now gained information which could be used against these apostles who had too permissive an attitude toward "freedom in Christ." Either Herod or the chief priests were in a position to dispose of such troublemakers as Peter and John.

A decision concerning the correlation of Acts 11:27-30 and 12:25 with Galatians 2:1-10 must rest in part upon chronological considerations. The initial problem in this respect is the dating of Agrippa I's death. This event is generally reckoned as having occurred in 44 on the basis of Josephus's statement (*Antiquities* xix, 8.2; cf. *War* ii, 11.6) that he reigned three years under Claudius, following four under Gaius, 37–41 (cf. *Antiquities* xviii, 6.10). Confirmation of the year 44 as Herod's death date is found in his coinage. The final confirmed coin dates from the eighth year of his reign and in all likelihood was issued to celebrate Claudius's victory over the Britons in 43. [15] When Claudius returned to Rome after an absence of six months, the Senate voted an annual festival to commemorate his triumph (Dio, *History* lx,21.2–22.2; 23.1). Josephus (*Antiquities* xix,8.2) relates that Herod died four days after being stricken on the second day of a festival honoring Caesar. Zahn [16] perceived that the festive games were held after news reached Caesarea of Claudius's safe return from Britain. The celebration and the issue of a victory coinage could have occurred in the late spring of 44; a delay far into the summer would be unexpected. Herod had imprisoned Peter during the days of Unleavened Bread (Acts 12:1ff.). Perhaps with the onset of warmer weather, Herod went down to Caesarea after Peter escaped, and here he died (Acts 12:18-23).

Upon the death of Herod Agrippa, Claudius sent Cassius Longinus to Syria as legate and Cuspius Fadus to Judea as procurator (*Antiquities* xix,9.2; xx,1.1). Both Cuspius Fadus and Cassius Longinus were in office when a dispute arose with leaders in Jerusalem concerning the custody of the high priest's holy vestments. This controversy would be timely before the Passover season. A Judean delegation was sent to Rome and, upon the intervention of the younger Agrippa, Claudius delivered to the ambassadors a favorable letter dated June 28 (Latin version of *Antiquities* xx,1.1-2; cf. xv,11.4) when Claudius was tribune for the fifth time and consul for the fourth time. Since the office of tribune was renewed each year, the letter is datable in 45. From a Caesarean coin of 45–46 we know that Cassius Longinus was then legate. These data indicate that Cuspius Fadus and Cassius Longinus were in office by the early spring of 45. The next procurator, Tiberius Alexander, was succeeded by Ventidius Cumanus at the death of Herod, king of Chalcis, during the eighth year of Claudius (*War* ii,12.1; *Antiquities* xx,5.2). As Claudius was proclaimed emperor on January 24, 41, Tiberius Alexander must have been in office until 48.

According to Josephus (*Antiquities* xx,5.2; cf.2.5; iii,15.3), it was under Cuspius Fadus and Tiberius Alexander (*epi toútois:*[17] cf. Eusebius, *H.E.* ii,12.1) that Helena, queen of Adiabene, and later her son relieved a famine in Jerusalem. Since Josephus and the Talmud mention the benefactions of Helena and her sons, Izates and Monobaz, it is reasonable to suppose that their aid to the needy did not cease before the ending of the famine during the procuratorship of Tiberius Alexander. If she relieved a famine during, or beginning with, the procuratorship of Fadus, the earliest possible date of her arrival in Jerusalem would be Passover, 44. She had come to worship at the temple and to present her thank offering, presumably at a festival (Josephus, *Antiquities* xx,2.5). As she was able to send her servants to Alexandria and Cyprus to buy wheat and dried figs, their mission must have occurred during the spring and summer sailing season. The distribution would have occurred shortly after the death of Herod Agrippa.

However, if the year of 44 is thought to be too early to be possible, then the chronology implied in *Antiquities* xx,5.2 by Josephus is inaccurate or misleading, as Andres M. Tornos has established;[18] for Helena's trip to Jerusalem, he has shown, must be dated in the context of events in Adiabene and Parthia. Josephus gives other information about the date of the trip of Helena to Jerusalem which scholars have generally overlooked. He refers to the death of Artabanus, king of Parthia, which is universally dated between 38 and 40. In Parthia a civil war broke out between the sons of Artabanus: Vardanes and Gotarzes. The first coins of Vardanes are dated June, 42, or possibly August, 40.[19] Vardanes captured Seleucia after nearly seven years of independence (Tacitus, *Annals* xi,8; cf. vi, 42). His coins in Seleucia begin in 42–43, but in 44–46 the coins of Gotarzes and Vardanes alternate at Seleucia. Gotarzes captured the city about June, 44. The minting of coins with the name of Vardanes ends with that of *ca.* July, 45, but those of Gotarzes continue at Seleucia after January, 46.[20] These coins indicate that Vardanes was in firm control of Seleucia in 43 and parts of 42 and 44. This period must correspond with that during which a plot against them both led Gotarzes and Vardanes to a temporary reconciliation leaving the latter with supremacy. "Vardanes then visited the principal satrapies, and was burning to recover Armenia, when he was checked by a threat of war from Vibius Marsus, the legate of Syria" (Tacitus, *Annals* xi,10; Loeb transl.). Then followed a renewal of the civil war, the murder of Vardanes and the restoration of Gotarzes (*ibid.;* cf. Josephus, *Antiquities* xx,3.4). Now C. Vibius Marsus,[21] with whom Vardanes almost came into conflict, governed Syria from A.D. 42 until he was succeeded by Cassius Longinus following the death of Herod Agrippa (Josephus, *Antiquities* xix,6.4; 7.2; 8.1; xx,1.1). Because of the recall of Marsus in the summer or, at the latest, the fall of 44, Vardanes' anti-Roman ambitions must be dated before this time. The coins of Seleucia in the middle months of 44 also testify to the renewal of the Parthian civil war; but Vardanes would hardly be able to think of war against Rome once his conflict with his brother was renewed. If the summer of 44 is the latest possible date for Vardanes' external designs, his capture of Seleucia and the beginning of the hegemony which it demonstrates mark the earliest possible date for such plans. Since winter is the most opportune time to make military and diplomatic preparations for new adventures, it is reasonable to deduce that during the winter of 43–44 Vardanes was engrossed in seeking allies. This state of affairs is alluded to in the *Antiquities* (xx,3.4). After the death of Artabanus, Vardanes came to Izates and tried to persuade him to aid him in the war he was preparing with Rome. But Izates declined due to fear of the Roman strength and fear for the welfare of his mother and five young sons who had gone to Jerusalem to worship and for an education, respectively. If Helena hoped to arrive before Passover, a journey during the winter of 43–44 would be in order. Surely this precise evidence must control the interpretation of that concerning the procuratorships of Fadus and Tiberius Alexander, rather than vice versa, in ascertaining the date of Helena's famine relief.

A significant article, "The Universal Famine under Claudius," by Kenneth S. Gapp, presents an analysis of certain papyri from Thebutis, published by the University of Michigan in 1933. In this Egyptian city, grain prices were unusually high in August, September, and November, 45. "Since Egypt at this time was dependent upon the harvest of the previous Spring, a natural assumption is that the harvest of 45 was very poor." [22] Due to hoarding and speculation the famine may have extended from the fall of 44 to the spring of 46. As Gapp further clarifies, "A universal famine need not be explained by a general failure of the harvest. It is rather to be found in a general increase in the price of food, and in the universal inability of the poor to purchase food at the current price." [23] If the price of wheat rose substantially in Egypt, other lands would suffer as well. Another clue to the date is given by Orosius (*History* vii, 6.12). A most serious famine throughout Syria occurred in the fourth year of the reign of Claudius. Nothing prohibits the hypothesis of bad crops in Syria in 44 and in Egypt in 45. The two events are not necessarily simultaneous. Suetonius (*Claudius,* 18) related that famines characterized this emperor's reign. Helena's stay in Jerusalem occurred during the years 44, 45, and possibly 46. That it may have been of some length is indicated not only by her directing of relief operations but also by her building of three pillars near Jerusalem and by the education of her grandchildren there (*Antiquities* xx,4.3).

Since Josephus describes the famine as extending over two reigns and causing many deaths, its length must have been considerable. There are two curious references in the New Testament to a three-and-one-half-year drought which caused a great famine (Luke 4:25; James 5:17-18) during the time of Elijah. But the Old Testament references (1 Kings 17:1 and 18:1) report a drought ending during the third year. Why did both of the New Testament references add an extra year? Perhaps the methods of calculating time differed. Or, could the three-and-one-half-year drought thus mentioned be an allusion to the one under Fadus and Tiberius, which was interpreted by the Jerusalem church in terms of the one under Elijah? Just as the Lord provided for Elijah by means of ravens (1 Kings 17: 6-7) and the widow in Zarephath (1 Kings 17:9), so he cared for the saints in Jerusalem through the aid from Antioch. Just as Elijah was sent, not to the widows in Israel, but rather to Zarephath in Sidon (1 Kings 17:8-24; Luke 4:25-26), so now the gospel was being preached to the Gentiles, since "no prophet is acceptable in his own country" (Luke 4:24). Just as the synagogue rose in wrath and expelled Jesus from Nazareth, so disciples suffered in 44 at Jerusalem. James teaches that "the prayer of a righteous man has great power. . . . Elijah was a man . . . like . . . ourselves" (5:16-18). He prayed first that it not rain and then that it might rain. As verses 16-20 are addressed to the readers in the second person, the "ourselves" includes James. He, like Elijah, was a righteous man capable of effective prayer like Elijah's. Epiphanius (*Haer.* 78,14) records a tradition (probably derived from Hegesippus, a second century Syro-Palestinian Hebrew convert)[24] that once when the earth was suffering from drought, James the Just prayed by uplifting his hands to heaven and rain then came down. Hegesippus (Book V, *ap.* Eusebius, *H.E.*ii, 23.4ff. from R. M. Grant, *Second Century Christianity* [London: SPCK, 1957], p. 58) described the piety of James the Just in these terms: "Alone he entered into the temple, and was found kneeling on his knees . . . so that his knees grew hard as a camel's because he was always kneeling on them, worshipping God and asking forgiveness for the people." Such a righteous man of prayer was comparable to Elijah.

If the Judean drought lasted for "three-and-one-half years" and was associated with the Gentile mission and Jerusalem persecution and the Antiochene relief, it would most satisfactorily be dated in 44, 45, and 46. Droughts begin in the summer and end in the winter. Accordingly, we suggest that the barley and wheat crops failed during the springs of 44, 45, and possibly 46. Only in the spring of 47 (46–?) was there a sufficient crop to end the famine. When the inadequate late rain beginning in November, 43, caused the barley and wheat seedlings in Syria and Palestine to dry up or blow away, it became obvious that a food shortage was coming. Due to hoarding and speculation, food prices in Jerusalem rose immediately. The price rise particularly squeezed the resources available under the "consumption communism" of the saints (Acts 4:32). Acts 11:28-30 does not tell of aid in response to a known need during the height of a famine, but of a ministration sent because of prophecy concerning a coming famine. Zahn commented on the timing of the relief: "If the indefinite prophecy of a single prophet was sufficient to lead to the collection of a charitable fund, any indication that this prophecy was about to be fulfilled could have led to the resolution to send money at once to the poor Judeans." [25] Could there be a hint of this in Paul's choice of the word *spoudázo* (literally, to make haste or speed), in his reference to remembering the poor (Gal. 2:10)? Whoever has foreknowledge of a major commodity shortage is tempted to hoard before prices rise further. It is not known whether the Jerusalem community used the Antiochene gift to make a large grain purchase immediately. But it would have been potentially disastrous for the Antiochenes to delay in sending help as soon as the fulfillment of divine warning was at hand. Accordingly, their help must have preceded the receipt of the relief for which Helena was responsible when she found starvation in the center of her new religion. The Christians in Jerusalem were thus better prepared for the famine than the Jews. Since it took some time for Paul's churches later to raise a fund for "the saints," we need not imagine a hastily collected fund. It is possible that Agabus prophesied before the reign of Claudius, as the famine "took place in the days of Claudius" (Acts 11:28). The expectation of famines in many places may have been occasioned by Caligula's attempt in A.D. 40 to set up his statue in Jerusalem's temple or by the famine in Rome in 41. Luke, by placing the account of the persecution of certain church leaders between the arrival and departure of Barnabas and Paul, evidently intended to describe the setting of their visit. Since Paul himself dated his second visit in 44, it would be precarious to date the famine visit three or four years later. Had the Antiochenes waited that long, there might have been no church left at Jerusalem to receive the aid when it was sent!

According to Acts 12:1-3, after the receipt of relief, Herod "killed James the brother of John with the sword; and when he saw that it pleased the Jews, he proceeded to arrest Peter also." A well-founded tradition has John suffering the same fate as his brother. [26] It is understandable that a tyrant like

Herod would on occasion seek to please the mob and to exploit public disapproval of certain Christian leaders. If he was concerned enough about Christians to persecute them, he must have been keeping them under close surveillance. Evidently his spies and informers had recently come upon some condemning information; scandalous rumors about certain leaders of the sect might circulate publicly and arouse enmity. But what occasioned this outburst of anti-Christian sentiment? Obviously the famine did.

Famines were one of the signs of the End commonly mentioned by apocalyptic writers and preachers. They appear as such a sign in the apocalyptic discourse attributed to Jesus. The sons of Zebedee were essentially apocalyptic in their outlook. [27] With the fulfillment of the prophecy of famine, their eschatological enthusiasm may have boiled over. They easily could be offensive to some of the Jews who did not believe and to Herod they would be a menace as he sought to keep public order at the time Jerusalem was teeming with visitors. The presence of such a multitude could only have forced food prices up further. But Jerusalem Christians, by virtue of "tainted money" received from uncircumcised Gentile converts, were relatively secure. Famines readily arouse men's passions to seek a scapegoat. The Christians at this time must have been influenced by what Jesus said in the Nazareth synagogue, words which were remembered by his brothers, at least: "There came a great famine over all the land; and Elijah was sent to none of them but only to Zarephath, in the land of Sidon . . ." (Luke 4:25-26). Could Peter, John, and James have considered the famine as a sign that the gospel should be preached to the Gentiles?

Be that as it may, Paul and Barnabas at this time did receive the right hand of fellowship from Peter, James, and John in order to go to the Gentiles, on the sole condition that they (continue to) remember the poor of Jerusalem (Gal. 2:9-10). The spies, who exposed the fact that Titus was uncircumcised (Gal. 2:3-4), could misconstrue the Gentiles' intentions and lay the groundwork for stimulating public outcry against the church. Only the circulation of ugly rumors about certain Christian leaders could account for public approval of Herod's treatment of its leaders. It would have been easy to start a report that while law-abiding Jews went hungry, Jerusalem

Christians feasted from the "sale" to the Gentiles of the exemption from circumcision. That is, Paul and Barnabas were, because of the money they brought, being authorized to continue their virtually unconditional mission to the heathen. The Jerusalem community had accepted a "bribe" from the uncircumcised for the privilege of communion! By this lowering of standards, the church had broken with exclusive Judaism as the Hellenists had earlier. Since the Hellenists had been expelled from the Holy City and their leader, Stephen, had been stoned, why shouldn't the Jerusalem church suffer for officially renewing or cementing communion with a Gentile-infested church at Antioch founded by these same Hellenists and led by the renegade Paul?

John suffered both as an unruly apocalyptic preacher and as one of those who gave the right hand of fellowship to Barnabas and Paul. For the latter offense Peter also was responsible. Moreover, was not Peter accountable for the Gentile mission because he defended his behavior in the conversion of the centurion Cornelius (Acts 10:1–11:18)? The Cornelius affair had prepared the way for the favorable reception of Paul and Barnabas in Jerusalem. James, the Lord's brother, was less suspect because of his greater reluctance in permitting Gentile freedom. Actually, if the Western reading of Galatians 2:9 ("Peter and James and John") is correct, it implies that it rather was James, the son of Zebedee, who was involved. The Alexandrian reading ("James and Peter and John") would then be a correction in light of Acts 15:13-22.

THE JERUSALEM COUNCIL

The identification of the settings of Acts 11:27–12:25 and Galatians 2:1-10 has the merit of clarifying the cause of Herod's persecution, of explaining why Peter, James, and John were all still alive and active in Jerusalem (i.e., before the dispersion of the Twelve), and of avoiding the problem of explaining Luke's interpolation of a narrative of Herod's persecution of the church and his death. On the other hand, several unresolved difficulties beset attempts to equate the accounts of Acts 15 and Galatians 2:1-10. [28] The Council of Acts 15 had nothing to do with the approval of Paul's apostolic mission. Rather,

he then came to Jerusalem, not moved by revelation and eagerness to remember the poor as in Galatians 2:2 and 10, but as
an irate apostle to the Gentiles with the right to present his
case (Acts 15:2-3, 12-13) along with Barnabas and Peter. The
influence of the Holy Spirit on the movements of Paul, which
Luke points out elsewhere in Acts, is replaced in 15:2 by a
resolution of the church at Antioch in response to dissension.
Whereas, according to Galatians 2:2 (cf. 6, 9), Paul lays his case
privately before the leading authorities, Acts 15:2, 4, 6, and 12
have Paul and Barnabas publicly address the apostles, elders,
and multitude concerning the great success of the Gentile mission. Moreover, Paul insisted that the Jerusalem leaders imposed
on him no additional restrictions, obligations, or conditions
concerning the propagation of his gospel among the Gentiles
(emoi gàr . . . oudèn prosanéthento) (2:6; cf. 10), but Acts 15
narrates how new food restrictions were imposed. It would be
dangerous for Paul to try to mislead his readers concerning
apostolic regulations.

The problem begins to untangle when we recognize that
Galatians 2 relates the sanctioning of the Gentile mission, whereas the decision in Acts 15 shows how Hebrew and Gentile believers resolved the later problem of table fellowship. The decisions
recorded in Galatians 2 are thus further removed from a final
settlement than those described in Acts 15. The latter agreement was more of a triumph for Paul than the former. The
attempt to compel Titus to be circumcised is not consistent with
the sentiments expressed at the "Council." Nevertheless, the
speeches in Acts 15:7-21, which set forth the general positions
taken by Peter and James, were equally relevant for the second
and third visit by Paul. Luke merely found it more convenient
and artistically appealing to mention them in this context,
where final action was taken on Jewish regulations for all the
faithful in Syria and Cilicia.

Acts 15:1-2 (cf. 24, 28) appears to be a parallel account of
Galatians 2:11-14. Common to both narratives is the presence
of Paul and Barnabas at Antioch when someone from the circumcision party came from Judea, where James led the church,
and troubled Gentiles by trying to compel them to live like
Jews. This caused dissension on the question of salvation by
works of the Law. When Paul said that "men came from

James" and that Peter feared "those of the circumcision," he implied that at this time James was accommodating to circumcised Jews *and* Christians. During Peter's absence from Jerusalem after his arrest and escape (Acts 12), the circumcision party in Jerusalem must have grown substantially in power or assertiveness as the full consequences of the Gentile mission became clear — more and more were joining the church who were voluntarily following less and less of the Law. Growing Judaizing intransigence and reaction were due also, in part, to fear of further persecution in Jerusalem by Jews and of hindrance to the evangelization of local Jews, if Gentile converts were allowed to neglect the Law. Peter feared, then, possible Jewish persecution, the loss of conversions, the "excommunication" of Antiochene Christians by those in Jerusalem, and/or a split in the Jerusalem church itself. The events mentioned in Galatians 2:11ff. followed the Jerusalem meeting in 44, and preceded the formal gathering described in Acts 15:6ff. Paul's rebuke of Peter makes sense only before this Acts 15 "Council," whose decisions were binding in Antioch (15:23), where the dispute arose. Peter and Paul could hardly quarrel about the practical issue of whether Hebrews could eat with Gentiles if it had already been effectively decided by the Acts 15 gathering. Rather, their personal disagreement on table fellowship had virtually forced the convening of the apostles. The issue was pressing because of the importance of the common meal in uniting the church. That this Council followed, and was intended to resolve, the conflict at Antioch is the opinion of a majority of investigators. It is highly unlikely that, following the decisions at Jerusalem, the envoys from Judea would have been able to create so much trouble at Antioch or that Peter would have vacillated. But if the conflict at Antioch occurred after the right hand of fellowship had been given to Paul, he could rebuke Peter for failing to perceive the consequences of Paul's gospel (Gal. 2:14a, 16ff.) and of his mission among the Gentiles (Gal. 2:11-12, 14b-15). Peter "stood condemned."

Peter stopped his practice of eating with Gentile believers out of fear of members of the scandalized circumcision "party" in Jerusalem after the arrival of their envoys (Gal. 2:12). Barnabas and the rest of the Hebrew believers then followed Peter in withdrawing from table fellowship. Paul bitterly complained that thereby Peter was seeking to Judaize and to compel the Gentiles to live as Jews (Gal. 2:14-15), i.e., with regard to food laws. In the words of William Sanday, the issue was "on what terms are they to mix together in common social and religious intercourse?" [29] For it was the Gentiles' ignorance or neglect of regulations on the choice, preparation, and serving of food which would most ostensibly justify the separation of all the Hebrews ("even Barnabas") from their fellow believers at common meals. There is much evidence [30] of the Jews' fear of consuming unclean foods received from the Gentiles. The scribes and Pharisees criticized Jesus for eating with sinners, and the circumcision party reproached Peter for eating with the uncircumcised, however reluctantly. The almost universally preferred text [31] of Acts 15:29 (cf. v. 20; 21:25, where the reader is reminded of the regulations) reads: "abstain from what has been sacrificed to idols and from blood and from what is strangled [32] and from unchastity." At least the first two requirements are beyond question. In either case, the chief barriers to general table fellowship were thereby removed. Hebrew believers could then resume eating with Gentiles once they no longer ate improperly slaughtered animals, i.e., those sacrificed to idols or containing remnants of blood and hence of life (as in the case of their strangulation), [33] and once fornicators were excluded from fellowship. Marc Philonenko finds evidence that originally the last prohibition was of pork (choireia) rather than porneia. [34] Even so, fornication was often associated (1 Cor. 10:7-8; Rev. 2:14) or identified (Exodus 3:15-16; Judges 8: 27, 33) with idolatry. Earlier the Christian's eating of forbidden types of animals was sanctioned by virtue of Peter's vision of a sheet and of various animals and by his audition of the revelation, "Rise, Peter, kill and eat. . . . What God has cleansed, you must not call common" (Acts 10:10-16; 11:5-10; cf. Mark 7:19). This vision had made it possible for him to eat initially with Gentiles. The fundamental problem was how to separate the clean from the unclean. [35] How could Hebrew believers preserve their purity when eating with Gentiles who had been polluted by fornication and the use of sacrificial foods from idols? Contamination received from demons was deemed contagious. Second Corinthians 6:14–7:1 illustrates well the Hebrew aversion for what was pagan, unclean, and unholy.

The Jerusalem Council, in the eyes of the church at Antioch, solved the problem of the terms of Gentile-Hebrew fellowship. In the eyes of Jerusalem it made clear the minimal conditions for Antiochene, Syrian, and Cilician Gentiles as church members. The Gentile believers were asked to cease offending the sensitivities of their Hebrew brethren. Paul did not allude to, or feel *bound* to enforce in his churches in Galatia, decisions or arrangements which were originally intended to be locally valid for "Gentiles in Antioch and Syria and Cilicia" (Acts 15:23). Actually, according to Acts 16:4 Paul had already delivered the Jerusalem decisions to his churches in Asia Minor on his second trip. Thus they were already known in most of Galatia as interpreted by Paul. The apostle doubtless was pleased with the restoration of Gentiles to table fellowship at Antioch, and he must have considered it a fair, practical, and convenient compromise; for in 1 Corinthians 8:1-13; 10:23-33; and Romans 14:13-23 he plainly taught that one should not offend and cause his weaker neighbor to stumble in the matter of food offered to idols. Although appeal to the Jerusalem decisions would have been relevant in dealing with this problem in pagan-Christian relations at Corinth, Paul was silent. Why? There was no sanctioning in Jerusalem of his teachings that "food will not commend us to God" (1 Cor. 8:8), that "all things are lawful" (1 Cor. 10:23), that "everything is indeed clean" (Rom. 14:20), and "why should my liberty be determined by another man's scruples?" (1 Cor. 10:29). Paul could, in writing Galatians, draw no useful argument from the fact that Gentiles were asked by the Council to conform to more of the Torah, even if these rules were considered by rabbis to belong to those given to Noah and hence to be binding on all men. [36] Paul saw the human weakness in those who could not eat food offered to idols, whereas the Council saw the weakness in the Gentiles who could not obey the whole Law. Nevertheless, Paul sought, on his own grounds, to preserve a partially kosher table at the common or private mixed Gentile-Hebrew suppers in his churches; the Galatian Judaizers found no cause for complaint on this matter. Hence the issue did not have to be discussed by Paul anew when writing to the Galatians. The issues raised by the Judaizers in Galatia were not really answered by the Jerusalem Council; its decisions were not relevant enough to be mentioned by Paul. If the "decrees" were intended to enumerate all the minimal laws for admitting Gentiles to church baptism and *membership* (an intention clearly in the mind of the Western editor of Acts 15), then Paul would have cited them. But the decisions pertain only to table *fellowship,* in response to a special historical situation. Thus the decree was not directed to the whole church, and reference is made to the great burden which unauthorized Jerusalemites had been seeking to impose.

Still another reason may be offered for Paul's silence on the visit at the time of the so-called Jerusalem Council. Since he was enumerating his Jerusalem visits in order to demonstrate that he was not subject to the apostles and elders there and that his teaching was not dependent upon theirs, he needed to mention only those visits which took place before he first preached his gospel to the Galatian readers. There is no indication that his Judaizing opponents in Galatia were accusing him of preaching a gospel different from that which he first brought. Hence it would have been superfluous in this controversy for Paul to mention a visit to Jerusalem occurring after his first trip to Galatia.

It is true that Acts 15:1-5 poses the issue under dispute at Antioch in terms of circumcision rather than of food laws. Several explanations can be offered. By the nature of their principles, the circumcision party wished the Gentile converts to keep kosher table laws as well, and they would have had more success in enforcing the latter than the former at Antioch. Male Gentile converts would be far more willing to eat kosher food than to be circumcised! There is no difficulty in supposing that the envoys raised the demand for circumcision and also objected to indiscriminate eating practices. Both matters were deemed to involve equally essential teachings of the Torah. The Jerusalem Council, sensing the adamant opposition in Antioch to compulsory circumcision as requisite for church membership or for salvation, wisely decided to drop the question after some discussion. The decisions make no reference to it. But in effect this was a decisive victory for Antiochene Gentiles; time was on their side. Indeed, because no decision was reached, Judaizers could raise the same war cry later in Galatia. The Council did not suppress the circumcision party; it was still free to try to convince individuals to accept Jewish practices voluntarily. Moreover, Luke referred to the more challenging problem of circumcision (15:1-5) rather than to the food question, which he treated as having been already resolved in principle (10: 10-16; 11:3-10, 17-18). His omission of reference to the dispute between Paul and Peter and his failure to mention the cause of Paul's disputes with Barnabas and Mark correspond to his emphasizing in 15:1-2 the matter on which Paul and Barnabas agreed (against the Judaizers), rather than the subject on which they split.

The Acts 15 Council provided a "modus vivendi," but left several problems unresolved; it thereby provided the basis for the later theological battles between Paul and the Judaizers. Although circumcision was not made a requirement of church membership for Gentiles, its potential value or desirability for them was left an open issue. The principles underlying the formal Jerusalem decisions were deliberately left vague, since the apostles were deadlocked on the theological question of freedom from the Law, i.e., how much of the Law is necessary for salvation? The decisions were sent to the Gentiles only (Acts 15:23), not to the Hebrew Christians (21:25). Paul apparently left the latter in his churches responsible for the personal decision of how free they were from the Law; he did not encourage them to change their manner of life (1 Cor. 7: 17-19). But when pressed, he taught that Hebrew believers should continue circumcision (Gal. 5:11). Peter and James, as far as we know, never approved of Paul's allowing converted Jews the right of evangelical freedom if they preferred to exercise it.

At the time of the Jerusalem Council (Acts 15) there were two parties encountered by Paul and Barnabas: (1) the circumcision party, which held that because belief in Jesus was only an added, supplementary law, the Gentiles for their salvation had to practice the whole Torah, including circumcision and a kosher table; and (2) the party of James and Peter teaching that, because God was now bringing Gentiles to acceptance of the gospel, they need to keep only the bare minimum of the Law requisite for religious and table fellowship with Hebrew Christians. The Lord would judge whether the individual Gentile had followed enough of the Law to be saved. The second party triumphed, but it was, after all, only a party of mediation. The theological principles of Paul and Barnabas concerning a new covenant (wherein faith was a substituted path to salvation) were not endorsed by the mediating party. Although Paul might be pleased with the practical modus vivendi, its assumptions were contrary to Pauline theology and really lent themselves to Judaizing interpretations. One could even say that at the Council, the Judaizers triumphed in regard to theological principles, while Paul won with respect to the practical problem at hand. A party strong enough to gain James's sanction for a mission to Antioch could not be defeated without an artful compromise. James's relations with the various Judaizers is an insufficiently studied subject, however.

The letter to Antioch does not even say that legal obedience is not *useful* for Gentiles' salvation. Rather, exemption is simply a concession so as not to trouble the Gentiles (Acts 15:19) with a greater burden (15:28). They are presented with only a bare *minimum* list of requirements for "doing well" in regard to foods (15:29). It is not surprising that the Judaizers interpreted the decisions to mean that it may not be necessary for the weak to practice the whole Law, including circumcision; but so much the *better* if those who are able do so. They claimed that there is a superior and surer way to salvation for those who trouble themselves to bear the burden of the Torah; they do *best* and not merely "do well." In fact, for "athletes" aspiring to perfection, it is necessary that they *prove* their ardor for their new religion. The issue between Paul and proponents of this Judaizing interpretation now became: Are circumcision and legal obedience meritorious and profitable for the "strong" who voluntarily bear the full burden? The speech attributed to James and the letter to Antioch lent themselves more to the Judaizing interpretation of the gospel than to the Pauline view. For this very reason Paul did not appeal to these statements when writing to the Galatians; these decisions were for Paul theologically worthless, more of an impediment than an aid to his case. Furthermore, his evangelical principles came from God, not from the human decisions of the "pillars" in Jerusalem. He mentioned his first two Jerusalem visits in order to demonstrate his independence. If he had acknowledged the full authority of those gathered to settle the earlier dispute at Antioch, he would have undermined his own authority; he would have granted something to his opponents' claim that he was a subordinate whose teachings and labors were subject to the approval of the apostles and elders in Jerusalem, who, allegedly, had delegated certain powers to him.

The question of circumcision was bound to come up on each of Paul's trips to Jerusalem following the first one. The terms under which Gentile converts would be received into the church was an unavoidable question for discussion as long as a significant body of Judaizers was influential. The case of Titus (Gal. 2:3-5) illustrates the tensions; but the textual uncertainty concerning *ois oudè,* "to whom not," (2:5) leaves unresolved the problem of whether Titus was circumcised or not. [37] The Western text (D, Irenaeaus, Tertullian, Victorinus, Pelagius, Jerome, old Latin version) which omits the two words provides earlier witnesses than the bulk of manuscripts which retain the words. Moreover, the otherwise inexplicable omission of the pronoun, *ois,* by other "Western" witnesses (Marcion, Ephraem, Ambrosiater, Syrᵖ) seems to be due to Marcion's adding *oudè* to the text he used. The earliest textual evidence thus indicates that Titus was circumcised. It is easier to understand the addition of the two words than their deletion, because from Marcion down to modern times investigators have been unable to believe that Titus actually submitted to circumcision as a momentary, gracious concession. In other words, the origin and propagation of the reading to the effect that Titus was not circumcised can be explained from the belief that Paul *should* not have yielded. Accordingly, Galatians 2:5 was altered to conform to a false deduction from 2:3, according to which Titus was not *compelled* to be circumcised. But what second century scribe would have sufficiently empathized with Paul and Titus in their dilemma of being confronted by the Christian Pharisees? Paul's position was weak and vulnerable. A circumcised Titus would be more acceptable to Hebrews and less embarrassing to Paul; the same considerations prompted the circumcision of Timothy (Acts 16:1-3). Because the latter's mother was Jewish and because Paul had more authority in Galatia than in Jerusalem, he did not have to be pressured into circumcising Timothy. In 1 Corinthians 9:20 he admits: "To the Jews I became as a Jew, in order to win Jews. . . ." In relating what befell Titus, Paul is on the defensive; his opponents were using the event in behalf of their own argument that he had submitted at Jerusalem to the apostolic authority. Paul's ambiguous language suggests that he was having difficulty explaining what happened. He does make it clear, however, that they did not yield in a matter of compulsion, as if to set a precedent for other Gentile converts. Nothing was added to the conditions for his mission (Gal. 2:6) ; he did not have to sacrifice the truth of his gospel (2:5). If an analogy is permissible, the circumcision of Titus was a suggestion which was voluntarily accepted, similar to James's exhortation that Paul associate himself with the seven-day vow of four men when he last brought relief to Jerusalem (Acts 21:20-27). Just as James's plan was prompted by the report that Paul was causing Jews to forsake circumcision (Acts 21:21), so the spying of the "false brethren," who spread the report that Paul's converts were uncircumcised, led to Paul's acceptance of the practical and temporary expedient of Titus's circumcision. His submission was personal and voluntary, and it made possible the continuation of the Gentile mission and the preaching of the Pauline gospel. Paul understood the outcome of this visit to Jerusalem to be that his authority, mission, and gospel were recognized by Peter, James, and John, and that his converts were freed from whatever Jewish practices they were not already following. But to many in the Jerusalem church it meant that Paul would not lead the Jews to give up circumcising their children (Acts 20:20-21) and that they would permit, if not encourage, his Gentile converts to undergo voluntary circumcision as their loyalty to the Torah grew. The case of Titus was subject to differing interpretations; hence Paul's opponents in Galatia considered it a precedent and argued from it at variance from Paul. There was at this time no formal definition of the comprehensiveness and degree of obligation of Gentile obedience to the Law. An informal accord (Gal. 2:6-10) was reached, but the underlying issues were left unresolved. Only the pressure of coming events and the development of Paul's theology revealed how little had been settled at this time. In Galatians 2 Paul was not so bold as to say that his converts' non-circumcision won the approval of the Jerusalem community. Rather, the tolerance and patience generally shown at Jerusalem were later regretted by the Judaizers. Few Gentile converts at Antioch followed Titus's example of voluntary submission to the knife. So many in Jerusalem later became alarmed that a protesting delegation was sent northward by the Judaizers (Acts 15:1-2; Gal. 2:12-13). In their ardor for the Law they came into theological conflict with Paul and Barnabas concerning the role of legal obedience as a condition of salvation. This sharp conflict at Antioch would have been impossible if there earlier had been a definitive decision in Jerusalem on Gentile circumcision while Titus was present. His momentary submission there had won enduring concessions to Paul's cause. That Paul had, in the opinion of Jerusalem Christians, allowed too much freedom from the Law is implied in his reception on the last trip to the Holy City. He is reminded of the decisions of the Council described in Acts 15 and is asked to bear witness to his acknowledgment that Hebrew converts were to remain loyal to the Law.

A logical sequence can be found in the suggested order of events. Peter, John, and James "perceived the grace that was given to" Paul by the Spirit that he "should go to the Gentiles" (Gal. 2:9). He had laid before them privately the gospel which he preached before the Gentiles (Gal. 2:2, 7). Although to report so might have helped his case in the face of the Galatian rebellion, Paul nowhere indicates that he had explained his teachings to the Jerusalem church as a whole or that his mission and preaching had received the general blessing of the community. Paul realized that the issue was too explosive to be faced publicly; he could not anticipate a favorable response. Thus he consulted only with the "pillars" and those "who were of repute" (2:6, 9). Because it was not their official status which was significant to him (2:6), Paul must have sought them out because they were thought to be perceptive. Could Paul have been so selective and secretive if the issues described in Acts 15 were already matters of public knowledge? Or, if his teachings were well known, would it have been necessary for the "false brothers" to put him and Titus to the test publicly? Because the Judaizing wing of the church would not have approved his gospel and mission, Paul was contented with a private agreement with the perceptive leaders. Would he have brought the uncircumcised Titus with him if the Judaizers had already been opposing him in Jerusalem on well-known issues? The secrecy of the agreement among the chief apostles was such that Paul's opponents in Galatia were misconstruing it and Paul had to explain what really occurred.

It was important for Barnabas and Paul to get tentative approval of the Gentile mission and Paul's gospel because their work was becoming more widespread; i.e., as Paul expressed it, "to make sure that what I had done and proposed doing was acceptable to them" (2:2, Phillips). When the "pillars" gave their assent, the way was cleared for a journey into Asia Minor. Thus, concerning the apostles to the Gentiles (Gal. 2:7-9), "the Holy Spirit said, 'Set apart for me Barnabas and Saul for the work to which I have called them'" (Acts 13:2). The very success of this mission was alarming to the Pharisaic believers in Jerusalem; the prospect of Gentile converts outnumbering the Hebrew Christians in the Diaspora created acute problems. Back in the Holy City James must have had a rebellion at hand when the Judaizers read the signs of the times. Peter and possibly James, who had been responsible for permitting a Gentile mission without the requirement of Jewish rites and a kosher table, were responsive to the feelings of those in Jerusalem who had not been a party to the right hand of fellowship privately given to Barnabas and Paul. After they returned from their first missionary journey and after Peter came to Antioch, there was no trouble at the church's common meals. But when "certain men came from James," then Peter withdrew from table fellowship (Gal. 2:12ff.). Jerusalem had learned that Gentiles were no longer such a small minority in the churches of Paul and Barnabas that they could be allowed to eat together. Peter's coming to Antioch must precede the Jerusalem Council because, following that gathering, it was Judas Barsabbas and Silas who were sent to Antioch to report on the Council's decisions (Acts 15:22, 27). Why would they, rather than Peter himself, be chosen to accompany Paul and Barnabas back to Antioch if Peter were soon coming anyway? Soon afterward, Paul, Silas, and Barnabas set out on new journeys and delivered the Jerusalem decrees (15:36–16:4). How could an unresolved conflict between Paul and Peter be squeezed into this interval?

SUMMARY

The only two chronological points of reference for the events of Paul's early ministry are his conversion in 31 and his famine relief visit to Jerusalem in 44. If these dates are accepted, his first Jerusalem visit is to be dated in 33–34 and his arrival in Antioch in the winter of 42–43. But the dates of his first two "missionary journeys" and of the Jerusalem Council cannot be approximated without reference to some event datable subsequent to 44. Fortunately such a terminus is available, and we will consider it in the next chapter.

3
Paul's Middle Years

The dating of what is customarily called Paul's second missionary journey is to be determined from the inscription found at Delphi, according to which Gallio's one-year term as proconsul has been ascertained as beginning in the spring of 51 or 52.[1] Paul had been in Corinth for eighteen months before Gallio arrived and the Jews brought Paul before him. Paul's arrival during the closing months of 49 or 50 can be calculated both from this information and from the fact that upon arrival at Corinth, he met Aquila and Prisca, who had recently *(prosphátos)* been expelled from Rome (Acts 18:2). Orosius *(History* vii, 6.15), claiming Josephus as his source, dated the imperial expulsion of Jews in the ninth year of Claudius (41-54).[2] The apostle's visit at Corinth must serve as our point of departure for dating preceding events in his journey, as we work backward through his itinerary.

Paul would have to cross over from Troas to Philippi (Acts 16:8-12) after navigation became safe in the late winter.[3] Only vague chronological data are available concerning the apostle's initial visit to Europe. He spent "some days" (Acts 16:12) at Philippi before a demon-possessed girl began "many days" of trouble for him (Acts 16:18; cf. 1 Thess. 2:2). From Philippi, Paul went to Thessalonica where he remained for three weeks (Acts 17:2). At Beroea many from the synagogue "believed" after examining Scripture "daily" (Acts 17:10-12). His work in Macedonia was followed by a visit to Athens (17:15). While waiting at Athens, Paul disputed "every day" (17:17). Because

Paul's stay at Thessalonica was cut short by persecution (17: 5-10), it is natural to think of his stop at Philippi and perhaps at Beroea as being of longer duration.

Regrettably Luke gives no information about the length of Paul's stay in Asia Minor as he traveled from Antioch to Troas. However, it is not hazardous to say that to "visit the brethren in every city . . . and see how they are" (15:36) and to tell of the outcome of the recent Jerusalem Council (16:4) were less potentially time-consuming tasks than initial evangelization. These tasks could have been satisfactorily accomplished if Paul left Antioch in the spring of 49 or 50. The sailing season had already opened, since Paul had thought of proceeding first to Cyprus; but, following a quarrel, Barnabas and Mark went there instead (15:39-40).

To estimate the date of the Jerusalem Council and the "first missionary journey" of Paul with precision is impossible. Following their return to Antioch from Jerusalem in the spring of 44, Barnabas, Paul, and Mark may have been reluctant to undertake another long trip immediately. There is a hint of delay, if not of a prophetic rebuke for it, in their carrying out the work to which the Spirit had called them (Acts 12:25–13:3). The reference by Paul and Barnabas during their visit to Lystra in Lycaonia, to the living God who "did not leave himself without witness, for he did good and gave you from heaven rains and fruitful seasons, satisfying your hearts with food and gladness" (14:17), would be a timely one toward the end of the drought and famine under Claudius or if Lycaonia were less affected than Syria, Palestine, and Egypt. Most investigators think that the journey was spread out over parts of at least two years [4] or two sailing seasons (13:4, 13; 14:25-26). These could be 45, 46, or 47; the latter two years would allow a more even chronological distribution. The interval, "no little time," between their return to Antioch and the arrival of the Judean Judaizers (14:28–15:1) sounds longer than the "some time" (15:33) and "after some days" (15:36) between the subsequent "Council" and the "second missionary journey"; yet Luke or his source did not feel the need to be more specific. Some time was necessary for the Judean Judaizers to become aware of the success and implications of the Gentile mission in Asia Minor. Paul (Gal. 2:11-12) hints that Peter had not been very long in Antioch before the dispute arose, but nothing is said in this context about the journeys of either Peter or Paul. An estimated date of 48–49 for the related trouble at Antioch and the synod at Jerusalem would not go too far astray.

Paul's second journey in Asia Minor took him further afield, as we noted, to Corinth. After his appearance before Gallio, he tarried "many days" (Acts 18:18) before departing for Syria. It is rather unlikely that he would venture to cross the stormy Aegean before February (53 or possibly 52). Stopping off at Ephesus, he had time only for a brief visit to a synagogue; but he promised to return (18:19-21). His intention to celebrate the Passover in Jerusalem is clear enough (18:18, 21-22) from the Western and Antiochene reading, "I must by all means keep the approaching feast in Jerusalem. . . ." "He went up and greeted the church" (Acts 18:22; cf. 15:2-3; Luke 18:31; 19:28) before he went down to Antioch. If he were in Caesarea already, Paul would not "go up" to the church there; rather, this movement is parallel to his going "up" *(anabaino)* to Jerusalem from Caesarea in Acts 11:2; 21:12, 15; 24:11; and 25:1, 9. "The church" in Acts 12:1, 5; 13:1; and 15:22 seems to mean the church of Jerusalem. Travel from Jerusalem to Antioch was considered "downward" in 11:27 and 15:30. In going to Jerusalem, Paul would naturally land at Caesarea whereas in proceeding to Antioch, he would land at Seleucia (Acts 13:4). It may be that Paul gave to James a "report on missions" at the end of this second journey, just as he did at the end of the third (Acts 21:19) and probably the first (15:12). His haste in proceeding from Asia to Jerusalem in order to celebrate a holy day is paralleled in Acts 20:16. The Nazarite vow which led him to cut his hair (18:18) was redeemable in Jerusalem. After proceeding there from Caesarea, he returned to Antioch, [5] where he spent an indefinite period of "some time" (18:22-23). Thus, he could have departed for Ephesus in the late summer of 52 or 53 or the following spring. The later date is the more probable in light of better weather (cf. Acts 18:23; 19:1) and Paul's need for rest. Antioch was still the apostle's home base (Acts 11:25–15:41). Nothing even prohibits his passing as much as a year and one-half there; the interim between his first and second journeys was at least that long. Acts 18:21 does not indicate that Paul promised to return quickly to Ephesus. In any case, his absence from Ephesus could not be much less than a year, because Apollos had come and gone and a church had been gathered (18:24–19:1).

GALATIA

Did Paul visit and write to the churches of northern Galatia, which was conquered by the Celtic Galatians in the third century B.C.? Or was his contact limited to the inhabitants of the southern part of the more inclusive Roman province of Galatia, namely, Lycaonia, Pisidia, and eastern Phrygia?

Paul's own use of the word "Galatia" is significant. "The churches of Galatia" are mentioned in Galatians 1:2 as the recipients of the Epistle, and in 1 Corinthians 16:1 as potential donors to the "collection for the saints." Since we learn from Acts 20:4 that the representatives bringing their contribution were Gaius of Derbe [6] and Timothy, who had been commended to Paul by the brethren in Lystra and Iconium (Acts 16:1-2), "the churches of Galatia" include at least Iconium, Lystra, and Derbe. The recipients of the Letter to the Galatians were familiar with the obligation of Paul's converts to "remember the poor" of Jerusalem (Gal. 2:10). The omission of delegates from North Galatia (Acts 20:4) need not signify the lack of Christians in this area, but it does cast some doubt on Paul's establishment there of churches which were strong enough to send a contribution.

As a Roman citizen, Paul customarily named groups of churches geographically according to their location in Roman provinces, [7] namely, "the churches of Asia" (1 Cor. 16:19), "the churches of Macedonia" (2 Cor. 8:1; 11:9; Phil. 4:15; cf. Rom. 15:26; 1 Thess. 1:7-8; 4:10), and "Achaia" (1 Cor. 16:15; 11:10; 2 Cor. 9:2), and "the region of Syria and Cilicia" (Gal. 1:21; cf. Act 9:30; 11:25-26). Alexander Southern writes that Paul "even does violence to the Greek language by forcing the Latin names for 'Philippians' (Phil. 4:15) and Illyricum (Rom. 15:19) into Greek, and passes by the proper Greek in each case." [8] In 2 Corinthians 9:4 he uses the term "Macedonians" to embrace the mixed peoples of Philippi and Thessalonica. Such usages tend to confirm that Paul was thinking of the Roman province of Galatia (1 Cor. 16:1). The issue, then, is one of specifying which churches of the province were included, if any, besides the ones which he had evangelized on his "first journey." It is natural to suppose that Paul understood "Galatians" (Gal. 3:1) to be the inhabitants of Galatia who were members of its churches (1:2). Proponents of the view that he was addressing only the true Galatians in the north central part of the province point to Galatians 3:1: "O foolish Galatians! Who has bewitched you . . . ?" This charge of being unperceptive and unthinking, however, would not be unnatural and misdirected if applied also to the other groups living in the province. Why would Paul single out for censure the Celtic Galatians, among all of those speaking Greek? Should Paul have said, if he wished to be comprehensive: "O foolish Pisidians, Phrygians, Lycaonians, and Galatians"? Certainly these groups, who had been incorporated in the province since 25 B.C., thought of themselves as Galatians in the political sense, at least sufficiently to understand the reference. In his animated writing Paul was not concerned about niceties of old tribal pride! Nor was he diligent in avoiding offense to his readers. Only a minority of the inhabitants of North Galatia, even in the cities, were Hellenized Celtic Galatians.[9] If Paul were addressing most members of a city church in the south by their imperial designation, however, there need have been no misunderstanding. Southern Galatia, especially Pisidia, was Romanized. Pisidian Antioch was a Roman colony.[10] Paul's addressees were Greek-speaking, and thus were able to identify with the beneficial Greco-Roman civilization of the imperial province of Galatia.

The two references to "the Galatian region (chóra)" in Acts (16:6; 18:23) are less clear, and consequently of less value in determining the addressees of Galatians. Acts 18:23 poses fewer problems and thus should be a standard for interpreting 16:6. Paul met the requests that he stay longer in Ephesus by promising to return after he sailed on to Syria (18:20-21). This gave him some motivation to return as soon as conveniently possible. If he left in the spring from Antioch for Ephesus, he may have taken the upper (mountainous) parts of the country (19:1), bypassing cities of the Lycus Valley, in order to escape much of the approaching summer heat and in order to reach Ephesus the sooner. No traveling companion and fellow evangelist, except possibly Titus, (see pp. 114-116) apparently accompanied him. Luke described the apostle's activity in terms of ministering to old, rather than new, converts. The itinerary is straightforward and direct: Antioch, the Galatian country, Phrygia, the upper parts, Ephesus. There is no need to extend *tèn Galatikèn chóran*" beyond Lycaonia Galatica (as distinct from Lycaonia Antiochiana)[11] and possibly Phrygia Galatia. The one term is simple and clear enough in the context. For the sake of variety Luke may have avoided repetition of *tèn Phrygían kaì Galatikèn chóran*" (16:6). *"Phrygían"* might refer to Phrygia Galatia and Phrygia Asiana (which together constituted Greater Phrygia) or to Asian Phrygia alone, through which Paul had to pass on the way to Ephesus. By passing through the Galatian country and Phrygia (*kathexes*, consecutively) for the purpose of strengthening all the disciples there (18:23), he followed the imperial highway through Derbe, Lystra, Iconium, and Pisidian Antioch. Apparently no known churches of the area were excluded from his itinerary. No parallel activity of any kind is associated with his passing through the upper country, where presumably he had no disciples. Thus in Colossians 2:1 Paul could write that the Colossians and Laodiceans still had not seen his face in the flesh; he bypassed the valley area where those cities were located. According to the Western text of 19:1, "When Paul wished according to his own counsel to go to Jerusalem,[12] the Spirit ordered him to return to Asia." This implies returning to Ephesus rather than to Jerusalem directly from Phrygia, whose easternmost city was regarded as either Antioch[13] or Iconium.[14] On the previous trip, because the Spirit had forbidden Paul "to speak the word in Asia," he had to detour from "the Phrygian and Galatian country" northward toward Bithynia near the border of Mysia (Acts 16:6). William Ramsay[15] argued forcefully that *"tén Phrygían kaì Galatikèn chóran"* refers to a single district *(chóra)*, the part of Phrygia belonging to the province of Galatia. If the *Phrygían* of 16:6 is an adjective, as is indicated by the use of the single article, *tén,* and the conjunction, *kaì,* then the reversal of the order in 18:23 is intelligible. As both "Phrygian" and "Galatian" are adjectival, no movement is implied and the sequence of terms is insignificant. In 18:23 "the Galatian country" would mean the area added to Galatia proper in the composition of the Roman province. However, it may be asked why, in Luke's usage, Lystra and Derbe are located in Lycaonia (14:6) rather than in Galatia. If his intent were not stylistic variation, then perhaps he was thinking of the Lycaonians as a people with a distinctive language (Acts 14:11), as in the case of people from Phrygia (2:1). On the eastern borders of Phrygia the various tribes had their own courts and popular assemblies (Strabo, *Geography* 13, 4.12). To Theophilus (Acts 1:1) "Lycaonia" was a more meaningful and precise description than "cities of Galatia." Nevertheless, the Phrygians and Galatians in 16:6 and 18:23 were not distinguished from each other by language. [16] Rather, the district of 16:6 was Galatian politically and Phrygian by population. The Phrygian and Galatian country (16:6) is not distinguished from, but rather is partially parallel to: (*a*) "the cities" where the Jerusalem decrees were delivered (16:4), (*b*) the churches which grew in faith and number (16:5), and (*c*) Derbe, Lystra, and Iconium, where the brethren recommended Timothy to Paul (16:1-3). Because 16:4-5 describes activity appropriate for all the churches (Acts 15:36, 41) which had been established by Paul and Barnabas, it would be impossible to consider these local, already existing groups to be mutually exclusive. The non-Phrygian cities of Lystra and Derbe, though included in *"tèn Galatikèn chóran"* (18:23), were not referred to in the restrictive description, "Phrygian-Galatian" (16:6). After he went "through" Syria and Cilicia, Paul "came also" to Derbe and Lystra, cities of Lycaonia (15:41–16:1); then they "went through" (16:6) the Phrygian and Galatian country (Iconium and Pisidian Antioch). Because he was moved by the Holy Spirit not to preach in Asia, Paul had to turn northward after leaving Phrygia Galatia. Approaching Mysia, he had to pass through a portion of Asian Phrygia, including Nakoleia and Dorylaeum, [17] which could be described as *katà tèn Mysían*. The Bithynian cities of Nicea and Nicomedia were bypassed, due again to the message of the Spirit (16:6-7). No such Spirit-led shift from Derbe, Lystra, and Iconium to the Phrygian-Galatian territory is indicated. Iconium is mentioned in 16:2 and is implicit in 16:6. A clear transition would be appropriate if a long journey into North Galatia were being narrated. It would be unbecoming for Luke to mention casually Paul's initial journey through the Phrygian and Galatian country without a word describing the apostle's activity and reason for being in this mission territory. Certainly Luke's mention of the Galatian country and Phrygia in 18:23 does not encourage one to interpret 16:6 as a reference to a separate and new area.

One of the major difficulties in the North Galatian hypothesis is the omission of any reference in Acts 16 and 18 to the cities in the area which Paul supposedly visited, or to his preaching and founding of churches there. It is not credible that Luke, on the one hand, related where the Spirit told Paul *not* to go (16:6-7) while in the area, and, on the other hand, Luke was so hasty in getting Paul to Europe or so lacked writing space that he took no note of the length and breadth of Paul's fresh area of Spirit-directed evangelization (cf. 16:9; 19:1 Western). If Luke did know of the gathering of disciples in the North by Paul, he did not deem it significant enough to mention it. Such an estimate would hardly be compatible with the importance of events in the churches of Galatia which were addressed by Paul. The silence of the second century *Acts of Paul* concerning the apostle's supposedly extensive work in the North is just as telling. If the author, an elder in Asia Minor (Tertullian, *On Baptism,* 17), showed no knowledge of, or interest in, Paul's hypothetical work to the North, the existence or extent of such work is all the more doubtful.

Because Paul is known to have been active in the southern part of the Roman province of Galatia, this area has the greater claim of being the one revisited by Paul (Acts 15:36) and addressed in his Epistle. A judgment in its favor requires far fewer unverified assumptions. The North Galatian hypothesis is possible, but hardly necessary. The burden of proof rests upon the proponents of the North Galatian hypothesis; but their case is undermined by the lack of reasons for excluding South Galatia. If Paul had passed through much of this southern area before writing Galatians, why must we postulate a detour to the North?

Nevertheless, it is possible that "on his second missionary journey Paul passed through the western edge of old Galatia, there finding or making a few disciples but founding no churches." [18] Such was the sound opinion of Ernest Burton. Luke may have considered these disciples too inconsequential to mention, or he may have lacked information about them if these believers did not grow in numbers or in "the faith." That Paul on his second journey may have encountered and strengthened a few believers in or near Pessinus is indicated because "the word of the Lord spread throughout all the region" of Pisidian Antioch (Acts 13:14, 49). Pessinus is less than one hundred miles to the north of Antioch. Later, while Paul was teaching at the hall of Tyrannus, Luke relates (Acts 19:10): "all the residents of Asia heard the word of the Lord." Colossae, Laodicea, and Hierapolis in Phrygia received the gospel, not from Paul, but from Epaphras (Col. 1:7; 4:13) on Paul's behalf. Thus, if Luke did intend to give any information about the evangelization of inhabitants of North Galatia, we might infer that Paul's converts were the first to tell them of Christ. Possibly this happened early enough for Paul to find, or at least learn of, believers on his third trip through Asia Minor. Yet, even if he did visit them in Pessinus and possibly Nakoleia at this time, it does not follow that he wrote to them. From Pisidian Antioch the Word may have spread westward into Phrygia by the time of Paul's third journey through there, for in Acts 18:23 it is related that he passed through, "strengthening all the disciples." This more individual designation, which differs from the strengthening of "churches" in 14:22-23; 15:41; and 16:5, suggests that he found some unorganized and possibly unbaptized believers. Yet this clue, too, offers no basis for holding that Paul wrote to the Celtic Galatians.

The North Galatian hypothesis encounters several problems in the exegesis of Paul's Letter to the Galatians. The readers are expected to be surprised that "even Barnabas" was carried away by deception at Antioch (Gal. 2:13). His status as co-worker with Paul is emphasized (Gal. 2:1, 9-10). The South Galatians were well acquainted with Barnabas from his first tour with Paul (Acts 13:14–14:24). When Paul wrote that the readers had received him "as an angel of God, as Christ Jesus" (Gal. 4:14; cf. 1:8), he may have been alluding in part to the acclamation Paul and Barnabas received at Lystra: "The gods have come down to us in the likeness of men!" (Acts 14:11). Secondly, Paul gives no evidence of addressing a mixture of older and newer churches. The readers were assumed to be uniform in their conversion experience and spiritual development in response to Paul's difficult preaching (Gal. 3:1-5; 4:13-16). They did not come to believe through the natural spread of the new religion from neighboring churches. Thirdly, Paul had visited his

"churches of Galatia" on at least two separate occasions: "I
preached the gospel to you *tò próteron* (originally, the first
time) " (4:13). Between the initial visit (4:13-14) and the time
of writing, he had been in contact with the readers (4:16, 20).
His bodily infirmity was annoying to his listeners, not habitually
or whenever he visited Galatia, but in the beginning, on the
occasion of his first visit to Galatia. One with such a physical
illness was more apt to traverse South Galatia than the rugged
North. A second visit may be deduced also from 1:9 ("As we
have said before, so now I say again"), 5:3 ("I testify again"),
and 4:16 ("Have I then become your enemy . . . ?"). That he
was on intimate terms with his readers is apparent from 4:19-
20. But if Paul had found Christians in North Galatia, he had
seen them only on the second journey through Asia Minor and
they had not first heard of Christ through his preaching.
Fourthly, Paul laments that his readers were so *tachéos* deserting
Him who had called them and turning to a different gospel
(1:6). This word could mean "quickly, hastily, precipitately"
(cf. Luke 14:21; 16:6; John 11:31; 2 Thess. 2:2; 1 Tim. 5:22)
in receptive response to "some who trouble you and want to
pervert the gospel of Christ" (Gal. 1:7) ; or it may imply "soon,
shortly" (1 Cor. 4:19; Phil. 2:19, 24; 2 Tim. 4:9), i.e., since he
warned them, "If any one is preaching to you a gospel contrary
to that which you received, let him be accursed" (Gal. 1:9). Or,
better yet, in light of the context, it can mean both "suddenly
and soon." Paul did not think his churches were so susceptible
to a false gospel. If Paul had recently preached to them the
true gospel and cautioned against any other, this Galatian visit
must have been made no more than one or two years earlier.
But a possible visit to Pessinus (North Galatia) in 49 or 50 was
several years before the penning of the Epistle.

THE DATE OF GALATIANS

How is the Letter to the Galatians to be dated?[19] Obviously
it dates after the dispute between Paul and Peter at Antioch
(Gal. 2:11 ff.) in 48 or 49 and after at least two visits to the
Galatian churches. The second visit in 49 or 50 was followed
by a third in 53 or 54. That the latter was already a matter of
history could be deduced from other considerations. When Paul's

opponents drew false conclusions about his preaching of circumcision (Gal. 5:11), the reference may well have been to the apostle's circumcision of Timothy on the second journey (Acts 16:3; cf. Gal. 2:3-5). Although Paul expresses the wish to be present with the Galatians in their crisis (4:20), he makes no promise about a return visit for personal intervention. This is curious in light of his method of directly confronting troublemakers in other situations (2 Cor. 10:2; 12:14). There is no hint in the Letter to the Galatians that he is imprisoned, and even imprisonment did not dispel Paul's hopes for visiting Philippi (Phil. 1:25-26; 2:24) and the Lycus Valley (Philem. 22). Thus Rome and Caesarea, where he was in prison, can be eliminated as places of writing. So may Antioch, since it was from here that he started off on each of his three journeys through Asia Minor. Barnabas, who was with Paul until their second journey (Acts 11:25–15:41), was unnamed in the greetings of Galatians 1:1-2. When writing to the Galatians, Paul had already completed his first two trips. The third was pending during his stay in Antioch in the winter of 53–54 (52–53?). He would hardly write then, omitting reference to his plans and projected arrival (cf. Rom. 15:22 ff.; 1 Cor. 16:5-9; 2 Cor. 12:14; 13:1; Phil. 2:24; Philem. 22). Therefore, by elimination, the Epistle must have been written sometime during his first stay at Corinth or else between his return to Ephesus and his final trip to Jerusalem. He would scarcely write during that trip itself, however, and omit all reference to the collection (except for Gal. 2:10) and the presence of Gaius and Timothy, the Galatian representatives (Acts 20:4). The reference to "all the brethren with" Paul (Gal. 1:2) suggests a large group of believers little known personally to the readers. Since Paul was not surrounded by fellow workers while he was traveling (apart from the last Jerusalem trip), one naturally thinks of his being established in a larger church at the time of writing. His involvement in more important work in Corinth or Ephesus (e.g., teaching in the hall of Tyrannus: Acts 19:9) sufficiently accounts for his reluctance to return to Galatia so soon. The dating of Galatians in Paul's Ephesian period gains confirmation from the readers' acquaintance with Titus,[20] a Gentile (Gal. 2:3) convert of the apostle (Tit. 1:4) who had been a delegate from Antioch to Jerusalem (Gal. 2:1). His appearance by Paul's side when he was dealing with Corinthian problems suggests that he accompanied Paul from Antioch to Ephesus on his third journey through Galatia. Another method of dating Galatians is to ascertain which other Pauline Epistles bear the greatest resemblance to it in situation and thought. The earlier, eschatologically oriented First and Second Thessalonians are far removed from the Galatian controversy. Raymond T. Stamm has succinctly summarized the abundant similarities of Galatians to the Corinthian correspondence:

> The points of comparison are (*a*) the disparagement of Paul by his enemies; (*b*) obsession with the theme of strength in weakness; (*c*) the defense of the gospel; (*d*) the attitude toward the law; (*e*) the remedy for factions; and (*f*) the need to balance freedom with responsibility.[21]

Likenesses of the Letter to the Galatians to the Letter to the Romans are often noted by commentators; that Romans offers a more fully developed and reasoned treatment of grace, freedom, and the law is generally admitted. The priority of Galatians to First Corinthians (16:1-6) and Second Corinthians (8:4; chap. 9; cf. Rom. 15:26)[22] may be indicated by references to the collection for the saints in Jerusalem. In 1 Corinthians 16:1 Paul prefaces his directions with the statement that he had already likewise charged the churches of Galatia. Some reference is to be expected in his letter to the Galatians, though not necessarily the original directions. In Galatians 2:10 he alludes to his obligation, as an apostle to the Gentiles, to remember the poor. Now, if this reference implies that the readers knew about the obligation,[23] it would be puzzling that no follow-up for a project already under way appears, as in 2 Corinthians 9. On the other hand, if Galatians 2:10 implies no knowledge of the collection on the part of the readers, then a relatively early date for the Epistle would be probable. It is possible, though, that when Paul first sent directions, his messengers reported back on the situation in Galatia which evoked Paul's response in the letter. In such a case the collecting itself would be placed in some doubt and Paul might wait until the danger passed before he pressed the delicate matter of fund-raising for Hebrew Christians of Jerusalem (cf. 2 Cor. 12:14-18). More likely, Paul himself had given directions to the Galatian churches on his last trip. In any case, the Epistle was written before the collection for the church in Jerusalem was well under way.

If Galatians 4:13 implies that Paul had visited the Galatians not long before, it would be increasingly untenable to date the Epistle after the first few months of 55. Moreover, Paul shows less knowledge of the background of his Judaizing opponents in Galatians (3:1; 5:8, 10) and less stereotyped condemnations of them (Rom. 16:18; 2 Cor. 11:13-15, 18; Phil. 3:2, 18-19) than he does in later warnings. A more precise date (fall or winter of 54) may be obtained from the fact that the Galatians had been misled into observing years (Gal. 4:10), i.e., the Sabbatical year which was scheduled to be celebrated in 54–55.[24] Trouble arose with the arrival, soon after Paul's departure, of the time-observant Judaizers. Paul wrote as soon as he learned of their limited success in convincing the Galatians of the necessity of circumcision (5:2-3; 6:12-13).

THE ASIAN MINISTRY

The dating of Galatians at this time accords well with Paul's stay at Ephesus from the late spring of 53 or 54 to Pentecost (1 Cor. 16:8), 56. In his reported farewell address to the Ephesian elders at Miletus, Paul emphasized his unceasing labors among them "for three years" (Acts 20:18, 31). During this period he spoke boldly in the synagogue for three months (19:8), lectured in the hall of Tyrannus daily "for two years" (19:9-10), and sent Timothy and Erastus to Macedonia while himself delaying a time in Asia (19:22). According to the ancient manner of reckoning, it is possible that the duration of Paul's Ephesian ministry was no more than two years. After the cessation of an uproar started by Demetrius, the silversmith, Paul departed for Macedonia (20:1). Arriving in Greece, he remained three months before leaving for Jerusalem (20:2-3). Possibly Paul evangelized parts of Asia intermittently during his Ephesian residence. But Acts 19:10 attributes the spread of the gospel to Paul's lectures in the hall of Tyrannus (19:9), and Polycarp, in his letter to the Philippians (chap. 10), admitted that his own church at nearby Smyrna lacked direct apostolic foundation. That no churches were early established between Ephesus and Troas may be deduced from the apostle's plan to visit (only) Corinth and Macedonia before going to Jerusalem (2 Cor. 1:16). By the time 1 Corinthians 16:19 was written, Paul could send greetings in behalf of "the churches of Asia."

CORINTHIAN CORRESPONDENCE

Paul's correspondence with the Corinthians gives valuable, though ambiguous, information concerning this period. The letter containing 1 Corinthians 16:8 and 19 was written from Ephesus. Even if one disputes the unity of the letter, there is no reason to doubt that all of its theoretical components were written at Ephesus. Access to Paul had been possible for the Corinthian Sosthenes (1 Cor. 1:1; cf. Acts 18:17), Chloe's people (1 Cor. 1:11), and Stephanas, Fortunatus, and Achaicus (1 Cor. 16:15-18; cf. 1:16); they had delivered to the apostle information concerning Corinthian church affairs (1:11; 5:1; 11:18).

Paul sent Timothy, who had been by his side, to the Corinthians (1 Cor. 4:17; 16:10). His apprehensions about the reception of Timothy (16:11) may have been justified, since his co-worker had returned to Paul as planned (1 Cor. 16:11) when 2 Corinthians 1:1 was written. In this passage he is associated with Paul just as Sosthenes had been in 1 Corinthians 1:1. Because the Corinthian letters make no further mention of Timothy's labors across the Aegean, it is natural to identify this mission with that mentioned in Acts 19:22 in the company of Erastus, who had connections with both Ephesus and Corinth (Rom. 16:23; 2 Tim. 4:20). Because the Corinthians were expected to receive their first (canonical) Epistle before Timothy arrived, it is likely that the letter was dispatched by sea and Timothy went overland through Macedonia. Timothy's arrival in Macedonia and Achaia (Acts 19:22) may be deduced from his role in preceding Paul in his journey to Macedonia and Achaia (19:21; 20:1-2) before going to Jerusalem. First Corinthians 16:1-11 perhaps also associates Timothy's trip with the collection. Accordingly, we might date First Corinthians between the time Paul planned the Jerusalem collection (16:1-4) and the time he left from Ephesus for Macedonia. There is no indication in First Corinthians that Paul had already visited Corinth twice; the verses in 2:1 and 3:1-2 imply a single visit.

In 1 Corinthians 4:18-21 Paul threatens to come "with a rod," rather than "with love in a spirit of gentleness," to deal with the arrogant talkers, if necessary. His plan to come soon *(tachéos)* is ostensibly to be equated with his intent to leave Ephesus for Macedonia and Corinth after celebrating Pentecost (1 Cor. 16:

5-8). This language suggests that he was writing a few months before leaving and perhaps that a visit to Corinth on the way to Macedonia was being considered even at this time. In 11:34 he promises to resolve remaining problems when he comes; evidently he did not expect to wait long before being able to give directions in person. However, in 2 Corinthians 1:15-16 Paul describes a different plan which he had failed to fulfill as promised: "I wanted to visit you on my way to Macedonia, and to come back to you from Macedonia and have you send me on my way to Judea." The readers are expected to know the background or purpose of this trip. Second Corinthians 8:4–9:15 represents an advanced stage in the collection, and 1 Corinthians 16:1-2 a very early stage. Likewise, according to 16:3-6, Paul has not even decided whether or not to accompany the bearers of the gift to Jerusalem; these plans give evidence of being earlier than those in 2 Corinthians 1:16, where his intention to proceed to Judea is expressed. When Paul did not carry out his new plan of visiting Corinth on the way to Macedonia from Ephesus, he reverted to the original one, and he proceeded from Ephesus directly to Troas, Macedonia, and Achaia (Acts 20:1-3; 2 Cor. 2:12-13), where he spent the winter (Acts 20:3; 1 Cor. 16:6).

The temporary change in plans was occasioned by Paul's second and "painful visit" at Corinth (2 Cor. 1:23; 2:1-5), during which someone painfully wronged him (2 Cor. 2:5-8; 7:12). He did not wish a quick recurrence of mutual pain; this he explained to be the reason for not keeping then his promise of a return visit. His next trip was to be his third to Corinth (2 Cor. 12:14, 20-21; 13:1-2, 10). After he wrote the severe letter, in which he *threatened* to come soon a third time to Corinth, memories of the painful second trip led him to decide definitely against returning so soon. Earlier, before the second trip, he had been happily anticipating any coming visit (1 Cor. 16:5-7; 2 Cor. 1:15-16); the alienation from the painful visit had not yet occurred. When Paul opened himself to the charge of fickleness or vacillation *(elaphria)* (2 Cor. 1:17), he had first decided to visit Corinth only at the end of his Macedonian journey; then he decided to go there first and made such a promise, but finally he reverted to his first plan. Evidently in the harsh letter after his painful visit Paul had not notified the Corinthians about *when* to expect him. Because Paul was uncertain, Titus, his messenger who bore the severe letter to the church (2 Cor. 7:5-12), before leaving apparently had been instructed by Paul to meet him subsequently at Troas or Macedonia (2 Cor. 2:12-13) if the apostle did not arrive at Corinth within a specified period of time. Paul did not accompany Titus to Corinth, but in Macedonia he learned of the response to his harsh letter. A stern letter thus took the place of the projected visit (13:10); the use of the aorists, *ekrina* and *egrapsa* (2 Cor. 2:1, 3), indicates that Paul decided not to go, but wrote instead at the same time. Even on his second visit itself he was threatening, but indefinite, about another trip (see 2 Cor. 13:2: "if I come again").

Concerning the harsh letter, Paul said: "I wrote [to you] as I did, so that when I came I might not be pained by those who should have made me rejoice. . . . I wrote you out of much affliction and anguish of heart and with many tears, not to cause you pain but to let you know the abundant love that I have for you" (2 Cor. 2:3, 4). "For this is why I wrote, that I might test you and know whether you are obedient in everything" (2 Cor. 2:9; cf. 7:12). "I made you sorry with my letter" (2 Cor. 7:8). Sending a letter could fulfill the same chastening purpose as another visit. Second Corinthians 7 indicates that Titus carried the harsh letter and was to report back to Paul on its effect on the Corinthians. In the context of referring to his stern letter, he expressed his relief: "God, who comforts the downcast, comforted us by the coming of Titus. . . . We rejoiced still more at the joy of Titus, because his mind had been set at rest by you all" (7:6, 13). Titus had brought news of the Corinthians' repentance. Romans 15:25-27 confirms the success, at least, of their collection for "the saints at Jerusalem." The bearer of this harsh epistle was one who was in the best position to inform Paul of its effect. It was Titus to whom the apostle looked expectantly for news. From 2 Corinthians 2:12-13 we learn: "When I came to Troas to preach the gospel of Christ, a door was opened for me in the Lord; but my mind could not rest because I did not find my brother Titus there. So I took leave of them and went on to Macedonia." When the two met there, Titus was coming from Corinth, and Paul from Troas and, presumably, Ephesus. By using the indefinite article, *eis tèn Troáda,* and by speaking of a door's opening there, Paul indicates that his local mission area was not limited to the port itself.

There was thus time for Titus to carry the painful letter to Corinth and then to bring a report back to Paul in Macedonia. After completing the mission, Titus returned to Corinth to complete the collection (2 Cor. 8:6, 10, 16-24). Prior to both of these journeys Titus had visited Corinth without burdening or taking advantage of the church there (2 Cor. 12:16-18). The defense of his handling of the Jerusalem relief collection is suggested by *"panourgos dolo humas elabon* [being crafty I took you with guile] . . . *epleonéktesa humas* [did I defraud you?]." Possibly Titus's role in regard to the collection was familiar to the readers because he had initiated "this gracious work" (2 Cor. 8:6, 10). It would be hazardous to identify his mission in 12:16-18 with that mentioned in 2:13 and 7:6, 13 because, in the judgment of Alfred Plummer, "St. Paul would not make so difficult a task as that of putting to an end a rebellion against his authority still more difficult by coupling with it a request for money." [25] In 2 Corinthians 2:18 Paul assumes that, unlike himself, Titus has been above suspicion with regard to the collection, presumably because he accepted no money from them. If Titus had been accused together with Paul, his name could not have been used so casually to defend the apostle's intentions. Second Corinthians 7:13-16 implies that Titus on his first visit to Corinth had not been there long enough, or at the right time, to understand why Paul boasted about the readers, in spite of their propensity to rebel.

Ever since Johann Semler in 1776 argued that 2 Corinthians 10:1-13:10 was a separate letter and Adolf Hausrath in 1870 developed the hypothesis, scholarly opinion has been sharply divided [26] on the identity of the "harsh epistle." Almost universally those who divide Second Corinthians at 10:1 identify the last four chapters with the severe letter, or a portion thereof. This view has been set forth most forcefully by Paul W. Schmiedel,[27] James H. Kennedy,[28] and Kirsopp Lake.[29] The first nine chapters picture the apostle's reconciliation with the Corinthians; in mild language he expresses his joy, comfort, and confidence in his readers' faith, knowledge, love, earnestness, loyalty, and repentance. On the other hand, in the last four chapters the apostle's relations with his readers appear to be as strained as ever, as he defends his authority against false apostles. His tone at times is indignant, sarcastic, threatening, and discouraged as he reproaches his readers for their short-comings. Such a loss of confidence in his beloved converts was sufficient motive to write to them "out of much affliction and anguish of heart and with many tears" to let them know his abundant love for them (2 Cor. 2:4). It would have been poor strategy for Paul to open Second Corinthians with a conciliatory approach and, following an unexpected transition (9:11–10:2), to terminate with self-righteous irritation and accusations. Moreover, in the first nine chapters, but not in the last four, "boasting" *(kauchasthai, kaúchesis, kaúchema)* is used in a favorable sense. How is it possible to maintain the unity of Second Corinthians in light of the abrupt change from optimism to pessimism? In the closing chapters there is no evidence for conjecturing that disturbing news had arrived after Paul had already written the opening chapters, or that Titus gave Paul the bad news only after the first nine chapters were penned, or that Paul was separately addressing different segments of the church,[30] or that a bad meal or sleep between writing sessions had occasioned the return of unpleasant memories. Rather, in three pairs of parallel passages (10:6 and 2:9; 13:2 and 1:23; 13:10 and 2:3), Paul uses a much more positive tone in the early chapters than in chapters 10 and 13. The use of the past tense in 1:23; 2:3 and 9, versus the present tense in 10:6; 13:2 and 10, likewise suggests that the latter chapters were actually written and sent before the opening chapters of the canonical Epistle.

Scholars arguing for the integrity of Second Corinthians generally conclude that the stern letter was totally lost or destroyed, perhaps because the Corinthian church was ashamed to publish the harshest apostolic criticisms of its own problems or its insulting members (cf. 2 Cor. 2:5-10). In reality the same motive could have led, with even more plausibility, to the non-copying of the severest and most personal parts of "the painful letter." Parts can be lost or neglected as readily as the whole; it is no easier to explain a total loss than a partial one. But the segment preserved as 2 Corinthians 10–13 was worth copying for its general "anti-heretical" value, as well as for its defense of Paul's authority. That the canonical second Epistle was edited before being published is a hypothesis [31] which squares well with the fact that Clement of Rome, when writing to Corinth, evidenced no knowledge of it, although he abundantly quoted

First Corinthians. Second Corinthians' relative slowness in circulating indicates that there was ample time for editorial work before it was "published" as a unit. No manuscript evidence of the original independence of chapters 10–13 is to be expected.

The rival apostles admitted that Paul's "letters are weighty and strong" (2 Cor. 10:10). This might imply more than one letter had already been written to the Corinthians. But these opponents may have been acquainted with the Letter to the Galatians, and the Corinthians remembered Paul's writing to the Thessalonians. Still there can be no doubt that Paul had written to Corinth even before the canonical First Corinthians was penned. For, in 1 Corinthians 5:9-11 he corrects a misunderstanding for his earlier warning against associating with "anyone who bears the name of brother if he is guilty of immorality or greed, or is an idolater, reviler, drunkard, or robber." While the message of 1 Corinthians 6:12-20 is to "shun immorality" (6:18) and that of 10:1-22 is "to shun the worship of idols" (10:14), to include these ethical passages in the early, lost letter is a dubious procedure. [32] As Paul explains its content, "I wrote to you in my letter not to associate with immoral men; not at all meaning the immoral of this world" (5:9). To shun immorality, to shun immoral brethren, and to shun the immoral of the world are quite distinct matters. However, the widely held hypothesis [33] that 2 Corinthians 6:14-7:1 is a portion of the lost letter is worthy of serious consideration. The preservation and editing of chapters 10–13 are analogous. Such a charge as "Do not be mismated with unbelievers" readily could have led to the Corinthians' misunderstanding (1 Cor. 5:10-12) of Paul's intended warnings. As S. M. Gilmour succinctly states concerning 6:14-7:1, "It differs in style and content from what precedes and follows it. And its categorical imperatives, its rhetorical questions, and its angry tenor are such as might have been characteristic of Paul's first lost letter." [34] The appeal, "Or what has a believer in common with an unbeliever" (6:15), could justify the Corinthians' interpretation, namely, the duty to dissociate from "the immoral of this world" (1 Cor. 5:10). A further reason for doubting the originality of the context of 2 Corinthians 6:14-7:1 is that "the passage has a self-contained, independent character, forming a unit intelligible in itself, like a short homily." [35]

A strong case has been made for the non-Pauline origin [36] of the passage. Six of its words are otherwise alien to the New Testament, and two more, which appear in Old Testament citations, are also not found in the New Testament. The expression "every defilement of body and spirit" (7:1) is not Pauline, and their cleansing is not effected by separation from unclean persons, according to the apostle (cf. Rom. 8:9–14; Gal. 2:20; Phil. 1:21-22). He was not opposed dogmatically in principle to living as a Gentile unbeliever (1 Cor. 9:21); under certain conditions it was permissible to be married to them (1 Cor. 7:12-14), eat their meats with them (1 Cor. 10:27-29), and admit them to church services (1 Cor. 14:22-25). "You would need to go out of the world" to avoid association with immoral outsiders (1 Cor. 5:9-10, 12). The sweeping intolerance of the commands *exélthate, aphorísthete,* and *me haptesthe* (2 Cor. 6:17) reflects a non-Pauline, monastic-priestly mentality. The passage's many affinities with Qumran material [37] has led Joachim Gnilka to describe it as a "Christian bit of teaching stemming from Essene tradition" [38] and as a composition of an unknown Christian rather than Paul. For Joseph A. Fitzmyer "the evidence seems to total up to the admission of a Christian reworking of an Essene paragraph which had been introduced into the Pauline letter." [39] Both scholars reject Karl G. Kuhn's pioneering suggestion that Paul quoted and Christianized an Essene text [40] for the question remains why he should have chosen this unsuitable passage to intrude in the context of 2 Corinthians 6:11-13 and 7:2. We would suggest that the passage was considered Pauline by the compiler of Second Corinthians and that it had been accepted and preserved as Paul's in the archives since being received or found by the Corinthian church. As letters were forged in Paul's name (2 Thess. 2:2; 3:17), it is possible that the section in question either was written in his name during the last two or three years of his life or was discovered later [41] as the purported lost first letter (1 Cor. 5:9). In either case the compiler of Second Corinthians may have considered it that first letter.

Between the writing of this first letter and that of the canonical First Corinthians at least a few months must have elapsed. Paul had learned of a misinterpretation of the first letter. The Corinthians had written asking questions concerning marriage, virgins, eating meat from idolatrous sacrifices, spiritual gifts, probably about the collection for Jerusalem, and a return visit by Apollos (16:12). Chloe's people had reported on the existence of party strife. The dating of our First Corinthians depends partially upon one's opinion of the chronological reliability of Acts 19. According to 19:21-22, Paul's Ephesian ministry was drawing to a close when he resolved "to pass through Macedonia and Achaia and go to Jerusalem" and when he sent ahead Timothy. This setting partially corresponds to that of 1 Corinthians 16. As Paul planned to depart soon after the coming of Pentecost (16:8), he may have hoped to have this letter delivered before the end of the sailing season in October, 55.[42] Some exegetes think that the allegory in 1 Corinthians 5:7-8 was written with an eye toward the coming Passover season. However, the keeping of the feast by the preponderantly Gentile readers is not literal and temporal, but spiritual and perpetual. Paul had already sent Timothy (1 Cor. 4:17) via Macedonia when he dispatched the letter. When Timothy returned via Corinth (16:11) and reported on the success of the intruding apostles, Paul paid a quick but painful emergency visit there, probably in March or April. Back in Ephesus again, he expressed his vexation through writing the letter which is partially preserved in 2 Corinthians 10–13. He threateningly reaffirmed his plan to pay another visit, now the third (12:14; 13:1). Although he spoke conditionally *(eàn eltho)* in 13:2, his departure from Ephesus was imminent *(hetoîmos ego elthein)*, possibly about the time of Pentecost (unless the riot had forced him to leave earlier). If it is fitting to integrate Acts 19 into the chronology at this point, the "wide door for effective work" which opened for Paul at Ephesus not long before he wrote First Corinthians (16:9) is identifiable with the fruits of demon exorcism (Acts 19:11-13). The silversmiths' riot, which Luke places just before Paul's departure, is perhaps alluded to in 2 Corinthians 1:8-10, though Acts 19:29-31 does not picture Paul as despairing of life as if under a sentence of death. The riot may well have occurred during the annual festival of Artemesia in April or May.[43]

No exact chronological information can be extracted from 2 Corinthians 8:10 or 9:2, where Paul refers to the Jerusalem collection as having begun a year ago. Not only could this be the Roman, Jewish religious, or Jewish civil year, but it is far from clear whether 1 Corinthians 16:1ff. represents Paul's first exhortation to take up a collection. Here he is more likely answering a question about his earlier request (cf. 1 Cor. 7:1, 25; 8:1; 12:1). The most natural conclusion is that about twelve months earlier Titus had initiated the collection (2 Cor. 8:6; 12:18). First Corinthians and 2 Corinthians 10–13 would then be datable less than a year before 2 Corinthians 1–9. There is a high probability that 2 Corinthians 1–9 was written from Macedonia (2 Cor. 2:13; 7:5-6; 8:1; 9:2-5) in the late summer of 56, for he spent three months in Achaia (cf. 1 Cor. 16:6) before leaving for Jerusalem via Philippi, where he passed the days of Unleavened Bread (Acts 20:1-6).

THE EPISTLE TO THE ROMANS

There is virtually unanimous agreement that Paul wrote Romans just before he went to Jerusalem. He states his situation and plans in Romans 1:8-15 and 15:16-32. He reports that Macedonia and Achaia have contributed to the collection (15:26).

In all probability chapter 16 also was written at Corinth soon before Paul departed for Jerusalem. Gaius, his host (v. 23) who sent greetings, can be identified with a convert he baptized at Corinth (1 Cor. 1:14). Erastus (v. 23) later "remained at Corinth" (2 Tim. 4:20). Phoebe was deaconess at the nearby port of Cenchreae (Rom. 16:1-2). Timothy, Sosipater, and Lucius (if he is to be equated with Luke) accompanied Paul when he left Corinth (Acts 20:4-5).

The available evidence supports a widely held opinion of scholars,[44] first suggested in 1829 by David Schulz, that most of this sixteenth chapter was addressed to Ephesians, perhaps as an appendix to another letter, rather than to the Romans. What city would be more likely than Ephesus to contain twenty-six acquaintances, including Paul's "beloved" Ampliatus, Stachys, Epaenetus (his first Asian convert: 16:5), and Persis; his "kinsmen and fellow prisoners" Andronicus and Junias; his "fellow worker" Urbanus; his "kinsman" Herodion and his own "mother"? Andronicus appears among the disciples at Ephesus in the Acts of John (chap. 31ff.). Aquila and Prisca are found in Ephesus before and after this writing (Acts 18:18, 26; 1 Cor. 16:19; 2 Tim. 4:19); they were well enough established to have a house church when Romans 16:5 was written, just as they had one in Ephesus some sixteen months earlier when First Corinthians was penned. Paul was more likely to commend Phoebe, who had helped him, to a church which he knew, than to one where he was a stranger. E. J. Goodspeed observed that as a woman she needed hospitality in one of the family circles.[45] How would Paul know that all of these friends were in Rome and who was in certain house-church groups (vv. 14-15)? But had he been in Ephesus less than a year before, he would have such information about Ephesus. How are we to understand: "all the churches of Christ greet you" (v. 16) and "all the churches of the Gentiles give thanks" (v. 4)? Most plausibly Paul is referring to the churches which he had visited since leaving Ephesus for Corinth via Macedonia (Acts 20:1-2; Rom. 15:19, 26); the churches of Asia had recently greeted the church of Corinth (1 Cor. 16:19). Above all, the tone of the warnings in vv. 17-20 is pastoral, intimate, hortatory, authoritative, polemical, and therefore appropriate for a church, such as the Ephesian, where Paul was familiar. The rest of Romans is irenic (1:7-13; 15:14-15), and he did not wish to "build on another man's foundation" (15:20; cf. 2 Cor. 10:15). Had he known of false teachers in Rome, there was ample opportunity in the first fifteen chapters to speak of the threat. Such a threat may have already existed at Ephesus (1 Cor. 16:8-9; Acts 20:29-30). The bitterness of Paul's outburst in Romans 16 presupposes specific opponents and existing troubles.[46] The readers of 16:17-20 were expected to understand which false teachings were to be avoided. The Ephesians would understand Paul's obscure derogatory characterizations, but the Romans would be partially baffled. The apostle ended no other epistle with a sudden attack on error. His attitude toward food questions in chapter 14 is altogether different from that in 16:18. Finally, if it were Paul's intent to emphasize his personal contacts in Rome, he would have made some early reference to its leaders (Col. 1:6-9; cf. Philem. 2).

It is apparent from the variant readings of Romans 1:7 and 15 that the Roman church was not, or at least was not considered, the only recipient of the Epistle. The words *"en Rôme"* were omitted in one or both verses by Origen,[47] Ambrosiaster, 1908, G and g. Whereas the reading *"en agápe Theou"* appears in G d, the mixed reading, "in Rome in the love of God," is witnessed to by Pelagius, Ambrosiaster, D, and the Vulgated

MSS. Amiatinus and Fuldensis. [48] Marcion could not have exercised the mention of Rome in order to turn it into a general epistle since the Marcionite Prologues call it, "to the Romans." Marcion did not even consider Ephesians to be a general letter; rather, he believed it was addressed to the Laodiceans. Moreover, Marcion was never criticized for suppressing the mention of Rome.

The preservation of chapters 15 and 16 [49] may have been due to the superior Alexandrian [50] Pauline corpus. At least the only ante-Nicene evidence of knowledge of these last two chapters is found in P[46] Origen and Clement of Alexandria. In the West there is no evidence that they were known to Marcion, Irenaeus, Tertullian, and Cyprian.[51] The chapter headings of such Latin codices as Amiatinus and Fuldensis [52] point to the existence of a Latin text ending with 14:23 and the doxology of 16:25-27. In three Vulgate manuscripts (17040 and 17043 of Munich; i-2/9 of Monza) the benediction intervenes between 14:23 and the closing chapters.[53] In MSS 17040 and 17043 the intrusive blessing takes the strange form, *"Gratia cum omnibus sanctis."* The simplest explanation of the origin of a blessing at this point is that its original absence was felt to be inappropriate for a text lacking the last two chapters; so, a proper closing benediction was added. No Greek manuscript has a blessing after 14:23. Dom Donatien de Bruyne [54] was probably correct in attributing the *"Gratia cum omnibus sanctis"* to Marcion.

In the East, in particular, Syria, the final doxology (16:25-27) was known only at the end of chapter 14 by Chrysostom, Theodoret, Oecumenius, John of Damascus, Theophylact, and Euthemius. Its manuscript and version witnesses include the Harklaean and Curetonian Syriac, the Armenian and Gothic, K, L, many Greek lectionaries and more than 200 minuscules. As most of these witnesses were under the influence of the recension of Lucian of Antioch, it is a reasonable conclusion that his late third-century text placed the doxology at the end of the fourteenth chapter. Other witnesses besides this Antiochene Koine text of Paul's Epistles have been studied by P. Corssen [55] at this point. In reconstructing the text of the ancestor of "Z" from D F G he found that the final two chapters came from a different source than the rest of the Epistle (with its essentially "Western" readings) because they contained almost as many peculiar readings as the first fourteen chapters together. The doxology is absent from F, G, and g; but G and g leave a blank space after 14:23 sufficient for inserting it, as if the copyist who produced the Greek model of F and G knew manuscripts which inserted the doxology there. Since the doxology is far more appropriate for the end of a letter than at 14:23, where it breaks in abruptly, it is proper to add an ancestor of G to the Antiochene witnesses of an archetype ending at 14:23 plus 16:25-27. Such a text, which was known both in Syria and the West, both in Latin and Greek, must have been relatively ancient.

On this issue Origen has provided the most significant information. Commenting on Romans 16:25-27 (trans. Rufinus; Migne, *P.G.* 14, 1290), he said of Marcion:

> He entirely removed *(abstulit)* this paragraph *(caput hoc)*, and not only this, but also from this place *(et non solum hoc, sed ab eo loco)*, where it is written, "but everything which is not of faith is sin," even to the end, he cut away *(dissecuit)* all. In other copies, however, that is in those which have not been corrupted by Marcion, we find this paragraph differently placed. For in some codices, after the place which we mentioned above, that is, "but whatever is not of faith is sin," then follows immediately *(statim cohaerens habetur)*, "but to him who is able to establish you." But other codices have it at the end, as it is now placed.[56]

Origen, then, knew of Catholic, non-Marcionite texts in which the doxology appeared after 14:23. Moreover, Marcion and presumably his Apostolikon omitted the doxology altogether. As Origen was speaking of the Marcionite text as he knew it in his own day, it is natural to conclude the Marcion's followers likewise omitted the doxology. If we believe Origen's statement that this passage was not in Marcion's Bible, it is hazardous to conjecture that it originated among his followers.[57] For, if they had invented the doxology, the church would not have pointed out that even Marcion himself lacked it; the church would not quickly accept this addition to its own texts if it had a Marcionite theological bias. Jacques Dupont shrewdly observes: "It is rather striking to see Origen, who claims to inform us on the Marcionite text, to use as catholic text copies altered by Marcion, if indeed it be he himself or his followers who eliminated from the epistle mention of Rome and added the doxology." [58] There are no analogous cases of corruption of catholic texts by later Marcionite additions to Marcion's Apostolikon. While Irenaeus, Tertullian, and Epiphanius frequently charged Marcion with altering the

New Testament text, they did not blame on him the excision of the doxology and the last two chapters. Are we to assume that Marcion's hypothetical removal of the last two chapters explains Irenaeus's and Tertullian's failure to quote them and that his or his disciples' addition of the doxology quickly led the catholic editors of texts used by Origen and the P[46] scribe to adopt the Marcionite doxology? The chronological problem is severe if the latter question is answered affirmatively. How would the Marcionite hypothesis explain the location of the doxology after 15:33 in the early third-century Egyptian P[46], our earliest Pauline manuscript? Gunther Zuntz [59] has found that "the proto-Alexandrian [manuscripts] as a group have solidly withstood this [Marcionite] infection," and that Marcion preserved many genuine readings. When he and the early fathers and catholic manuscripts agree in the text, their combined witness shows either that the reading is genuine or very early indeed. Such is the case with the omission of the last two chapters of Romans; Irenaeus, Tertullian, Cyprian, and Marcion were using such a current, inherited edition. Possibly conclusive proof that Marcion did not know chapter 16 is to be found in the fact that many manuscripts of the Marcionite Prologues say that Paul sent the epistle to the Romans from Athens. Such a tradition is not readily compatible with the Corinthian connections of 16:1, 21-23.

While it has been postulated that Marcion cut away the last two chapters because of their Old Testament quotations, he did not usually omit such citations in the rest of his canon. On the other hand, he may have rejected the doxology because the "only wise God" of the gospel is equated with the God of the prophetic writings. For Marcion "shamelessly blasphemed him who was proclaimed as God by the law and prophets. . . . From the Father, who is above the God who made the world, Jesus came. . . . He destroyed the prophets and the law and all the works of the God who made the world" (Irenaeus, *Adv. Haer.* i, 27.2). The thought of the doxology is more Pauline than Marcionite. The apostle held that there was a veil on the face of the Jews when they interpreted Moses (2 Cor. 3:13-16). The Old Testament truth which is unveiled by turning to Christ the Lord is specified in Romans 1:1-5 and 3:21-23. But in neither the Romans' doxology nor in Pauline thought is it stated that the Old Testament prophets announced the divine eternal plan for the cosmic Christ. The closest parallels to the doxology are found in Ephesians (1:9-10; 3:3-6, 9) [60] and Colossians (1:26-27), where reference is made to the hidden mystery of Christ which has now been revealed (Rom. 16:25-26). The authenticity of the doxology has been well defended by F. J. A. Hort [61]; but it is tempting to find it in the influence of the author of Ephesians.[62]

That the doxology is Pauline (in some sense) and definitely pre-Marcionite is further confirmed by its presence in the Chester Beatty Codex (P[46]) following 15:33. This ancient manuscript marks the break at the end of chapter 15 and the doxology with a diagonal line before continuing with the last chapter. Ostensibly the copyist of P[46] knew a form of the letter which ended at this point. This observation agrees well with the hypothesis that only the first fifteen chapters were sent to Rome and that chapter 16 was not originally an integral part of Paul's Letter to the Romans. While 15:33 is a benediction, it is unlike any ending in the Pauline epistles. Rather, it prepares the way (cf. 2 Cor. 13:11; 1 Thess. 5:23; 2 Thess. 3:16) for the closing doxology as found in P[46]. As suggested above, the apostle appended Phoebe's letter of introduction to a record of his gospel (Rom. 1:1-6, 15-17), which he wished the Ephesians to have. In P[46] we thus have evidence of a very early recension ending at 15:33 with the doxology. It is only a remote possibility that a *post*-Apostolic doxology would be appended to all known editions or recensions of Romans (i.e., at the end of chaps. 14, 15, and 16) except that of Marcion, who was accused of omitting it.

Three illuminating quotations concerning the location of the doxology now follow. The first is from Kirsopp Lake:

It is very unlikely that this was originally anywhere else than at the end of the Epistle, wherever that was: therefore all the manuscripts which insert it after xiv. 23 are really evidence for the existence of a short recension, and confirm the witness of Tertullian, Cyprian and the Latin *Breves* and *Capitulatio*.[63]

According to T. W. Manson:

The insertion of the doxology after xiv. 23 produces a break in the continuity of the text. . . . The natural inference is that when the doxology was attached to xiv. 23, it was attached to a form of the text which ended at that point.[64]

In their commentary William Sanday and Arthur C. Headlam wrote:

> A careful examination of the first thirteen verses [of chap. 15] shows conclusively that they are closely connected with the previous chapter. The break after xiv. 23 is purely arbitrary, and the passage that follows to the end of ver. 6 is merely a conclusion to the previous argument, without which the former chapter is incomplete. . . . No theory therefore can be accepted which does not recognize that xiv and xv. 13 form a single paragraph which must not be split up.[85]

As the truncation of the last two chapters was pre-Marcionite, the break of the intimate, original connection between 14:23 and 15:1 must have been due to the accidental loss of the last two chapters in the manuscript or perhaps due to the copyist's running out of writing material. If, under such circumstances, Paul himself or a co-worker such as Timothy had authorized the transmission of such a shortened version plus a closing doxology, then the subsequent wide circulation of this "edition" would be more intelligible.

Under what circumstances was the short recension circulated? One approach to this problem is to correlate each "edition" with the inclusion or omission of references to Rome (1:7, 15). The inclusion of these references in the Chester Beatty Papyrus, which omits the personal, non-Roman greetings of chapter 16, indicates that the first fifteen chapters with the doxology were sent to Rome by the apostle. On the other hand, some of the witnesses to the omission of "Rome" in 1:7 and 15 are direct or indirect witnesses of the fourteen-chapter recension: Origen, G, g, Amiatinus and Fuldensis. This correlation in such diverse sources suggests that the shortest form of the Epistle was not sent to Rome but was intended to circulate in several churches unvisited by Paul (1:7-15). In this respect it resembles Ephesians.[66] Because the context (1:7-15) requires the name of some community, and as 14:23 properly leads into 15:1ff., it is natural to think of the fifteen-chapter edition, which was addressed to Rome, as having priority.

The following historical conclusions may be drawn. Paul sent to Rome chapters 1–15, ending with the doxology. This was his primary writing. At the same time he sent to Ephesus a needed (Acts 20:29-30) copy of the summary of his gospel, but with the doxology located at the end of the note which chapter 16 constitutes. Nothing prohibits the writing of this note to the Ephesians even before the penning of the letter to Rome. Both were dispatched in the custody of Phoebe (16:1-2) at the outset of the sailing season. In this case the doxology could have been originally written for chapter 16. In any case, the Ephesians received the note and the copy of the Roman letter simultaneously; consequently they were preserved together. The origin of the fourteen-chapter epistle and its probable doxology is a matter of conjecture. It apparently arose during the apostle's lifetime and with his authorization, since the editor did not exclude the possibility of Paul's visit (1:10-16) to the area for which it was to serve as a circular letter of introduction. Why did not the editor delete this promise together with the reference to Rome? The only known occasion for a Pauline journey to churches previously unvisited by him was when he hoped he would be released from his Caesarean imprisonment.[67] The truncation at the end of chapter 14 might be the result of the loss of the ending on the copy which Paul had taken with him to Jerusalem (in order to explain his teaching there). The resemblance of the doxology to material in Ephesians and Colossians might signify that it was written at the time of these epistles in order to close the general letter. Its transfer to the end of the other two recensions by later scribes would follow. But it is a moot question for which edition the doxology was originally written; a case can be made for each edition.

It would be natural for the sixteen-chapter Ephesian edition to be put into circulation in an Ephesian-sponsored collection of the Pauline corpus (see Appendix), which found its way to Egypt, where Clement of Alexandria, Origen, and the P[46] scribe knew the longer recension. The Roman recension was also known to the Egyptian P[46] scribe. The fourteen-chapter recension was the most widely known or quoted "edition" in the ante-Nicene church. Its primary groups of witnesses are "Western," Syrian and Antiochene-Byzantine. Ignatius of Antioch, though citing Romans 1:3 (ad Smyrn. 1:1) and 6:4 (ad Eph. 19:3), made no reference to Paul's act of writing to the Romans as he himself did to commend their faith; yet, such a comparison to Paul might be expected (cf. ad Rom. 4:3). The recipients of the short recension lived in the unvisited area stretching from Caesarea to Phrygia. Phoenicians and south Syrians in particular might be readers; they were being evangelized by Paul's fellow workers (Col. 4:10ff.; Philem. 24). Paul visited friends at Sidon on the way from Caesarea to Rome (Acts 27:3). Taken together, this evidence suggests Antioch to be the place where the short recension was "published." From here originated the "Western Text" of the gospels and the Letters of Paul and John. [68]

PHILIPPIANS

Paul's Letter to the Philippians poses problems not unlike those encountered in Second Corinthians and Romans. The only partition theory [69] which we find convincing enough to elaborate on concerns the alien section beginning with 3:1b. Étienne Le Moyne in 1685 was the first to observe the beginning of another letter at this point. There is an abrupt change of subject and mood; whereas the first two chapters are among the most intimate, tender, and rapturous which the apostle ever wrote, chapter 3 has a bitter and irate tone. As Kirsopp Lake pithily commented: "Is it natural to say 'rejoice in the Lord' and then suddenly say 'Beware of dogs'?" [70] Various endings of the interpolated section have been proposed: 4:1, 3, 9, and 23. But J. Hugh Michael has presented textual evidence that the splice lies between 3:19 and 20; [71] many reliable witnesses for 3:20 read the colorless dè rather than gár. There is no real connection between 3:18-19 and 21. The eschatological hope (3:20-21), however, is not only a source of rejoicing (3:1a), but also a reason for "stand[ing] firm . . . in the Lord" (4:1). There are several parallels of 4:1-9 with the first two chapters: epipothéo (1:8; 4:1); stékete (1:27; 4:1); chaírete en kurío (3:1; 4:4); and missions of Epaphroditus (2:25; 4:18) following a period in which the Philippians had not helped Paul (2:30; 4:18). His pride in them is stated in 2:16 and 4:1. He deals gently with their disunity (1:27; 2:2-3, 14; 4:2).

Philippians 3:1b-19 may be approximately dated by virtue of its resemblances to letters which Paul wrote after he settled in Ephesus and before he was imprisoned in Caesarea. The parallels include:

Philippians	1 Corinthians	2 Corinthians	Romans	Galatians
3:3-4	1:29, 31			
3:14	9:24			
3:17	4:15-17; 11:1			4:12
3:5		11:22		
3:10		4:10-11	6:3-5; 8:17	
3:4-7		11:18-31	11:1	

Philippians	1 Corinthians	2 Corinthians	Romans	Galatians
3:7-8	1:5-7			
3:3-4			2:28-29; 4:11-12	
3:18-19; 3:3			8:5; 16:18	6:12-14
3:9			3:21-22; 9:30-32	2:16, 21; 3:21
3:2		11:13		5:15

This striking number of parallels would seem to date Philippians 3 before the Captivity Letters. Paul's call to self-imitation (3:17) is found in 1 Thessalonians 1:6; 2:10; 2 Thessalonians 3:7; Galatians 4:12; and 1 Corinthians 4:16; 11:1; but it is altogether absent from his later epistles.

Only three visits by Paul to Philippi are mentioned in the New Testament (Acts 16:12ff.; 20:1-6; 2 Corinthians 2:12-13; 7:5-7; Philippians 4:15; 1 Thessalonians 2:2); two of them occurred after Paul last left Ephesus. When he wrote in Philippians 3:18, "For many, of whom I have often told you *(pollákis elegon)* and now tell you even with tears, live as enemies of the cross of Christ," one supposes that he has had much more contact with the Philippians than the first visit. Whoever locates the writing of 3:18 in Ephesus bears the difficult burden of establishing both sufficient occasions of Pauline instruction and the pertinence of the harsh, stereotyped warnings at the time of Paul's first visit. A second clue is found in 3:1b: "To write the same things to you is not irksome to me, and is safe for you." What were these instructions duplicating? It was hardly the exhortation to rejoice; neither would a spontaneous reminder be irksome, nor the absence of joy unsafe. Nor was it likely the first two chapters, in which Paul shows no concern over his readers' safety *(asphales)* [72] from false teachers. And it was probably not an earlier lost letter to the Philippians which warned against the same false teachers; for the teachers thought it might be tedious and wearisome *(okneron)* for Paul to honor their request that he repeat his warnings, and he would have said, "write you again." There was no more apt to be a recently written letter to another church, because a copy of it could be sent or left instead of writing Philippians 3; and, we might expect him to write, "the same things to you *also*." Rather, if "to write the same things" is not paired with something else which the apostle had written, then it is to be differentiated from an oral warning. Victor P. Furnish [73] suggests that *"ta auta"* refer to supplementary and clarifying admonitions to be transmitted *orally* by Epaphroditus and Timothy when they visit Philippi. But this hypothesis assumes the integrity of chapter 3 to the letter. [74]

A more adequate basis for interpreting 3:1*b* is 3:18, where Paul refers to his own oral *(elegon, légo)* warnings. If what Paul has said and now is saying (3:18) is the conclusion of his warning (3:1*b*ff.), then what he writes is supplementary to his own past and current preaching in their presence. "To write" and "to say" are equated in 3:18. Such a situation may have existed during Paul's visit to Philippi during the days of Unleavened Bread (Acts 20:6). Doubtless he had described his troubles at Corinth (2 Cor. 10–13; cf. 1–9) when he passed through Philippi on his way from Troas to Corinth about eight months earlier. After revisiting Corinth, he would not fail to warn the Philippians again, as he soon warned the Ephesian elders (Acts 20:28-31). However, the bitterness of Philippians 3 would be more intelligible if it mirrored Paul's unrested mind (2 Cor. 2:12) as he awaited news from Titus about the rebellion at Corinth. As the apostle himself testified, "When we came into Macedonia, our bodies had no rest but we were afflicted at every turn — fighting without and fear within" (2 Cor. 7:5). The Philippians would be eager to add no unnecessary burden to the tired, downcast apostle, and he would be in a mood to attack viciously those who so upset him. Accordingly, Paul may well have written Philippians 3:1*b*-19 during his second visit as a summary of his oral warnings at the request of the Philippians, so that they might have a record. He deemed the written statement to be an added safeguard.

SUMMARY

The only fixed point of time in Paul's ministry in the Aegean area is the proconsulship of Gallio in the spring of 52. The apostle had arrived in Corinth eighteen months before he appeared before Gallio. After his dismissal from Gallio's court, Paul stayed in Corinth some time longer, then made his way back to Jerusalem and Antioch. He set out again, visiting the churches in Galatia and Phrygia before settling in Ephesus for a two-year stay. From Ephesus, he wrote Galatians during the

Sabbatical year of 54-55. Four letters to Corinth followed during the next two years, and from that city in 57 he wrote the letter to Rome and sent a copy with an appended personal note to Ephesus. He traveled back through Macedonia in 56 and left from Corinth for Jerusalem in 57. Captivity awaited him in the Holy Land.

4

Paul's
Captivity
Letters

Did the "Captivity Letters" of Paul (Philippians, Colossians, Philemon, and possibly Ephesians, 2 Timothy 4:9-22, and Titus 3:12-15) emanate from Ephesus, Caesarea, or Rome?

EPHESUS

The Ephesian hypothesis has won a large number of adherents [1] in the present century. Nevertheless, besides this erudite support, the thesis has little to recommend it. Why do none of the Captivity Letters allude to contributing to the forthcoming Jerusalem collection, which was so important in Paul's thinking at this time? Timothy and Titus were agents in arranging the collection, and the Philippians were major contributors (Rom. 15:26; 2 Cor. 8:1-5; cf. 9:2). How could Paul write from Ephesus requesting prayers from the Colossians that God might open a door for the word (Col. 4:3; cf. Eph. 6:19-20), unless his activity described in Acts 19:8-10 is altogether misleading? The gospel did not penetrate Colossae until Paul first had been successful in Ephesus. It would be indeed a curious situation if Colossae had already been evangelized by Epaphras (Col. 1:7) while Paul at Ephesus was still praying for a door to open, as if he had been imprisoned since arrival! However, by the time of the writing of Philippians (1:12-14), this prayer for spreading the gospel had already been answered. Thus if Philippians and Colossians were both written from the same place, Colossians would be the earlier. This is partially confirmed by the impression from Philippians 1:5 and 4:10-11, 15-16 that the church there had been established for some time. The dilemma posed by these problems is that Philippians would be later than Colossians, but that *both* would be written before Paul proposed the Jerusalem collection, that is, some time before Paul wrote 1 Corinthians 16:1. For here he appears to be answering the Corinthians' questions about the collection, and he had already instructed the Galatians. But such a chronology would be untenable. In writing the Letter to Philemon, by referring to himself as an old man *(presbutes)* (v. 9), Paul shows that he has aged. Also in writing Philippians (1:23) he expresses the desire to depart and be with Christ, "for that is far better." In writing to Rome and Corinth, when did he intimate that his work might thus be drawing to a close? Rather, in 2 Corinthians 1:8-10 he thinks of life as precious, and he praises God for delivering him from the peril of death. Moreover, if Colossians be early, is it to be seen as almost contemporary with Galatians, which was also written from Ephesus? The Christology of Colossians and Philippians can hardly be placed two years before that of First and Second Corinthians and Romans. In fact the tone and outlook of the Captivity Letters differ vastly from those of the Epistles to the Galatians and Corinthians which were penned at Ephesus. Nor can the partially realized eschatology of Colossians [2] be intelligibly dated so early. It would not be consistent to hold, on one hand, that Colossians and Philippians were written early during the stay at Ephesus (in order to account for Paul's prayer for an open door and his failure to mention the collection), while alleging, on the other hand, that they were written toward the end of his stay (in order to account for his increasing age and more developed Christology and eschatology).

The references to Paul's fellow workers are poorly suited to the Ephesian hypothesis. What happened to all the Ephesians [3] greeted in Romans 16:3-16? How could Paul be left alone here (2 Tim. 4:11) in need of money from Philippi (Phil. 4:10ff.), or would he reckon Timothy as the only sympathetic, unselfish colleague (Phil. 2:19-21)? Why should Prisca and Aquila be greeted in 2 Timothy 4:19 and be unmentioned elsewhere if they were in Ephesus at least from the time of Paul's arrival (Acts 18:18, 26) until after he wrote 1 Corinthians 16:19? The

Captivity Epistles were scarcely written during Timothy's mission from Ephesus to Macedonia and Corinth (Acts 19:22; 1 Cor. 4:17; 16:10), because he joins Paul in the greetings of Col. 1:1; Phil. 1:1; and Philem. 1. Why is Luke present with Paul in Colossians 4:14; 2 Timothy 4:11; and Philemon 24, but otherwise absent from Ephesus as far as we know? For he is unmentioned in First and Second Corinthians, and the "we-sections" of Acts do not extend to the description of Paul's residence at Ephesus.

Proponents of the Ephesian hypothesis conjecture conveniently that, despite the silence of Acts, Paul was imprisoned in the capital of Asia (cf. Rom. 16:7; 1 Cor. 4:9-13; 15:30-32; 2 Cor. 1:8-10; 4:8-12; 6:4-5; 11:23-25; Marcionite Prologue to Colossians). Though his serious troubles there could have taken many alternate forms, and though none of his letters written at Ephesus indicate that he was writing as a prisoner, the possibility of a relatively short imprisonment cannot be excluded. But the real question is: was he imprisoned for a *long* time (Phil. 1:12-14; 2:25-30; Col. 4:18; Philem. 13; 2 Tim. 4:16-18, 21) on capital charges (Phil. 2:17; cf. 1:23)? Was he incarcerated long enough before writing to the Philippians to permit the recovery of the almost fatally ill Epaphroditus (Phil. 2:25-30), who had brought funds collected for the apostle from Philippi after news of his imprisonment had been received? Epaphroditus was troubled because the Philippians had already heard of his illness while aiding Paul as a fellow laborer in the work of Christ. In his Captivity Letters Paul shows no such bitterness about his sufferings as is found in 2 Corinthians 1:8-10 (cf. 1 Cor. 16:9). In such desperate circumstances at Ephesus, it is highly unlikely that his enemies and troubles would have permitted him the privilege of writing letters, collaborating with his assistants in spreading the gospel for which he was imprisoned (Phil. 1:7, 12-13), and making converts in Caesar's household (Phil. 4:22). Moreover, if Paul suffered a lengthy imprisonment at Ephesus, there would have been insufficient time left out of his "three years" (Acts 20:31) there to allow for his three months of synagogue preaching (19:8), two years of teaching in the hall of Tyrannus (19:9-10), the fruits of his contact with the exorcists (Acts 19:11-20; cf. 1 Cor. 16:9), his activity in initiating the Jerusalem collection (Acts 19:21-22; 1 Cor. 16:1-12), his quick trip to Corinth (2 Cor. 1:23; 2:1-5; 12:14; 13:1-2), and his trouble with the silversmiths (Acts 19:23-41). It might also be necessary to squeeze into Paul's chronology a promised visit to Phrygia, the residence of Philemon and Onesimus (Col. 4:7-9, 12-15; Philem. 1, 5, 23). It would be just as dubious to squeeze into Paul's Ephesian ministry, or a few months afterward, nearly all of his letter writing. Did almost none of his surviving letters date from the last six or seven years of his life, the very period in which his churches were better established and would be inclined to save the communications from their absent founder?

If in writing 1 Corinthians (1:2; 16:19), 2 Corinthians 1:1, and Romans 16:5 Paul referred to the churches of Asia and Corinth, why are no such allusions found in Philippians? Why did not Paul send greetings in the specific name of his local church itself in his Captivity Epistles? Surely an angry tone, such as that with which Galatians ended, is not the explanation. The recipients of the Captivity Epistles were well enough known to the Ephesian community, for, according to Acts 19:10, all the inhabitants of Asia heard the Word while Paul taught at Ephesus.

In summary, the Captivity Epistles are too different from Romans, Galatians, and First and Second Corinthians to belong to the same brief period of writing.

ROME

If the increasing popularity of the Ephesian hypothesis is unjustified, its support is understandable partially as a reaction against the weakness of the traditional view that Paul wrote during his Roman imprisonment. It is sometimes urged that the fugitive slave, Onesimus, would be more apt to escape from Colossae to Ephesus than to Rome. The distance to Rome and the necessity to go mostly by sea do constitute minor difficulties. But would Paul ask Philemon (v. 22) in Colossae to prepare a lodging for him if the journey from Rome and the need to revisit such intervening troubled churches as Corinth, Philippi, and Ephesus made the time of such a stay at Colossae highly indefinite? After an absence of at least five years, Paul, on the way from Rome to Colossae, could hardly pay but a brief visit to his churches of Achaia, Macedonia, and Ephesus.

The names of Paul's companions while imprisoned raise problems for the Roman hypothesis. Would Aristarchus, Mark, and Jesus Justus have been Paul's agents in working among the Roman Jews (Col. 4:10-11) if this were Peter's prerogative (Gal. 2:9)? Why is Cephas unmentioned? Did Timothy, Luke, Aristarchus, and Tychicus all stay with Paul from the time of his departure for Jerusalem (Acts 20:4-6) until he wrote the Captivity Epistles during his Roman imprisonment? Only Luke the physician and Aristarchus accompanied him to Rome (Acts 27:2-4). There is no indication that Tychicus and Timothy went to Rome. Tychicus is twice mentioned as a messenger, first to Colossae (Eph. 6:21), then to Ephesus (2 Tim. 4:12). Second Timothy 4:11-15, and 19-21 presuppose that this beloved "son" and co-worker was sent on a journey through Asia, Troas, and Philippi (cf. Phil. 2:19; Col. 4:10). Paul wrote a second letter to Timothy from Rome (2 Tim. 1:17). This verse was not from the same epistle as 2 Timothy 4:9-22, if both sections be genuine fragments. For in 1:16-18 Onesiphorus, if alive, is present at Rome, while in 4:19 he is greeted with his family back at Ephesus. [4] In 1:15 Timothy is supposed to know that all the Asians have abandoned Paul, but the purpose of Timothy's and Tychicus's missions includes enlisting their aid (2 Tim. 4:12, 14-15, 19).

Other problems beset the Roman hypothesis. Are we to assume that the Philippians had no desire and opportunity to aid Paul from the time they first helped him until he was imprisoned in Rome (Phil. 4:10-18), or that Paul is sarcastically criticizing the Philippians for waiting a long time before helping him again? Paul recalls their earlier gifts while he was in Thessalonica and Corinth. On the other hand, it is apparent that much time had already passed (*ede totè anethálete*) (Phil. 4:10) and Paul was not in special need at Ephesus, where a community of believers awaited his return from Jerusalem (Acts 18:21–19:1). But, on the other hand, the reference would be no more suitable for Rome than for Ephesus. Some four years passed between Paul's departures from Corinth and Ephesus; it was yet another four before he was confined in Rome: a rather lengthy interval for the Philippians to leave the apostle to other resources.

Is it proper to imagine that Paul gave up his plan to visit

Spain (Rom. 15:24, 28) in order to return to the East after the
ending of his Roman imprisonment? He is quite hopeful of
visiting Philippi (Phil. 2:24) and Philemon (v. 22). It would
perhaps be attributing too much vigor to the aging apostle
(Philem. 9) to think of his going, or planning to go, in both
directions. He never again saw the elders of Ephesus (Acts 20:25,
38) after the farewell at Miletus, though the tradition of his
exile in Spain is quite credible. [5] If it be justifiable to presume
that Paul in Rome still had his heart set on Spain, it is strange
that his Captivity Letters are not only silent, but even present a
contrary image. Wherever Paul planned to go, he must have
been uncertain about the outcome of the judicial process in
Rome. Appeal to Caesar was a last resort when Paul was faced
with the threat of being sent back to Jerusalem (Acts 25:9-12).
Once this appeal had been made, he had less cause for optimism
about release.

Also against the Roman origin of Colossians and Ephesians
is the failure to mention the Laodicean eathquake in A.D. 60
(Tacitus, *Annals* xiv, 27), which almost destroyed the city.
Eusebius's Chronicle (ed. Schone, II, 154–155) dated the earthquake in 64. But nothing precludes two destructive upheavals
during a period of seismic activity in such an unstable area. [6]
Paul expressed no commiseration or concern, and Nympha's
house was still standing in Laodicea (Col. 4:15). Would not
Epaphras (Col. 1:7; 4:12) have told Paul of sufferings in Phrygia? Philippians, Colossians, Philemon, and Ephesians all suggest that Paul's relations with his churches were good. They
cast no light on Paul's lament from Rome in 2 Timothy 1:15-17
that "all who are in Asia turned from me" except Onesiphorus.
The attitude of local believers where Paul was imprisoned,
which can be deduced from the Captivity Epistles, is also incon-
sistent with his Roman experience. The local church (Phil. 1:
14-18) contained some brethren who were unresponsive to Paul's
presence, though most were roused to confidence and zeal in
preaching. Presumably fear, timidity, and uncertainty had made
the church stagnant and ingrown before his arrival (Phil. 1:14).
Some local preachers of Christ were motivated by envy, strife,
loveless rivalry, and partisanship, as they sought to add to Paul's
afflictions in imprisonment (Phil. 1:15-17). However, Paul
praises the faith of the church at Rome (Rom. 1:8, 12; 15:14) as

if it were not in need of renewal, and he anticipated a favorable reception there (1:10-13; 15:23-24, 28-32). When Paul arrived, he was well received by believers and Jewish leaders (Acts 28:15-28).

For two years Paul paid for his own room in Rome and preached without hindrance to all who came to him (Acts 28: 30-31). He was evidently at liberty to write letters and communicate freely with fellow workers. However, in Colossians 4:3 Paul asks for prayers that "God may open to us a door for the word, to declare the mystery of Christ, on account of which I am in prison." Evidently he was lacking in effective opportunities for work at this time, due either to severe restrictions on his preaching and teaching, or to being shunned by the local believers.

Nevertheless, in due season the door for evangelization did open, and converts were made among the "whole praetorium" (Phil. 1:13) and "those of Caesar's household" (Phil. 4:22). Four of them are probably named in 2 Timothy 4:21: Eubulus, Pudens, Linus, and Claudia. Such a group could in principle be found in the provinces [7] as well as in Rome. The "praetorium" most often meant the provincial governor's residence and the attached military barracks; "Caesar's household" was the entourage of servants in the imperial and military administration. Paul lived in an *oikia* staffed by imperial servants and protected by a praetorian guard. Now, Ephesus was merely the capital of a Senatorial province, and at Rome he lived in his own hired dwelling *(misthoma)* for two years and welcomed everyone coming to him (Acts 28:30). Wherever Paul was living, he was paying for his own room and board. Are we to imagine that he rented a room in the imperial palace on the Palatine or in the nearby barracks of the palace guard, and that Nero allowed the free preaching of the gospel in his own household and the free access of Christians? It is unlikely that part of the imperial residence would be designated by a military term at this early time. Or are we to discredit the testimony of Luke, who accompanied the apostle to Rome? Or should we think that Paul lived in the fortified barracks of the military camp *(castra praetorianorum)* outside the northeastern wall of Rome? This apparently was never called a "praetorium" and was not under immediate imperial control. [8] No evidence exists that at this time the *praefectus praetori* at Rome was responsible for prisoners from the provinces who had "appealed to Caesar."[9] It is more accurate to hold that when he wrote the Captivity Letters, he was imprisoned in the residence or the headquarters of a provincial governor who was under direct imperial control. Here he would have opportunity to come into contact with the governor's guard and a staff of male and female imperial servants. Here, too, he would bear witness at his hearings before the procurators and Agrippa (Acts 23:35–26:32).

CAESAREA

In light of the cumulative hindrances to the acceptance of either an Ephesian or Roman origin of the Captivity Epistles, it is necessary to look with more favor upon Caesarea as a possible location. Only a relatively small percentage of investigators[10] have held this view since it was proposed in 1700 by H. E. G. Paulus and in 1829 by D. Schulz. Its most eloquent recent defender was Ernst Lohmeyer.[11] It avoids all the pitfalls of the alternate hypotheses. The Jerusalem collection was a thing of the past. The Laodicean earthquake belonged to the future. During a year of confinement before beginning this new group of letters, Paul doubtless had profitably used the time on his hands to penetrate further into the mysteries of the incarnation and the church. In a city where he was little known and where he had not preceded his arrival with a letter of introduction, such as the letter to the Romans, he would naturally be at somewhat of a loss in finding open doors for work. Here he experienced a continuous two and one-third year (Acts 24:26ff.) imprisonment which must have exhausted his patience. Here he was at liberty to communicate with all his associates (Acts 24:23; cf. 27:3) and thus to write letters; yet he was bound in chains (Acts 24:27; Eph. 6:20; Phil. 1:7, 13-16; Col. 4:18; Philem. 10, 13). At Caesarea, too, Paul was guarded at Herod's praetorium (Acts 23:35; cf. 24:23).[12] It is easy to imagine that many members of this palace in the capital of Palestine either inquired about the issues between Paul and the Jews, or they were so informed by Paul's visitors and fellow evangelists. Quite possibly the earlier conversion of a Roman centurion at Caesarea by Peter (Acts 10:1–11:18) had at least facilitated the spread of the gospel in the praetorium. When Paul tells the Philippians that events in his life had advanced the gospel, he means that all those who lived or worked in the praetorium "and . . . all the rest" had come to know that he had been imprisoned for Christ's cause (Phil. 1:12-13). Those who learned what he preached include his accusers, Felix and his wife Drusilla and those present at his interrogations (Acts 24:1-26), "all the saints . . . especially those of Caesar's household" (Phil. 4:22), and those in the area who heard the preaching by Paul's brethren (Phil. 1:14ff.; 4:21).

Caesarea would be an attractive place of refuge for Onesimus. By escaping to a different Roman province, he was unlikely to be recognized. Here Roman officials would be less on the lookout for runaway slaves than in Rome or Ephesus. Unless his master thought Onesimus was going to see Paul, no one would expect him to go to Caesarea. This city had the disadvantages neither of the remoteness of Rome nor the closeness of Ephesus. It was quite accessible by boat from Attalia, near Perga in Pamphylia, and it was only about half the distance to Rome. Onesimus could reach Attalia from Phrygia just as easily as he could Ephesus. However, a discussion of the relative safety and accessibility of Caesarea, Rome, and Ephesus is not really relevant to the issue at hand. Onesimus's intent was not simply to escape slavery; otherwise he would have avoided Paul and his contingent, who could inform Philemon of his slave's whereabouts. Through such common acquaintances as Epaphras he might be traced, or by them or by Paul himself he might be sent back to Philemon. He may even have followed Epaphras to Caesarea. His real intent was to serve Paul (Philem. 11-14), whether the apostle were in Rome, Caesarea, or Ephesus. He would have tried to go wherever Paul was; he chose Caesarea because he learned that the apostle was there. Surely Paul did not meet him by accident; possibly it was Epaphras himself who brought the slave to Paul. Surely Onesimus knew of the apostle, who addressed Philemon as "our beloved fellow worker." The coming of Epaphras to Paul (Col. 1:7-8; 4:12) presupposes that the believers in Colossae (including Onesimus) knew Paul's whereabouts.

How is the attitude of local Christians to Paul to be understood? At Caesarea was located an older church (Acts 8:40;

chap. 10), most of whose members earlier had wished Paul well
(Acts 21:8, 12, 16). But the church was so close to Jerusalem
that some must have had a reserved and suspicious attitude
toward him. Jewish pressures (cf. Acts 24:27; 25:2-3) on the
Palestinian church forcing them to side with or against Paul
must have made many embarrassed local Christians indifferent
or hostile to the apostle. His presence at Caesarea during his
imprisonment could only cause trouble in the community. Those
who considered his presence a hindrance to missionary work
among the Jews would not fail to point to the apostle's stub-
bornness in failing to respond to the words of the Holy Spirit
through the mouth of Agabus, the very prophet whose warning
of a forthcoming famine had earlier led to the Antiochene relief for Jerusalem (Acts 11:27-30). "The people there begged
him not to go up to Jerusalem. . . . And when he would not be
persuaded, we ceased and said, 'The will of the Lord be done'"
(Acts 21:12-14). There is reason to believe that on the previous
occasion on which Paul went to Jerusalem bringing relief, a persecution of the Jerusalem church followed (Acts 11:27–12:25).
Was it by coincidence that, learning of the apostle's pending arrival, Agabus "came down [there] from Judea" while Paul and
his companions were staying at Caesarea? Be that as it may, his
refusal to obey the Spirit had the inevitable results of (1) dividing the Caesarean church in regard to its members' attitude
toward him, (2) putting those members favorable to him, as in
the case of the Philippians, under a moral obligation to support
him, and (3) causing restrictions on local evangelization of
Hebrews. Possibly some of the circumcised evangelists (Col.
4:11) working with Paul were considered intruders in the local
work of proselyting, though these co-workers may have been
preaching elsewhere, such as in Phoenicia (cf. Acts 15:3; 21:
3-7; 27:3). In writing that only Mark, Jesus Justus, and Aristarchus (Col. 4:10-11) were his fellow workers among the circumcision, he hints that other Hebrew Christians were not helping
him or were not cooperating with his evangelizing in the area.
It is not surprising that Paul does not have a kind word (Phil.
1:14-18) for all local leaders. The greetings sent to the Philippians (4:22) are from "all the saints" (cf. 2 Cor. 13:13), but
most of all from Caesar's household; the latter are his closest
associates. Although the amount of local aid which Paul could

count on was probably insufficient under the circumstances, the Philippians no longer lacked an opportunity to take care of Paul (Phil. 4:10-11) during his period of want. They had recently heard of his imprisonment, which reminded them of his experience at Philippi (Acts 16:23-24; 1 Thess. 2:2) ; he was suffering anew for the gospel (Phil. 1:29-30). A bribe-hungry procurator like Felix (Acts 24:26) did not offer virtually free hospitality to the apostle for two years, hence the new opportunity for the Philippians to help him (Phil. 4:10-11). Would the generous Philippians not hasten to aid the apostle as soon as they learned of his "struggle"?

Analysis of the whereabouts of Paul's associates during his imprisonment is favorable to a Caesarean origin for the Epistles. Jesus called Justus, [13] Demas, and Crescens are unknown elsewhere and are of no significance in this context, except for the fact that they are absent from the Romans 16 greetings. This absence casts a suspicion of doubt about their presence in Ephesus or wherever the chapter was received. Timothy, Luke, Aristarchus, and Tychicus accompanied Paul to Jerusalem (Acts 20:4-5) and in all probability to Caesarea, in order to aid his defense and to comfort and work with him. There is no reason to believe that the others who went to Jerusalem remained for long with Paul. Aristarchus was a Thessalonian who, together with Luke, accompanied Paul when he left Caesarea for Rome (Acts 27:1-2). There is thus a presumption that the two of them remained with him for most of his Caesarean imprisonment. Since Timothy and Tychicus were useful for Paul as agents and messengers on important missions, it might be expected that they would remain with Paul at Caesarea until he had need of sending them somewhere. Besides these four companions, visiting emissaries and workers from Paul's churches, and an occasional Caesarean helper might be expected to be with the apostle from time to time during his Caesarean imprisonment. Would not Paul take advantage of his relative freedom to keep in close contact with his churches? The careful supervision of his churches while he was at Ephesus would hardly cease at Caesarea, though his need to write to them probably decreased with the passage of time.

Aristarchus was present with Paul when Colossians (4:10) and Philemon (v. 24) were written. In Philippians 4:21-22

Paul transmits greetings from all the brethren with him and all the saints, but not by name. In 2 Timothy 4:10ff. Aristarchus would not be mentioned among the deserters and possible messengers, since he was a fellow prisoner (Acts 27:2; Col. 4:10). Luke is mentioned as being with Paul in Colossians 4:14; 2 Timothy 4:11; and Philemon 24. Tychicus was apparently the bearer of Colossians (4:7) and Ephesians (6:21). The latter verse ("Now that you also may know how I am and what I am doing, Tychicus . . . will tell you everything") implies that the Colossians would receive Tychicus before did the Laodiceans, to whom the Letter to the Ephesians was ostensibly addressed (Col. 4:13-16). Since Colossae is east-southeast of Laodicea, it is legitimate to assume that Tychicus was coming from that direction. Such would be the case if he were proceeding from Caesarea via Attalia, but hardly from Rome or Ephesus. Because Ephesians, whoever wrote it, was not addressed specifically to the well-known church at Ephesus, there is no need to identify this mission with that of which Paul notifies Timothy: "Tychicus I have sent to Ephesus" (2 Tim. 4:12). Because Timothy was with Paul when Colossians (1:1) was written, he knew Tychicus's destination on this trip (4:7). From the fact that Paul had to notify Timothy of the departure and destination of Tychicus (2 Tim. 4:12), it may be deduced that Timothy left on his other mission before Tychicus did on his. As to Timothy himself, he coauthored Colossians (1:1), Philemon (v. 1), and Philippians (1:1). Though he was with Paul when these letters were written from prison, Philippians 2:19 expresses Paul's hope to send Timothy to Philippi shortly (tachéos) and personally to follow tachéos afterward (2:23-24). If the situation in Philippians is to be related to that in 2 Timothy 4:9-22, the sequence of events would be: the writing of Philippians, the dispatch first of Timothy, then of Titus, then the letter to Timothy.

The best test of the historicity of this sequence is to try to relate meaningfully the names and locations of Paul's companions in 2 Timothy 4:10ff. to those in the other Captivity Letters. Demas is known to have worked with Paul only during the period in which Colossians 4:14, Philemon 24, and 2 Timothy 4:10 were written. Since in the latter he is accused of deserting Paul because of a love for the world, it must have referred to a situation subsequent to that found in Colossians and Philemon. Mark was with Paul when Colossians (4:10) and Philemon (v. 24) were written, though according to the former verse the prospect of Mark's visit to Colossae is held out. By the time 2 Timothy 4:11 was written, Mark had proven himself very useful in serving Paul, presumably on the mission to Colossae. That he was in this general area, where Timothy could pick him up, may be deduced from the other towns which Timothy was visiting (4:12-15, 19-20). Mark must have left Caesarea before or with him, as Timothy is expected to know his whereabouts. As to Titus, who had gone to Dalmatia (2 Tim. 4:10) after Timothy had left Paul's side, he was only carrying out Paul's instructions to go to Nicopolis, a city of Epirus not far away from Dalmatia and Illyricum (Rom. 15:19). This message was conveyed to Titus by Artemas or Tychicus (Titus 3:12). Because Tychicus could have easily stopped off at Crete to see Titus (1:5) on the way from Caesarea to Ephesus, and because we know that Tychicus left after Timothy's departure, the natural conclusion is that 2 Timothy 4:10 could have been written after Philippians 2:19. References to a fourth associate of Paul suggest the same conclusion. After the departure of all of the apostle's available co-workers, Luke alone was left with him (2 Tim. 4:11). The impression conveyed by this passage is that Paul earlier had been surrounded by co-workers, one of whom had been Luke. Among those who earlier had returned home from Paul's side were Epaphroditus (Phil. 2:25-30; cf. 4:18) and probably Epaphras, a native of Colossae who had evangelized his hometown, Laodicea, as well as Hierapolis and who had brought Paul news of local problems before himself being imprisoned (Col. 1:7; 4:12; Philem. 23). If Epaphras survived his imprisonment, the need for him back in Phrygia would have called him home. The only other worker mentioned in Colossians, Philemon, and Philippians who does not reappear in 2 Timothy 4:10ff. is the Hebrew believer, Jesus Justus, who joins in the greetings only of Colossians 4:11. That Paul would soon be left alone except for Luke (2 Tim. 4:11) was anticipated by him when he wrote Philippians 2:19-23. Here he states that he has no one like Timothy to send to the Philippians; the others "all look after their own interests, not those of Jesus Christ." The charge *"tà heauton zetousin"* (Phil. 2:21) is reminiscent of *"agapésas tòn nun aiona"* (2 Tim. 4:10).

Hence Paul did not mention them by name in Philippians 4: 21-22, though when he later wrote to Timothy, he related where Demas, Crescens, and Tychicus had gone.

Nevertheless, whatever the merits of the case for Caesarea, a number of objections have been raised to this hypothesis. F. F. Bruce writes: "Rome was a more natural place than Caesarea for Paul to receive visitors from all parts and have news of his converts in the Aegean world." [14] All roads lead to Rome rather than to Caesarea. But does it follow that such visitors as Epaphras and Epaphroditus would be more apt to bring news of trouble or to bring financial aid, respectively, to Rome than to Caesarea, even though Caesarea was closer and the need to visit Paul required the traversing of any distance? "All parts" of "the Aegean world" and of Asia were closer to Caesarea than to Rome, and the object of visits to Paul involved more than the passing along of news by casual visitors.

Secondly, Ernest F. Scott objects: "In Caesarea he was not in serious danger. . . . The Caesarean imprisonment was tedious and irksome, but it would not justify the tone of martyrdom which pervades the Epistle to the Philippians." [15] Although it is true that in Philippians 2:17 he speaks of the possibility of being poured out as a sacrifice, his tone may have been affected by his own desire to depart and be with Christ (1:23), by the near death of Epaphroditus (2:26-28), and by a dangerous turn of events, such as the recall of Felix. Whereas he would have released Paul upon receipt of a satisfying bribe (Acts 24:26), Felix might be tempted by Jewish bribes to send Paul to Jerusalem. Moreover, the attitude of Festus, his successor, could prove fatal. He might well return Paul to Jerusalem for judgment and potential punishment so that the danger of a murderous plot was also real (23:12-15; 25:1-3). F. F. Bruce perceived:

> Why did Paul appeal to Caesar? He did not do so while Felix was in office, presumably because Felix had virtually decided on his innocence and was simply postponing his formal acquittal and release. One day, Felix's procrastination would come to an end. . . . So Paul might have hoped. But with the recall of Felix and his supercession by Festus a new and dangerous situation was developing. . . .[16]

Paul knew that if he were to be tried by the Sanhedrin, its inevitable verdict (i.e., that he was a renegade and apostate) could lead to fatal consequences (Acts 25:9-11). At Rome, however, Paul would be far more secure from being put to death by the Jews (cf. Acts 28:17-31). Paul's attitude in Philippians is actually one of great vexation, uncertainty, and hope for release (1:19-20, 25, 27; 2:23-24). He was not despairing. On what other occasion during his long imprisonment could Paul's sense of closeness to death or release be so intense?

Thirdly, it is often objected that no reference is made to Philip as a comfort or fellow evangelist. Paul had stayed in his home on the way to Jerusalem (Acts 21:8). This is a difficult argument to press for those proponents of the Ephesian hypothesis, who have a similar problem for Aquila, Prisca, Erastus, and perhaps Apollos, and for the proponents of the Roman hypothesis, who have a problem with regard to Peter and perhaps Silas (cf. 1 Pet. 5:12-13) or Barnabas. [17] Whether Romans 16 was addressed to Rome or Ephesus, those greeted are likewise omitted from mention in the Captivity Epistles. The problem of Philip is more easily explained. As a long-resident evangelist (Acts 8:40) of Caesarea and as host to Paul there (21:8), he was exercising a proto-episcopal function (1 Tim. 3:2; Tit. 1:8). As an independent and responsible church leader, he would not be classified among Paul's fellow workers and "envoys." He could not be an errand boy for Paul. He was personally unknown in Paul's churches. Having his own full-time work in Caesarea, he would not be free to aid Paul. Moreover, since he was responsible for evangelizing local Jews and for appeasing a large Hebrew segment of his own church, he might find it more indiscreet to associate or sympathize with the suspect Paul, an apostle to the Gentiles, who was being well attended by his own followers. Because of especially tense Hebrew and Gentile relations in Caesarea (Josephus, *Antiquities* xx,8.7,9; *War* ii,13.7; 14.4-5; 18.1; vii,8.7), their reconciliation in Christ may have become all the more prized (Eph. 2:11-22; 3:4-9) by Paul and his co-workers. Nor would Philip be unjustified in feeling considerable resentment toward Paul, who had brought embarrassment and divisions to the Caesarean community as the result of stubbornly ignoring the word of the Holy Spirit through Agabus (Acts 21:11-14). Since Philip's daughters were also noted for prophesying (Acts 21:9), it is evident that Philip would highly esteem the prophecy received by Agabus. Would not Philip be among those who had an "I told you so" attitude toward the apostle? And how would Paul respond to this? Unless their sanctity repressed their human personality, Philip and Paul would have to remain largely aloof toward each other at Caesarea, in spite of their friendship. However, Philip might be able to help Paul in another arena. Is it coincidental that at a later date Philip and his daughters went to the same arena which was causing Paul so much anxiety? There is apt to be some connection between Paul's trouble with heretics in Asia and Phrygia and the work there by Philip and his daughters (Papias, Proclus, and Polycrates, *ap.* Eusebius, *H.E.* iii, 31.3-4; 39.9; v, 24.2). Perhaps Philip went there to deal with the dissidents of whom he learned through Paul and Epaphras at Caesarea. The theology of the Hellenists, among whom Philip was numbered (Acts 6:5; 8:5ff.), resembled more that of Paul than that of his opponents; such a comparison merits future study.

A fourth objection to the Caesarean origin is the doubt that Paul could have hoped to be released and to revisit his churches, presumably on the way to Rome and Spain. This criticism involves judgment concerning what Paul's plans would be *if* he had *not* decided to appeal to Caesar after the departure of Felix. Whether he would be freed or put to death in Palestine was the initial uncertainty facing the apostle. Since Colossians, Ephesians, Philemon, and Philippians, if written at Caesarea, would precede Paul's hearing before Festus and his appeal to Rome, his current legal situation during the time of the writing of these letters certainly cannot be assessed on the basis of his *subsequent* appeal to Caesar and transportation in bonds to Rome. Before his appeal, his plans may have been different. Nor, while imprisoned by Felix, would Paul necessarily think that he would linger in prison for over four years without a legal disposition of his case. For the written expression of his hope to visit Philemon (v. 22) and the Philippians (1:25-26; 2:24), Paul needed to have only one or two occasions, during his long imprisonment, in which he had either subjective or objective hope for release. Surely Paul was not at all times so lugubrious and pessimistic as (1) to believe that he was guilty in the eyes of Rome, and (2) to doubt perpetually both the justice given to Roman citizens and the efficacy of the church's prayers for his welfare. There is no reason to believe that the Caesarean imprisonment changed the apostle from a man of faith and hope into one of despair and resignation. The assumption is untenable that Paul never expected to be delivered by God and released by Felix. The sentiment of Luke, and hence perhaps of Paul himself, concerning the case for his release is expressed in the words attributed to Agrippa: "This man could have been set free if he had not appealed to Caesar" (Acts 26:32; cf. 28:18). Agrippa and Festus agreed that Paul was doing nothing worthy of imprisonment (26:31); Claudius Lysias had written to Felix that Paul in Jerusalem was "charged with nothing deserving death or imprisonment" (23:29). The Roman procurator Felix apparently from time to time sent for Paul and led him to believe that he would be freed upon payment of a sufficient enticement. Paul had a special cause for hope when Felix learned that his office as procurator was about to end. Acts 24:27 relates that "desiring to do the Jews a favor, Felix left Paul in prison" when he was succeeded by Festus. Whether this favor was at the cost of a sizable Jewish bribe which Felix could not obtain from the Christians is not stated, but it would be in accord with the procurator's greed. But Luke is quite clear about Felix's unwillingness to consider Paul guilty and to endanger his life. Paul may have hoped that before departing, Felix, who was by now well informed on all aspects of the cases for and against Paul, would spare his successor from the burden of repeating the investigations and hearings. There would be less likelihood, however, that Festus quickly would release Paul, since that would antagonize Jewish opinion at the outset and would make his reign more difficult. The incoming Festus, even more than the departing Felix, would prefer "to do the Jews a favor." Or we might say that Festus would do a favor to court public opinion, whereas Felix would do a favor to enrich himself. Accordingly, it would be a well-informed guess that Paul's hope oscillated during the reign of Felix and reached its height when he learned of the recall, but that Paul under Festus was plunged into insecurity and uncertainty, though not deprived of hope.

THE SETTING OF 2 TIMOTHY 4:9-22a

Insofar as Paul entertained the hope, if not the expectation, of being released, he would be laying plans for the future. But what were his present aspirations while lingering in the Caesarean confinement? In Romans he expresses his long-standing, but often frustrated, intent to visit Rome (1:10-15; 15:22-23; cf. Acts 19:21). His delay has been due to the need to complete the evangelization of the area from Jerusalem to Illyricum (Rom. 15:19-22; cf. 2 Cor. 10:13-16 for the same hesitancy to overextend his missions prematurely). Since, at the time of writing Romans 15:23, he had no room left for work where he was, he felt free to proceed to Rome and then onward to Spain (15:24, 28). However, he would change his plans if other significant opportunities for evangelization and confirmation were to appear. It was his policy to revisit churches which he had founded or in which there was serious trouble. It would be surprising if, on the way to Rome as a free man, he did not wish to see his converts after a long imprisonment, put their affairs in order, and say a final farewell. The prospect of returning from the West later was not bright. A visit to Phrygia (Philem. 22) for the first time and a return visit to Illyricum might be on his agenda.

There is evidence that Paul's plans were in a state of flux. According to Philippians 1:21-23 and 2:19-24, Paul was faced with the prospect of either martyrdom or release; he was waiting to "see how it will go with me." He was eager, but unable, to make definite plans. Two examples of adjusted plans may be found. When the apostle writes to Titus (3:12) that he has decided on his winter plans, he is indicating that previously his plans were tentative or different. Therefore, he has to notify Timothy of his recent decision. Also, Paul writes to Timothy (2 Tim. 4:13) to bring the cloak, books, and parchment which he had left at Troas. When would Paul have left them there except on the way to Jerusalem? Probably he did not originally expect to pass through Troas again on the way to Rome and Spain. At Troas, after a change in travel plans (Acts 20:3), Paul had met waiting representatives from Macedonia and Asia Minor (Acts 20:4-5). Probably the two from Asia, Tychicus and Trophimus, had been the ones intended to bring Paul's possessions with them from Ephesus. Paul then decided it would be safer to leave the things there rather than to take them to Jerusalem. After being imprisoned at Caesarea, he changed his plans. Whereas initially Paul would have had his possessions sent on to Corinth and Rome, now, when he hoped he was about to be released, he planned to stop at Troas in order personally to pick them up on the way from Colossae to Philippi, or he would have Timothy bring them on the way back from Philippi to Caesarea. Troas lies on this route of travel. However, after he appealed to Caesar, his chance of freedom to revisit his churches in the near future disappeared (Acts 25:11-12). Hence he had to request that Timothy pick up his cloak, books, and parchments (2 Tim. 4:13) for him. Accordingly, Second Timothy is dated after Paul's appeal to Caesar, whereas Philemon, Philippians, and Titus 3 belong to the prior period.

The events during the last five months at Caesarea can be fairly well fitted into place. Acts 24:27 seems to date the departure of Felix in the (late ?) spring of 59; *pleroo* indicates a full two years. Philippians was written not long before Felix departed, since, according to Acts 24:27, he was disposed to release Paul. Paul considered release to be the more likely prospect, but he knew the danger from a new procurator if the case were continued. Philippians shows the impatience of one who is oscillating between optimism and pessimism because his status is approaching a decision. At the other limit of time, Fair Haven in Crete was reached in October, after the Fast (of Atonement) had gone by. [18] New governors, according to Claudius's law of 43, had to leave Rome before the middle of April to take up their new offices (Dio Cassius, *History* 60.17.3). If the arrival of Festus is estimated to have occurred by June, Paul's first appearance before him is to be dated two weeks later (Acts 25: 1, 6: "after three days . . . not more than eight or ten days"). The defense before Agrippa probably was in August (25:13-14: "when some days . . ." and "many days"). Assuming that it would take a couple of weeks to prepare written reports for the journey (25:6), the departure from Caesarea could be placed in September. At least two or three weeks must be allowed for the difficulties in reaching Crete (27:3-12).

Paul's references to his first judicial defense *(en te próte mou apología)*, to his proclaiming the word to the Gentiles and to his rescue from the lion's mouth (2 Tim. 4:16-17) best fit the first hearing before Festus and his council (Acts 25:6-12). The terms *"apologeomai"* and *"apologia"* are used to describe Paul's defense (25:8,16). Though lacking witnesses, the apostle denied the charges and affirmed his faith that Jesus had risen from the dead and was alive. Festus was "at a loss how to investigate these questions" (25:20) about Jesus and about the Jewish Law and temple which the chief priests and elders had raised in order to obtain the right of adjudication in Jerusalem. Though sitting on the tribunal, Festus refused to judge or even to take up the case officially. He found that Paul "had done nothing deserving death" (25:25) ; i.e., "the accusers . . . brought no charge in his case of such evils as" Festus had supposed (25:18) and did not prove their charges that Paul had wronged the Jews, at least according to Roman law. "But Festus, wishing to do the Jews a favor" (25:9) and wishing to dispose of the case, suggested a trial in Jerusalem. Foreseeing the pressures and verdict in such an official trial and fearing death in an ambush on the way to Jerusalem (25:3; cf. 23:12ff.), Paul had no option but to appeal to Caesar. About Paul "the whole Jewish people petitioned" Festus, "both at Jerusalem and [Caesarea], shouting that he ought not to live any longer" (25:24). Paul sought to escape death on false, non-capital charges (25:11). He fittingly commented, "So I was rescued from the lion's mouth. The Lord will rescue me from every evil . . ." (2 Tim. 4:17-18). He had escaped a fatal transfer to Jerusalem. He had fought with wild beasts once before at Ephesus (1 Cor. 15:32) and despaired even of life (2 Cor. 1:8). Accepting Paul's appeal to Caesar following a conference with his council, Festus commanded Paul to be held until he could send him to Caesar.

Paul had now performed his first *apologia* since the arrival of Festus and departure of Timothy. He knew that his appeal to Caesar would necessitate another defense at Rome. On the other hand, it would be hard to imagine Paul's calling an *apologia* at Rome his first one, as if he had not made one in Caesarea or as if he expected that "Caesar" in Rome would give him more than one opportunity for self-defense by preaching his gospel before all the Gentiles (2 Tim. 4:16-17). At Caesarea Paul was given a second opportunity for making an *apologia* when King Agrippa arrived to welcome Festus (Acts 25:13ff.; 26:1-2). Paul may reasonably have anticipated his arrival and conference with Festus about Paul's case since letters had to be written indicating the charges against the prisoner being sent to Rome. Moreover, as Felix and his Jewish wife Drusilla were, upon arrival, interested in hearing Paul's views (24:24), so Paul may have hoped for a providential opportunity to address Agrippa and his sister Bernice when they arrived. Paul addressed him: "Because you are especially familiar with all customs and controversies of the Jews . . . I beg you to listen to me patiently" (26:3). The apostle proceeded to proclaim the gospel fully as he had done to all the Gentiles (Acts 26:2-23, especially 17, 20, 23). But at this second *apologia* (26:1, 24) Paul was no longer in danger of the lion's mouth.

Accordingly, 2 Timothy 4:9-22 is probably to be dated in August, 59. The brethren who were with Paul when he wrote to the Philippians (4:21) had largely departed (2 Tim. 4:10-11). The departure of Timothy is to be placed in June or July, before the first appearance before Festus. Paul earlier had intended to send Timothy to Philippi (Phil. 2:19, 22) "just as soon as I see how it will go with me," i.e., with Felix. But the departure of Felix settled nothing and the newly arrived Festus left for Jerusalem after three days, also without taking action. Impatiently sending Timothy on his mission, Paul was probably counting on other co-workers as witnesses; their departure was discouraging.

An explanation is necessary for Paul's later telling Timothy to do his best to come soon (2 Tim. 4:9, 11), at least before winter (4:21). This would befit a letter written in August. But did or did not Paul expect to spend the coming winter at Caesarea? Possibly Timothy, who by now knew of Paul's appeal to Caesar, may have understood Paul to say, "Come to me at Rome." This would be difficult, though not impossible. More likely, Paul did not foresee leaving for Rome so soon. Paul was not the one to decide when to sail for Italy, and Festus was probably more eager to get rid of Paul than Paul realized. Why else would such a risky long trip be begun in September? In Crete Paul advised against proceeding further (Acts 27:10), knowing from his own experience the dangers of shipwrecks (2 Cor. 11:25). The difficulties of leaving Caesarea at such a late date were certainly known by Paul and Festus. Paul had appealed to Caesar first in July, and when he wrote to Timothy, he was still lingering in Caesarea pending action by Festus

(Acts 25:21). Thus he had reason to believe that he would be spending the coming winter in Caesarea. Moreover, papers to accompany him would have to be drawn following his appearance before Agrippa and Festus in August. But Paul was dispatched sooner than he expected. Paul was apparently ill at the time of his leaving (27:3) : a further reason for his not anticipating an early sailing for Rome.

Can the setting of 2 Timothy 4:9-22 be further ascertained? Can sense be made of all of its allusions? After Paul had met his accusers face to face, first before Festus and later before Agrippa and Festus, then he became aware of the latest form of the Jewish charges against which he would have to defend himself at Rome. The missions of Timothy and Tychicus were probably intended partly to raise money for the apostle's appeal and to collect evidence and witnesses for his defense. Second Timothy 4:13 and 15 give such clues. The initial occasion of Paul's arrest was the supposition that he had brought Trophimus the Ephesian into the temple (Acts 21:29; cf. 25:8: "Neither against the law of the Jews, nor against the temple . . . have I offended at all"). In 2 Timothy 4:20 Paul informs Timothy that Trophimus had been left ill at Miletus. Since Trophimus disappeared and no mention is made of his apprehension, one may conclude that he had escaped from Jerusalem and returned home. Paul would have to discredit the testimony of Asian Jews concerning the time and circumstances of the alleged appearance of Trophimus in the temple (21:27-28). Regrettably Trophimus was now unable, because of illness, to return to testify in Paul's behalf. He was left ill at Miletus. Possibly, through the message of Tychicus (2 Tim. 4:12), Paul did not press the incapacitated Trophimus to come to his aid. But *apélipon* can mean "they left" as well as "I left." Because Trophimus was sick (possibly with fear), he did not accompany those who came in place of Erastus from Corinth [19] but who forsook Paul at his *apologia* (2 Tim. 4:16-17), as did his fellow workers (4:10-12). If Trophimus did not return as a witness, then it would be easier to understand Paul's lack of support at his first defense (4:16) and his need to appeal to Caesar. Second Timothy 1:15 records the later fact that "all who are in Asia turned away from" Paul, which implies that he had sought help or support from them and recently learned of its unavailability. The use of the aorist, *apestráphesán,* in that passage suggests a particular act in a definite circumstance in which unfaithfulness to the apostle was shown.

What other testimony could Asians who had not been in Jerusalem supply for Paul, whether in Caesarea or Rome? Phygelus and Hermogenes were two specific individuals on whom Paul had counted (2 Tim. 1:15). Paul had to be prepared to answer all charges brought by Asian Jews. Fortunately for him none of the accusers were present at his hearing: an absence to which he tersely calls attention (Acts 24:19; cf. 25: 7, 24). Since apparently no Asian Jews had in person brought charges against Paul, Paul's best defense would be that he had not taught at Ephesus against Judaism, and that his work was largely confined to Gentiles. Ephesian witnesses to this defense would carry great weight against charges by Jerusalem Jews as to what Paul had been teaching at Ephesus. It is highly unlikely that the Jews would now try to prove that Paul had caused rioting at Ephesus, for, as he had not been tried by Roman officials three years before (Acts 19:35-41), there would be little chance of prosecuting him now. Furthermore, Paul was now on trial for his life. Thus the area of possible Ephesian testimony is strictly limited. It may be conjectured that Phygelus and Hermogenes were Gentiles who were especially qualified to speak of Paul's activity among the Gentiles at the hall of Tyrannus, where all the residents of Asia had been free to hear him argue (Acts 19:9-10). The Jewish charges could plausibly pertain to Paul's disruptive teaching in synagogues (19:8-9). The Asian Tychicus (20:4) would be well qualified to get assistance from his own church; thus Paul sent him there (2 Tim. 4:12), as well as Timothy. Paul cautions the latter against Alexander, the (Jewish) coppersmith (2 Tim. 4:14-15; cf. Acts 19:33-34), perhaps because, as an opponent of the Pauline gospel, he would discourage potential witnesses for Paul among Hebrew believers. But it is not clear whether these two Alexanders are to be identified (see also 1 Tim. 1:20).

The charges against Paul and possibly against Aristarchus, his companion at Ephesus (Acts 19:29) and fellow prisoner in Caesarea (Acts 27:1-2), concerned primarily their teaching against the Torah and the chosen people (Acts 21:28; 23:29; 24:14; 25:8, 15, 18-19, 24-25; 26:2-3, 6-8, 20-23; 28:17). James may have concisely summed up the charges in Acts 21:21. Had or had not the apostle to the Gentiles so strayed from the *religio licita* of Judaism that he was to be considered the subversive founder of a new sect? [20] One of Paul's strongest lines of defense would be to present copies of his epistles (e.g., First Corinthians and Romans) for examination by "Caesar" in order to prove that he was not teaching against true Judaism. For this reason Paul urged Timothy to bring the books and especially the parchments. But just as Gallio at Corinth (Acts 18: 14-16) and Festus at Caesarea (25:20; cf. 28:18) felt that it was not within competence of their jurisdiction to judge in matters of the Torah, Caesar's court in Rome would likewise be unable to judge Paul's case according to Roman jurisprudence and would "throw the case out of court." Paul hoped this would happen after they examined his innocuous, irenic writings.

Why did Paul inform Timothy that "Erastus remained at Corinth"? Timothy and Erastus were together at Corinth when Paul wrote Romans 16:21-23. When writing later to Timothy from Caesarea, Paul was apparently looking to Erastus for some sort of assistance; but Paul had just learned from those who recently had arrived that Erastus unexpectedly was still at Corinth, rather than having proceeded elsewhere. As Erastus was a city treasurer (Rom. 16:23) who could have been the same Erastus sent to Macedonia and Corinth with Timothy (Acts 19:22) on a mission which included the task of organizing the Jerusalem collection, it is reasonable to posit, by analogy, that Erastus had planned a journey to bring money to Paul. The apostle thus explains to Timothy why no news or greeting is sent from Erastus; he was not among those who had been expected to arrive after Timothy had left Paul's side. If Erastus were not going to meet Timothy as planned, Timothy would need the news by way of Paul in Caesarea; but we should not anticipate in Paul's epistles information about perilous monetary transfers.

TITUS 3:12-15

Into this setting the Pauline fragment [21] in the Letter to Titus can be readily placed. If Titus himself had been in Crete earlier, 54-55 is the only plausible date. Having accompanied Paul on his third trip through Galatia in 54 from Antioch (Gal. 2: 3-5) to Ephesus, he seemingly disappears. He may have directed the Galatians to take up a collection and delivered the letter of instruction to them before he himself was sent to Corinth in 56 (2 Cor. 2:13; 7:6–8:23; 12:17-18). There are indications that Paul earlier had sent Titus to Crete to evangelize the island — before the mission on which he wrote to him. In Titus 3:14 Paul speaks of "our people"; he greets "those who love us" (Titus 3:15). In 1:5 "Paul" speaks of Titus's mending "what was defective" and appointing "elders in every town." Whether or not Titus had preached earlier on the island, it is altogether likely that he was there at some time. Although Titus 1:5 in its present form is probably editorial, the anti-Cretan editor (1:12) must have known of Titus's work on the island because he would not be inclined to give the false Cretans their own fictitious evangelist. That Titus was working among believers who were not personally known to Paul may be deduced from (1) the impersonal reference to "those who love us in the faith" (3:15); (2) the need to instruct "our people" to help cases of urgent need; and (3) the restriction of greetings to Titus by Paul and his companions (cf. Rom. 16:16; 1 Cor. 16:19; Phil. 4:21-22).

Titus apparently did not accompany Paul to Jerusalem (Acts 20:4-5), perhaps because of unpleasant memories of the first visit there (Gal. 2:3-5). He was last reported as being sent back to Corinth in the summer of 56 (2 Cor. 8:6) in order to complete the collection there, or at least to do so until Paul arrived, probably for the three winter months (Acts 20:3) of 56–57. Paul wrote the Letter to the Romans approximately in early March, 57, when it could be delivered by sea, and shortly before his departure for Jerusalem (Rom. 15:25). Titus is unmentioned in the Ephesian draft, which Phoebe carried (Rom. 16:1-2). Accordingly, there is a presumption that Titus departed from Corinth for Crete after completing the Corinthian collection, but before Paul wrote the Ephesian copy of Romans. The opening of the sailing season in February, 57, is a likely time of departure. Paul was planning to go to Rome from Jerusalem upon completing delivery of the collection on the day of Pentecost (Acts 20:16) and to take Titus with him from Crete. Hence he would wish Titus to get an early start for

Crete from Corinth where his presence was no longer needed. Other considerations confirm this mission to Crete. Tychicus and Artemis appear in Titus 3:12. At least one of the pair would have to be present with Paul whenever he wished to dispatch him to Crete. Tychicus, an Asian (Acts 20:4), is first mentioned as a bearer of his church's gift to the Jerusalem community. In Titus 1:5 *"kataleipo"* splendidly fits Paul's leaving Titus *behind* in Crete, rather than taking him along to Jerusalem, for Paul wanted affairs in the reputedly troublesome island (1:12-13) set in order by his trusted "partner" (2 Cor. 8:23) before moving on to Rome and Spain (Rom. 15:23-24). Following changes in Paul's plans as necessitated by his imprisonment and expected release, however, Titus was directed to join Paul at Nicopolis (Titus 3:12), where they could spend the winter before proceeding together on to Rome, as earlier planned.

The mention of Nicopolis has been a traditional barrier to understanding the setting of the Epistle to Titus. The most satisfactory setting for Paul's spending the winter at Nicopolis [22] would be in 59–60, while on his way from Jerusalem to Rome via a final tour of some of his churches in Asia Minor and Macedonia. This approximate date can be determined by the process of elimination. Paul did not even meet Apollos (Titus 3:13) until the latter had returned from Corinth to Ephesus (Acts 19:1; 1 Cor. 16:12). He would not have sent him to Crete until they had established a working relationship. Hence Paul could not have planned spending a winter at Nicopolis before that of 54–55 or of 55–56. But at this time Paul had hired the hall of Tyrannus for two years (Acts 19:9-10), and he was planning a collection for Jerusalem (1 Cor. 16:1-4). Thus these winters are eliminated from serious consideration. But from June, 56, to the Passover in 57 (Acts 20:1-6; 1 Cor. 16:3-7; 2 Cor. 2:12-13; 7:5-6; 8:1-6; Rom. 15:19; 16:1), Paul was in Troas, Macedonia, Illyricum, and Achaia. Since Titus had been dispatched to Corinth to complete the collection and to restore Paul's authority, Paul could hardly have written him in Crete asking him to come to Nicopolis for the winter of 56–57, which Paul spent at Corinth as planned. Furthermore, Tychicus must have remained at Ephesus until the collection was completed or until the apostle had arrived (Acts 20:3-5).

However, Paul's travels prior to his arrival at Corinth at the beginning of the winter of 56–57 give some clue to his interest in Nicopolis. He planned to pass through Macedonia the previous summer (1 Cor. 16:5, 8); Acts 20:1-2 has Paul going all through these parts before coming to Greece. In writing 2 Corinthians 10:13-16 from Macedonia during the late spring or summer, Paul indicated that he had not yet preached to lands beyond Corinth, but that he planned to do so soon. The allusion may have been both to Dalmatia and to Rome and Spain. Later, in Romans 15:19-20 he states that he has now preached the gospel as far around from Jerusalem as Illyricum, and therefore he is ready to come to Rome. He implies that his (recent) reaching of Illyricum [23] has freed him to proceed further afield. In this context Paul appears to be proud of the extent of his recent travels. Nicopolis lies not only within his Jerusalem to Illyricum circuit but also on a line from Corinth to Rome. The apostle could not accurately say that he had no more "room for work in these regions" (Rom. 15:23) if he had not visited Nicopolis on the west coast of Greece while journeying from Illyricum to Corinth. The lengthy period from Pentecost to December, 56, left Paul adequate time for traveling from Ephesus to Corinth via Troas, Macedonia, southern Illyricum, and Nicopolis. In writing to Titus, Paul may well have been contemplating a return visit; Titus is presumed to know *which* Nicopolis [24] is meant and why the visit was planned. Paul's purpose in (re-) visiting Nicopolis in association with Titus was not only to confirm the brethren, but also to get as close as possible to Rome and Spain after leaving Philippi and possibly Corinth. After spending the winter at Nicopolis, he could get an early start from there for Rome at the opening of the next sailing season. The city lay on the coastal route from Corinth to Brundisium. [25]

Why did Paul select Tychicus or Artemas as a future emissary to Titus on Crete? Tychicus was an Asian representative on the Jerusalem trip (Acts 20:4), and he appears as Paul's messenger to Colossae (Col. 4:7) and Ephesus (2 Tim. 4:12; cf. Eph. 6:21). Artemas, with whom he is associated, in all likelihood was native also to the general area of Ephesus. He bore some form of the name of the great goddess and patron of the Ephesians, such as Artemidorus, "gift of Artemis." He was also thought to be the first bishop of Lystra (lists of the Seventy by Pseudo-Dionysius, Pseudo-Dorotheus, and Abul-l-Barakat [Greek]). The available information suggests that Paul intended to send either Tychicus or Artemas to Titus from some port on the south or west coast of Asia. Since Paul while at Caesarea sent Tychicus to this area on an earlier mission, he would naturally be with, or not far away from, the apostle when he passed through Phrygia after his anticipated release. Paul thus ostensibly had planned to send one of the two to Crete as he was leaving Phrygia or Asia for Troas, Philippi, and Nicopolis. Both Paul and Titus thereby would reach Nicopolis before the advent of the winter season. In light of this plan we can understand the subsequent departure of Titus for Dalmatia (2 Tim. 4:10), i.e., southern Illyricum. The Pauline fragment, Titus 3:12-15, is best dated not long before the writing of 2 Timothy 4:9-22; at least they cohere and the former is prior. One reason for Titus's departure may be suggested. After two and one-half years in Crete, his further opportunities for evangelization and organization there were more limited than those in Dalmatia and Nicopolis, where the believers, converted three years earlier, were in need of visitation. Such was the case whether or not Paul's arrival was still anticipated. If Paul did come, Titus could easily reach him from neighboring Dalmatia. More likely, Titus had heard, perhaps through Tychicus, of Paul's appeal to Caesar and of the change in winter plans. Paul now was not going to revisit his churches. Titus decided, or followed the apostle's directions, to depart for Dalmatia in order to do alone the work in which Paul had hoped to participate. Paul did not speak with disapproval of Titus's move, in contrast to the case of Demas (2 Tim. 4:10). From Dalmatia, as from Nicopolis, Titus would be able to reach Rome as soon as possible the next February if the still imprisoned Paul wished a reunion.

The setting of the note to Titus can be further specified. Paul's inclusive greetings from "all who are with me" (Titus 3:15) resemble those of Philippians 4:21-22: "The brethren who are with me greet you. All the saints greet you. . . ." The group with Paul seems to be flexible and *ad hoc* in its composition; it is centered in Paul. The designation, "the brethren," would be inappropriate as a description of a local church, but fitting for his companions and associates during his imprisonment, at least before his relative isolation when writing 2 Timothy 4:10-12. The mission of Apollos and Zenas the lawyer (Titus 3:13-14) is also revealing. Doubtless they were the bearers of the note from Paul; they had been at the apostle's side at the time of writing. To whom else would the note be entrusted for delivery? If Apollos and Zenas were the ones in need of aid, they would be the natural carriers of a letter bearing Paul's request for support. Their mission was hardly a local one; they were on urgent business elsewhere. They were apparently personally unknown in Crete, as Paul had to justify assistance to them. Zenas had to be identified as a lawyer even to Titus; he nowhere else is mentioned among extant Pauline writings. Yet his mission was important. Later tradition (lists of the Seventy by Pseudo-Dorotheus and Pseudo Hippolytus) made him bishop of Lydda, i.e., Diospolis, a city lying between Jerusalem and Caesarea. What special need would Paul have of this lawyer and Apollos, and when? The major legal problem during Paul's long imprisonment was this: Was it the Roman court or was it the Sanhedrin which had primary competence and jurisdiction in investigating and judging the charges against him? Paul consequently would have need of an attorney experienced in similar (Palestinian) cases of conflict of jurisdiction. Apollos would be well-qualified, if not the best qualified believer, to speak on the relation of the old and new religions; i.e., he could demonstrate that in Jesus were fulfilled the promises of the Law and the prophets (Acts 18:28). He was eloquent and learned in Scripture (Acts 18:24), the future author of Hebrews, [26] and Paul's co-worker at Ephesus (1 Cor. 16:12). Surely he would be expected to play some role in helping to expedite the release of Paul or at least the hearing of his case. Now, if Apollos and Zenas were in Crete in transit from Caesarea, their destination would be Rome if we project their direction of travel. One occasion which might require such an urgent trip was when Felix was about to be succeeded by Portius Festus. This was a crucial legal juncture. At the same time, the leading Jews of Caesarea went to Rome both to accuse Felix of permitting his soldiers to loot their homes and to argue about their equality of privileges of citizenship in the city (Josephus, *Antiquities* xx,8.7 and 9; *War* ii,13.7). April or May, 59, would be as good a time as any for dating the letter to Titus. Such a time would be prior to the setback in Paul's fortunes when Festus arrived, prior also to his subsequent appeal to Caesar, his change of plans of visitation, the departure of his associates (including Timothy's to Asia and Philippi and Titus's to Dalmatia), and to the writing of 2 Timothy 4:9-22. This date would leave time for Paul and Titus to reach Nicopolis before winter, according to plan. It would also be when Paul was just as expectant of release as he was while writing Philippians. Whenever *(hotan)* "I send Artemas or Tychicus to you, do your best to come to me at Nicopolis" (Titus 3:12) is comparable in optimism to "I trust in the Lord that shortly *(tachéos)* I myself shall come also" (Phil. 2:24). Paul is not sure of when he will send a messenger to Titus, though it will be before the approach of winter. With the missions of Apollos and Timothy and the pending one of Titus, Paul was getting his plans under way. The embassy of Apollos and Zenas and then the imminent departure of Felix aroused the apostle's hope of release.

We do not wish to press the case of the genuineness and hypothetical setting of the Letter to Titus, since the case for the Caesarean origin of the Captivity Letters is to be judged independently. However, if the two hypotheses are mutually illuminating, so much the better. The assumption has been made that all these letters are from Caesarea, and they have been treated as a unit for purpose of analysis. In so doing we have failed (or neglected?) to uncover any need to locate elsewhere any of the Epistles, except another fragment of Second Timothy (1:15-18).

LATER DEVELOPMENTS IN PAUL'S THEOLOGY

One serious problem must be faced, however. If Paul's letters can be grouped and placed in proper sequence, we should expect these conclusions to correspond to some meaningful pattern in the unfolding of Paul's teaching. While such a systematic study is much needed, certain developments have often been noted. [27] The Christology and ecclesiology of Colossians (and of Ephesians, if it belongs to this period) are the most advanced of those of all Paul's letters. Is it permissible to locate them perhaps only a year and one-half after Romans, and before

Philippians? The dilemma can be escaped by positing interpolations in Colossians, [28] probably by the author of Ephesians. But such a radical solution is unnecessary once the occasions and purposes of Colossians and Philippians are compared. In writing to Colossae, Paul is combatting certain theological-cosmological speculations. Moreover, during his imprisonment he had ample time for meditating on the gospel and for maturing in his understanding of it. But Philippians 1; 2; 3:20-21; and 4 [29] are expressions of his love and solicitude for his community; his approach is one of encouragement and exhortation concerning the Christian life and suffering. He describes his own state of mind and plans and he thanks them for their gift. It is the most personal and the least theologically controversial of all his letters addressed to churches. As such it is not an especially fruitful source of information on tendencies in Paul's insight into the gospel. The *kenosis* theory of Philippians 2:5-11 does represent a significant advance in Paul's thought and in the use of earlier material incorporated in these verses, however. Further, it would be difficult to find elsewhere in Paul's letters as Christocentric an expression of piety as Philippians 1:21: "For to me to live is Christ." Only in Philippians 3:20 did he explicitly call Jesus, *"Soter"* (Savior). Paul's work in prison and among Caesar's household had progressed from the prayer of Colossians 4:3 and Ephesians 6:18-20 to the achievement noted in Philippians 1:12-14 and 4:22.

We have treated Ephesians as if it could, on the basis of its chronological setting, be included among the Captivity Letters. Whether or not this approach is sound must now be examined.

5

Ephesians

Many have questioned whether Paul ever addressed this epistle to the church in Ephesus, even though the title suggests such a destination. Because the Muratorian Canon (line 51), Irenaeus (*Adv. Haer.* v,2.3; cf.8.1; 14.3), Clement of Alexandria (*Strom.* iv,8.65; cf. *Paed.* i,18), and Tertullian (*Adv. Marcionem* v,11.17) believed the Epistle to have been addressed to the Ephesians, and because the Chester Beatty Papyrus (P[46]), Vaticanus, and Sinaiticus entitle it "to Ephesians" *(pròs Ephesíous),* there is no need to doubt that it bore such a designation in some of the earliest codices of Paul's collected writings. According to Henry J. Cadbury, "While independent it needed no localizing of addressees, but when associated with other 'Pauline' letters that did give locale, a similar differentiating title was supplied. *Pròs Ephesíous* was added, as *pròs Hebraíous* was supplied for another writing." [1] As F. W. Beare confidently points out, the same form (e.g., *pròs Romaíous, pròs Galátas*) "is inconceivable as the title of a single epistle circulating by itself; it is unintelligible except in relation to a collection." However, "the scribes who first used this title found nothing in the text of the epistle itself to guide them." [2] For, the most reliable array of textual witnesses (P[46], Vaticanus, Sinaiticus, 424, 1739, Marcion's text, [3] Origen, Basil, Ambrosiaster, and Jerome) establishes the likelihood that the words *en Epheso* were omitted originally in 1:1. The strange location of the words in the reading "who are in Ephesus" *(ousin en Epheso)* is a further witness to their being a gloss. Their insertion into the text by inference from the title on the codex is readily understandable, but no satisfactory motive for their hypothetical disappearance from 1:1 has yet been offered. The origin of the codex title itself for a letter borne by Tychicus (Eph. 6:21) is traceable to 2 Timothy 4:12: "Tychicus I have sent to Ephesus." Because Tychicus, the carrier of the Epistle, was sent to Ephesus by Paul during his imprisonment, it was deduced that the ultimate destination of both the Epistle and the bearer was Ephesus.

Nevertheless, the impersonal form and references of the Epistle were altogether inappropriate for the community of Ephesus. It would not be plausible for Paul to have the Ephesians primarily in mind when writing: "I have heard of your faith in the Lord Jesus and your love toward all the saints" (Eph. 1:15); or "Assuming that you have heard of the stewardship of God's grace that was given to me for you, how the mystery was made known to me. . . . When you read this you can perceive my insight into the mystery of Christ" (3:2-4); or "You did not so learn Christ! — assuming that you have heard about him and were taught in him . . ." (4:20-21). The salutation is brief and general. The impersonal tenor of the whole letter reaches its climax at the end, where no greetings are to be found. Nothing in the letter hints that Paul visited or preached to the readers. No allusions are made to plans for future personal contacts with them. James Strachan observed: "The writer . . . warms to his theme, but not to his readers. He gives no expression of his inner feelings." [4]

If the traditional bonds of the Epistle with the church at Ephesus are to be dissolved, the address, "To the saints who are also faithful in Christ Jesus" *(tois hagiois tois ousin kai pistois en Christo Iesou)* (1:1) must refer to believers living elsewhere than in Ephesus. As it stands, the phrase is at best awkward; [5] at worst it is unintelligible because it either is incomplete or suggests a distinction, rather than a total overlap, between saints and believers. Regardless of who the author of the Epistle was, he could be expected to follow the usage of Romans 1:7; Colossians 1:2; and Philippians 1:1 with regard to the Pauline placement of the geographical phrase *(tois ousin [en . . .])*, namely, either before *hagiois* or after *Christo*. The abundant similarities of the Epistle to the Colossians, including the parallel in Colossians 1:2, suggest that the original phrase may have been *"tois (en . . . ?) hagiois kai pistois en Christo Iesou."* In such a case, however, *tois ousin en Epheso* would be a clumsily inserted gloss based on the title, *pròs Ephesíous.* This insertion was only partially removed by the editors of the text underlying Vaticanus, Sinaiticus, and P[46]; presumably these editors found *tois ousin* intelligible and considered only *en Epheso* to have been a later insertion. This hypothesis, however, does not shed any light on the question of identifying the addressees or the question of whether there was an original address, *en . . . ,* which was lost or dropped.

THE ENCYCLICAL HYPOTHESIS

As long ago as 1598 Theodore Beza suggested that Ephesians was a circular letter intended for Ephesus and surrounding communities. In the next century Hugo Grotius included the Laodiceans among the recipients, and Archbishop James Ussher considered the letter an encyclical in which the first verse had a blank space to be filled in with the name of any church receiving it. [6] According to this hypothesis, *en Epheso* happened to survive in one of the copies. Rudolph Anger's *Über den Laodicenerbrief* in 1845 was a landmark in the development of this line of thought. During the twentieth century there has been little enthusiasm for Ussher's "blank-space" theory for several reasons. [7] In ancient usage no parallel is known. Why was *en* not included in all copies, thereby leaving only the name of the place to be inserted? If a copy were made for each intended community, why are no more names preserved in the textual variants of 1:1? Additional problems beset the encyclical or circular hypothesis. The New Testament general epistles carried along a certain route (Galatians, James, and First Peter) do not pose the same textual problem as does Ephesians. As Shirley Jackson Case commented, "Paul knows how to express himself clearly when he wishes to address one letter to several churches (2 Cor. 1:1; Gal. 1:2), and surely he would have been more explicit had he designed this for a circular letter." [8] Or if Ephesians were written by a devoted follower of Paul, his knowledge of Pauline practice would have guided him as to the form of the address.

Second Corinthians is addressed to "all the saints who are in the whole of Achaia," but it is intended primarily for the Corinthian church. Thus it appears that Paul might write to one community in particular even in a general epistle. When speaking of "the churches of Asia" (1 Cor. 16:19), he meant primarily Ephesus (16:8). One other piece of evidence also indicates that Paul, when writing primarily for the benefit of one community, intended his letter to be read in nearby churches. The Colossians were to be read a letter from Laodicea (Col. 4:16). Consequently, even though Ephesians was not an encyclical, Pauline practice suggests that it was to be read outside the church for which it was chiefly intended, at least if there were a group of nearby churches. A further concession may be made to the circular hypothesis, by virtue of the analogy of Ephesians to Romans. The name of a city could be removed from the text, as in Romans 1:7 and 15, ostensibly in order to make an individual letter more general when a copy of it was sent elsewhere. But we can only conjecture about the occasion of the origin of textual variants in these two verses.

LOCATION OF THE READERS

Several passages in Ephesians, nevertheless, indicate that the circle of readers was a geographically limited one. Their Gentile origin is manifest from Ephesians 2:1ff., 11ff.; 3:1-9; 4:17-22; 5:8. The recipients are distinguished from other believers (1:13, 15; 2:22; 3:18; 6:18). Several passages suggest a specific address. Paul remembered them in his prayers (1:15-16; 3:14). Tychicus was to visit them also and tell everything (6:21). They were interested in Paul's welfare (3:13; 6:19-22) and he in theirs (1:15ff.; 3:1, 13ff.). [9] Paul had heard of the readers' "faith in the Lord Jesus" (1:15). Such semi-personal elements are intelligible only if the readers are confined to a specific geographical area, and if the apostle had information about a concrete situation.

Where were the readers centered? Let us examine the situation envisioned. The recipients are not thought of as personal acquaintances of Paul. But they, "who have heard the word of truth, the gospel of [their] salvation, and have believed in him [Christ], were sealed with the promised Holy Spirit" (1:13;

cf. 4:30). In 3:1-9 Paul commends himself and the mystery which was revealed to him. This presupposes that his authority had been challenged by rivals, who were making converts of their own. Paul is portrayed as being in prison at the time of writing (3:1; 4:1; 6:20). When he says in 6:21, "Now that you also may know how I am and what I am doing, Tychicus the beloved brother and faithful minister in the Lord will tell you everything," he indicates that he is in the same situation as he portrayed in Colossians 4:7: "Tychicus will tell you all about my affairs; he is a beloved brother and faithful minister and fellow servant in the Lord." In fact, the next verse in each passage is identical: "I have sent him to you for this very purpose, that you may know how we are and that he may encourage your hearts." There can be no more explicit indication that Ephesians is portrayed as having been written at the same time as Colossians. Both sets of readers neither knew Paul personally nor knew of his present condition. Extensive parallels with Colossians exist, [10] though there are some differences in word usage. [11] The resemblances do confirm that the author of Ephesians looked upon his letter as a companion writing to — if not a commentary on — Colossians, which he deemed to be of special significance to his readers also. Where can we look for a Pauline letter of this description, which was written to converts who were not Paul's own and which was carried by Tychicus during Paul's imprisonment? According to Colossians 4:16: "And when this letter has been read among you, have it read also in the church of the Laodiceans; and see that you read also the letter from Laodicea." The letters had enough to say on mutually pertinent subjects to be worth exchanging. Now Paul was personally unknown among both the Laodiceans (Col. 2:1) and the Colossians (1:2-9), and in these two passages (cf. Col. 4:12-13) he expresses his same concern for both churches. They apparently faced common dangers (Col. 2:1) as described by Epaphras. In the words of Charles P. Anderson,

There are several indications in Colossians that the occasion of Laodiceans was very similar to that of Colossians. The very fact that Paul wanted both churches to read both letters implies that he felt each letter was relevant to the situation of each congregation. In addition, the close geographical proximity of the two churches makes probable their participation in a common religious and theological environment. More important, Paul shows by the manner of his expression that the two churches are in fact linked in his mind (2:1; 4:13). . . . The directive to exchange letters seems to imply that the purpose of the letters must have been nearly the same.[12]

On the other hand, if the similarities of the situation and message were so great, why would two separate letters need to be written? The Laodicean letter mentioned by Paul was already written, or at least partially drafted, when Colossians 4:16 was written.

Although the Letter to Philemon reached the Colossian church at the same time as Paul's letter to them (Col. 4:9), it would be very dubious to identify the letter *ek Laodikeias* (Col. 4:16) as the canonical Philemon. [13] The fate of Onesimus was hardly the business of various churches in the area, as if Paul wished to make it a public issue in order to bring ecclesiastical pressure to bear on one of the leaders! The Letter to Philemon was a tactful, private communication on a delicate subject. A further difficulty is that Marcion's canon included both Philemon and Laodiceans. As the lesser, private writing was preserved, it would be natural to expect that the letter *ek Laodikeias,* which was read at the apostle's request also at Colossae, would not be allowed to fall into neglect.

The tentative conclusion is that Ephesians, though of pedagogical value wherever Paul's gospel was not well known, is, or is intended to represent, that letter *ek Laodikeias.* Harnack is among the many scholars [14] who have held this hypothesis. Two forms are possible: Ephesians was written for the Laodiceans, or the Epistle was meant to circulate in an area of Asia Minor which included Laodicea. The churches of the Lycus and Maeander Valleys were the most likely readers. But it would be going beyond the evidence to hold that the letter was intended to be read in churches which were not visited by Tychicus on his mission (Eph. 6:21; Col. 4:7) or in those not in the same situation as those of Colossae, Laodicea, and Hierapolis (Col. 2:1-2; 4:13). If Ephesians were the Letter to the Laodiceans, the original copy was kept at Laodicea and it circulated from there. The fact that Hierapolis (Col. 4:13) is not mentioned again in 4:16 tends to argue against a wide, intended circulation of the Laodicean letter; just as significant is the lack of reference to Hierapolis in Colossians 2:1 as well. This verse may be our best clue to identifying the recipients of Ephesians: "I want you to know how greatly I strive for you, and for those at Laodicea, and for all who have not seen my face." The Laodicean letter was not primarily an encyclical; otherwise the designation of 4:16 would be a less specific and less local one. Indeed, from this verse it is natural to assume that the Laodiceans' copy was addressed to them alone. In 1:1 we might look for *en Laodikeía,* though no textual evidence supporting such a reading has yet been found. Colossians 4:16 tells of a letter from Laodicea which was read in the church of the Laodiceans. Few scholars think that it was written there. Charles Anderson asks pertinently: "In Colossians Paul sends greetings to the church in Laodicea. Why should he greet the Laodiceans if he were writing them a separate letter?" [15] Paul does not actually say that he had personally written this letter to the Laodiceans. Yet Marcion believed so when he entitled Ephesians, "to the Laodiceans." [16] Whether he derived this title from tradition or by his own inference is unknowable. [17] Probably for critical reasons, at least, he refused to accept the title *pros Ephesíous* as found on some codices.

Why, then, does not Ephesians bear the title "Laodiceans"? Possibly because of the deterioration of the Laodicean church (Rev. 3:14-22, especially 16: "I will spew you out of my mouth"). Does this most severe of John's criticisms indicate a break in fellowship and communion? If so, the name of the church was removed from the list of honored recipients of Pauline epistles. Marcion's use of this title would inhibit any remaining use of this title in Catholic circles. The evidently unexamined Marcionite "Laodicean" epistle was deemed heretical and thus "taboo" by the Muratorian Canonist. He and Tertullian considered such a title to be a Marcionite invention. Reasons for the origin of this alternative title, "to the Ephesians," have already been suggested. It is unlikely that the original letter survived when Laodicea was destroyed by an earthquake in 60. If the original copy were lost at Laodicea, a copy may have survived at Colossae, where it had been read (Col. 4:16), or at Ephesus. Wherever it survived, it is possible that it had already been turned into a generally circulating document by removal of *en Laodikeía* from 1:1. On the other hand, if the original letter to Laodicea were lost, and if no copies of it survived elsewhere, a replacement would be desired. An apocryphal letter to Laodiceans circulated among Catholics from the third or fourth to the sixteenth centuries. [18] But our canonical Ephesians may have already met this need of filling the gap suggested by Colossians 4: 16. The weakness of this hypothesis, though, stems from the apparent absence of the Laodicean title in ecclesiastical non-Marcionite tradition.

The issue at hand thus reduces itself to: Is our Ephesians the original letter *ek Laodikeías* or a later imitation thereof? In either case we have a local letter which was adaptable for general circulation among believers who did not know Paul. The question of originality is closely related to that of authorship.

THE WRITER

A comparison of the friendlier, laudatory, personal tone of Colossians and Romans with the abstract salutationless beginning and close of Ephesians, even though Epaphras had evangelized both cities (Col. 4:12-13), suggests that Ephesians was written by someone who was less diplomatic and gracious than Paul, by someone who was less capable, or at least less experienced, in addressing strangers. No individual message is found. There is no counterpart to Paul's greetings to Laodicea and to the house of Nympha (Col. 4:15). Even the history of the readers' successful evangelization (1:13, 15) is not mentioned.

The case against the direct authorship of Ephesians by Paul has won the adherence of a majority of modern writers. [19] Those who reject the Pauline authorship must account for its extraordinary resemblance to the apostle's thought and terminology; those who accept Paul as author have the equally difficult burden of explaining stylistic differences. [20] Unless one holds that Paul dictated the Epistle verbatim or wrote it with his own hand, the alternative explanations are (by degree of decreasing proximity to Paul himself) : Paul's giving liberty to a scribe or fellow worker to write an epistle conforming to Paul's general outline; a disciple's writing it independently from memory of the apostle's thought and terms; or a second generation writer's creating a work based on tradition and a thorough reading of Paul's collected epistles, Colossians in particular. The latter explanation [21] is satisfying only for one who is most impressed by differences rather than by likenesses in a comparison of Ephesians and Paul's undisputed letters. Even C. L. Mitton admits: "There is hardly a trace of mechanical reproduction. . . . Phrases from widely separated passages in Colossians are combined in Ephesians. . . . This is quite different from what one would expect if the author of Ephesians had worked with a copy of Colossians in front of him." [22] The very meaning of "literary dependence" and the need to invoke it as an explanation become less certain in the possible case that Ephesians was written by a disciple who had been by Paul's side when he wrote many letters and who had no opportunity to reread these letters. Since some of Paul's fellow workers were in this category and remembered well Paul's manner of expressing his thought, it is impossible to establish the strong likelihood of strict literary dependence. What meaning would "literary dependence" have, for example, if, say, Timothy, whose name is joined with that of Paul in Colossians 1:1, had the message of Colossians imprinted in his mind when writing Ephesians? The only way to demonstrate that Paul's collected letters were the inspiration and source of Ephesians would be to show that there were numerous or striking errors in interpreting Paul. Since the history of Christian theology reveals the ease with which this can arise, a second generation imitator could scarcely avoid blunders.

> It is, however, scarcely possible that the influence of Paul upon the author of Ephesians is purely literary. Certainly no other writer of the early centuries shows anything remotely comparable to this man's grasp of the fundamental Pauline ideas, or a like ability to bring out their universal implications. There is a kinship of thought here that is not to be explained on less intimate grounds than those of close personal discipleship.[23]

To these words of F. W. Beare we might add the question, why and how did the author snip phrases and clauses out of nine of Paul's letters without citing any longer sections than the one verse excerpt of Colossians 4:7-8 (cf. Eph. 6:21-22), which is a personal reference to Tychicus? Such a literary feat would be all the more amazing in light of his fitting Paul's words without serious flaw into new contexts. That the writer succeeded in producing a letter worthy of Paul is demonstrated by the conviction of so many scholars that Paul was the sole true author. In order to account for both likenesses to, and dissimilarity from, other Epistles, one might look for the cooperation of Paul and a close associate.

What type of religious background would best account for the author's own cast of mind? None of Paul's genuine letters approach Ephesians in the frequency of reminiscences of documents found at Qumran. Jerome Murphy-O'Connor [24] suggests that Ephesians was written under Paul's direction by a converted Essene. In summarizing the evidence for the Jewishness of the author, Beare calls attention to the Semitic flavor of such phrases as "children of light" or "of wrath," "sons of disobedience," and "works of darkness." [25] Earlier James Hope Moulton had called attention to these Semitisms and to "sons of men," which he explained as the result of the author's thorough acquaintance with biblical phrases. [26] Only in the synagogue would one be apt to learn the method of scriptural interpretation found in 2:13-17 and 4:8-9.

If Ephesians were written by a Jewish-trained disciple of Paul whose rather lengthy period of association with the apostle included the time when Colossians was written (inasmuch as the two epistles are so mutually illuminating), only six candidates appear: Tychicus, Aristarchus, Mark, Jesus who is called Justus, Luke, and Timothy. Jesus Justus is nowhere else associated with Paul, except perhaps in Acts 15:22-35. If he were Judas Barsabbus named Justus (Acts 1:21-23), we look in vain for evidence that Ephesians was written by an original disciple of Jesus Christ. There is no grammatical necessity to include Tychicus, Onesimus, Aristarchus, and Luke among "the only men of the circumcision" in Colossians 4:10-11. Aristarchus was a Thessalonian and Macedonian (Acts 19:29; 20:4), and like the Gentile Trophimus (Acts 21:28-29), Tychicus was an Asian (Acts 20:4). The role of Tychicus [27] was to comfort the hearts of the readers and to inform them about Paul's activities (Eph. 6:21), rather than to instruct them in the faith and interpret the lofty teachings of the Epistle. As to Mark, the "son of Peter" (1 Pet. 5:13), it is doubtful that the reputed author of the second Gospel, or the assistant (Acts 13:5) who was long separated from Paul (Acts 13:5, 13; 15:37-39), would be the author of Ephesians. Ralph P. Martin, [28] however, has called attention to enough linguistic and thought parallels in Luke–Acts to merit serious consideration of his hypothesis that Luke authored Ephesians. However, Luke–Acts is more removed from Qumran influence than is Ephesians, whereas the Lucan interest in joy and special concern for outcasts and sinners is not a distinctive mark of Ephesians. Moreover, might not Luke have been influenced by the author of Ephesians during their common association with Paul and vice versa? Timothy was Paul's closest and longest associate. No one else, therefore, had a comparable right and claim to be Paul's interpreter or amanuensis, at least as far as his message to the Colossians (Col. 4:16) was concerned. The more the likeness of Ephesians to the undisputed Pauline epistles is granted, the closer must have been the association of the amanuensis to Paul. No one was as well qualified for a role in writing Ephesians. Who knew Paul's mind better? Who was in a better position to echo Paul's phrases without having the apostle's collected letters before him? Timothy's name is joined with that of Paul in the addresses of Second Corinthians, Philippians, Colossians, First Thessalonians, Second Thessalonians, and Philemon. As co-authors they discussed and determined what they wished to say.[29] Timothy is the first fellow worker *(sunergos)* named in Romans 16 (v. 21). According to 1 Corinthians 4:17 he was a faithful exponent of Paul's universal teaching: "I sent to you Timothy, my beloved and faithful child (cf. 1 Tim. 1:2) in the Lord, to remind you of my ways in Christ, as I teach them everywhere in every church." To the Corinthians he preached "the Son of God, Jesus Christ" (2 Cor. 1:19). In Philippians 2:20-22 he writes: "I have no one like him *(oudéna gàr 'égo isópsuchon)*. . . . Timothy's worth you know, how as a son with a father he has served me in the gospel." This likemindedness lies in seeking the things of Christ. In 2 Timothy 1:5 Paul[30] writes: "I am reminded of your sincere faith. . . ." He tells the Thessalonians, "We sent Timothy, our brother and God's servant in the gospel of Christ, to establish you in your faith and to exhort you . . ." (1 Thess. 3:2). Paul even implies that Timothy is included among the apostles entrusted with imparting the gospel (1 Thess. 2:4-8; cf. 1:1). The technically correct title for Timothy in his role of announcing or preaching the gospel is "evangelist." In 2 Timothy 4:5 Timothy is exhorted: " . . . do the work of an evangelist, fulfil your ministry." The only other figure so designated in the New Testament is Philip at Caesarea (Acts 21:8). The author of Ephesians says of the ascended Christ: "And his gifts were that some should be apostles, some prophets, some evangelists, some pastors and teachers, for the equipment of the saints, for the work of ministry, for building up the body of Christ" (Eph. 4:11-12). Since the author of Ephesians had such edifying purposes in writing, he doubtless classified himself among these ministers of Christ. He had received grace "according to the measure of Christ's gift" (4:7). His explicit purpose in writing was to explain the gospel which he preached (3:3-10; cf. 1:15ff.). Whoever received from Paul a certain freedom in writing a summary of the Pauline gospel must have been a qualified "evangelist." Not only did Paul describe Timothy as a Christocentric servant of the gospel, but the author's use of the unusual term "evangelist" suggests his awareness of his own distinctive role.

Turning from a consideration of Timothy's spiritual qualities to that of his human personality, we find that he was genuinely concerned for the Philippians' welfare (Phil. 2:20b). He was a reliable judge of men's faith and love (Phil. 2:19; 1 Thess. 3:6-10). It was he who reported on the false apostles and their teachings at Corinth (1 Cor. 4:17; 16:10-11; 2 Cor. 1:1). In spite of his solicitude and discernment, he had deficiencies in self-confidence and the capacity to inspire personal confidence. Hence in 1 Corinthians 16:10-11 Paul asks the Corinthians to alleviate Timothy's fears about working among them *(hina aphóbos génetai pròs humas)* and not to despise him, presumably because of his shyness. He was deficient in social skills which were necessary to effectively lead the Corinthian church. In 2 Timothy 1:7 Paul advises his "beloved child": "God did not give us a spirit of timidity but of power and love. . . ." Timothy's lack of success in curbing the rebellion led at Corinth by false teachers required the more effective intervention of Paul and Titus (2 Cor. 7:5-16). A comparison of the personal warmth of Ephesians and Colossians reveals that the author of the former was not as cordial in writing to a strange church. He expected the readers to need comfort (Eph. 6:22), lest they faint at Paul's afflictions (3:13). If Timothy were largely responsible for the writing of Ephesians, his self-effacing nature might be confirmed by the omission of his name in the greetings. Since the occasion for writing was ostensibly that of Colossians and Philemon, where Timothy's name appears in the greeting, the omission can only reveal that he did not wish to draw potential attention to himself. He preferred to hide behind the authority of Paul, who was like a father to him. "Paul" modestly identifies himself as "the very least of all the saints" (3:8). Consistent with his reserved, timid nature would be a reticence in theological debate. In 2 Timothy 2:23 "Paul" advises him: "Have nothing to do with stupid, senseless controversies; you know that they breed quarrels." Behind this counsel probably lay the knowledge of Timothy as nonargumentative. Except for the brief and personal Letter to Philemon, no New Testament writing is more pacific than Ephesians, in spite of its touching on so many controversial questions. Yet Timothy was not timorous in judging and teaching revealed truth, as are many humans who are in other matters bold and self-reliant. There is no inconsistency in personality. The author of Ephesians had real fears of the devil and his cohorts (Eph. 6:11-12, 16), but found strength and protection in God, the truth of the gospel, righteousness and faith, and in the Spirit which is the word of God (6:10, 13-17). The author of 1 Timothy 1:18-19 knew that Timothy, being inspired by prophetic utterances, waged "the good warfare, holding faith and a good conscience." This is comparable to references in Ephesians 6:11-17 to putting on the whole armor of God and contending in spiritual warfare.

Timothy is described in Acts 16:1-3 (cf. 2 Tim. 1:5) as "the son of a Jewish woman who was a believer; but his father was a Greek." When Paul took him with him from Lystra or Derbe, he circumcised Timothy. Because his mother married a pagan and did not carry out the obligation to have her son circumcised, it is reasonable to conclude that she was not diligent in observing the whole Torah. But she and Timothy were considered Jews by the Jews in that area (Acts 16:3), and the author of 2 Timothy 3:15 remarked "how from childhood you have been acquainted with the sacred writings. . . ." Paul was more apt to have met them in the local synagogue than elsewhere. Under these conditions it would not be farfetched to imagine that Timothy did not esteem circumcision; nor did he consider it a necessary mark of his belonging to God's people, either in his pre-Christian or Christian stage. For he never voluntarily had himself circumcised before working with Paul; it was necessitated by potential Jewish pressures. Inevitably he experienced in his own life and family the uncomfortable tensions

of living as a Greek and living as a Jew; he was in a no-man's
land. If he had a major role in writing Ephesians, it is psycho-
logically understandable that he took much joy in the reconciliation of Jew and Gentile in Christ (Eph. 2:11-19; cf. 3:6).
"For he is our peace, who has made us both one, and has broken
down the dividing wall of hostility, by abolishing in his flesh the
law of commandments" (2:14-15a). His own unhappy recollection about being reproached by Jews as "uncircumcised" is
hinted at in 2:11: "Remember that at one time you Gentiles in
the flesh, called the uncircumcision by what is called the circumcision, which is made in the flesh by hands. . . ." Yet the
author of Ephesians always had an abhorrence of Gentile ignorance and ways of life (4:17-22; cf. 2:3, 12, 19; 5:5). The am-
biguity of his own racial status is revealed by the uncertainty
as to whether or not he was a Jew. [31]

Did Timothy write Ephesians at the same time Paul wrote
Colossians, or was it written long enough afterward (as a replacement for the lost letter to Laodicea) to leave traces of
a significantly later date? It cannot plausibly be dated after
85 if it were known to the authors of 1 Clement, Revelation,
First Peter, the Pastoral Epistles, and later to Ignatius and
Polycarp. The canonical letters to Timothy in the editorial
sections reveal a watered-down Paulinism which could have
been addressed to Timothy only after he passed from the scene.
The reference to the separating partitions (mesótoichon) in 2:14
would be most timely not long after Paul was charged with
bringing Trophimus into the temple (Acts 21:29). T. K. Abbott
commented on the word: "It seems probable that the figure was
suggested by the partition which separated the Court of the
Gentiles from the Temple proper, and on which there was an
inscription threatening death to any alien who passed it." [32]
The charge and separation itself would be of greatest concern
to the followers of Paul when he was imprisoned at Caesarea;
the wall was still standing at this time. But the reference would
become increasingly obscure to the Epistle's Gentile readers
after 70 and the destruction of the temple.

Numerous arguments have been brought forth for a post-
apostolic date of Ephesians, but none carries much weight. [33]
Literary dependence on the Pauline corpus is neither a fruitful
nor a necessary hypothesis if a close disciple wrote Ephesians

during the apostle's lifetime. Nor does the assumption that the readers are chiefly Gentiles (Eph. 2:3, 11; 3:1-6; 4:17ff.) signify a late development in the change in the racial composition of Paul's churches, any more than it does in Romans 11:13; 16:4; 1 Corinthians 12:2; Galatians 4:8; or 1 Thessalonians 1:9. These passages indicate an early preponderance of Gentiles rather than Hebrews. Nor does Ephesians 4:9 teach Christ's descent into Hades, [34] though it may have suggested the doctrine to the author of First Peter (3:19; 4:6). Nor is "devil" (diábolos) (Eph. 4:27; 6:11) a late word; it may be non-Pauline, but it occurs in the Septuagint and in Hebrews (2:14), as well as in the common source of Matthew and Luke. Nor is the reference to "the holy (hagiois) apostles" as the recipients of the revealed mystery and the foundation of the family of God (Eph. 3:5) necessarily post-apostolic; it may sound strange in the mouth of Paul about himself (1 Cor. 3:5-11; 15:3-10), in spite of his lofty concept of his authority (2 Cor. 10–12; Gal. 1–2), [35] but not in the mouth of Timothy, his "son" who was seeking to make known the apostle's authority (3:1-10). Such an intent could exist whether Paul were dead or in prison. He is classified among the Spirit-inspired apostles, presumably in the face of denials. Even in writing to the Galatians and Corinthians (1 Cor. 3; 2 Cor. 11:5; 12:11-12), Paul was upholding his authority in the face of its unfavorable comparison to that of the other apostles, especially Peter. Disciples may revere their teachers before they die or before a generation passes. Since all believers were hagiois in Pauline usage and in Ephesians (e.g., 1:1), the application of the term to the apostles themselves is natural.

Whether one judges Ephesians to have been written by Timothy at the same time as Paul wrote Colossians, or some time later, depends in part upon how great an advance is seen in the cosmic ecclesiology of Ephesians. Nothing prohibits Paul from having had the developed thoughts already in his mind; nothing prohibits his disciple who wrote Ephesians from having been the first to perceive and write down the implications of the apostle's thought even in his presence. Could not Timothy have been a more able thinker than is generally recognized? Doubtless Paul and his intimate disciple had more than an occasional discussion during Paul's long imprisonment; without such contact a miracle of successful interpretation of the apostle's teaching would be necessary.

To summarize: Ephesians is or purports to be the letter from Laodicea which Tychicus carried, together with Colossians and Philemon, to the Lycus Valley. There is some clarification or development by Ephesians of the Pauline teaching in Colossians, though the differences are not great enough to necessitate a long interim between the writing of each Epistle. The question is best left open whether Ephesians was written at the same time as Colossians or after the destruction of Laodicea by an earthquake in 60 and the consequent loss of the original letter which Paul had sent. The disciple of the apostle who best qualifies as writer is Timothy. If Ephesians is a replacement of a lost original, it would be a reconstruction from Timothy's memory with the added benefit of further developments. But if it is the original, we may presume that Paul did not write it with his own hand (Philem. 19) or dictate it to a scribe (cf. Rom. 16:22) while adding the greeting in his own hand (1 Cor. 16:21; Gal. 6:11; Col. 4:18; 2 Thess. 3:17) ; rather, he gave general instructions [36] or an outline to Timothy on the content of a letter of introduction (3:1ff.) setting forth calmly and clearly his position. J. H. Moulton suggested that Paul commissioned Timothy to draft a letter for churches other than that of Colossae. He "took Paul's thoughts and Paul's words, so far as he could reproduce them, and brought the draft to Paul. Paul then proceeded to amend his letter." [37] Timothy had a far less responsible role, we would suggest, in writing Colossians (1:1). Ephesians differs from the undisputed Pauline epistles in Timothy's degree of liberty in writing it. Ephesians was written as a more comprehensive and general statement of Pauline teaching concerning the mystery of Christ (Eph. 1:9-10; 3:3-5) ; portions may have had a liturgical origin or purpose.[38] If Ephesians were the original letter from Laodicea, Paul may have chosen Timothy to draft it; for he was the fellow worker who was most qualified to compose a positive supplement to the apostle's message in Colossians. One letter to Colossae and Laodicea would have sufficed for dealing with common problems unless Paul intended to deal with them in differing ways. But both communities would have been all the more edified if they heard from both co-workers.

6

Paul
in
Spain

Christianity was well established in Spain during the second century. Irenaeus (*Adv. Haer.* i,10.2) referred to "the churches which had been planted in Spain." Tertullian (*An Answer to the Jews,* chap. 7) boasted that "all the limits of the Spains" (*Hispaniarum omnes termini*) had been "subjected to Christ." This would include Hispania Citerior and Hispania Ulterior, with its provinces of Baetica and Lusitania. Cyprian (Letter 67; dated *ca.* 254–257) wrote concerning apostates of the Decian persecution, to the Spanish churches, including those of Leon, Astorga, Merida, and Saragossa. The Acts of Martyrdom of Fructuousus, bishop of Tarragona, describe the persecution under Valerian in 259. Nineteen bishops were present at the Synod of Elvira during the opening years of the next century. Its decrees presuppose considerable deterioration in church life. While none of these documents or writings attribute the evangelization of Spain to Paul, the question of his role in the local spread of the new religion persists. On the problem a large body of literature exists. [1]

PAUL'S LATER YEARS

Chronology is of some assistance in ascertaining the events in the final years of St. Paul's life. Paul's arrival at Rome is to be dated during the early months of 60. Among the proponents of this date have been William M. Ramsay, [2] Daniel Plooij, [3] and G. B. Caird. [4] The former English scholar [5] observed that in the year 57 the first and twenty-second of Nisan fell on a Friday, the day of the week when Paul left Philippi for Troas (Acts 20:6-7).[6] This line of reasoning makes the natural assumptions: (1) that the ancient method of counting parts of days as whole ones was followed; and (2) that Paul was able, by catching the first boat, to fulfill his wish to sail away from Philippi immediately after the days of Unleavened Bread (14-21 Nisan). The Passover week and the desire not to begin a journey from Philippi or Troas on the day of worship had influenced the party's travel schedule as it hastened to reach Jerusalem by the day of Pentecost (20:16). Since many other Hebrews probably had similar plans, the earliest possible sailing from Philippi may well have been made available for them.[7] Now, if Paul and his party were on the way to Jerusalem between Passover and Pentecost of 57, the elapsing of two whole years after his subsequent imprisonment at Caesarea would date the arrival of the new procurator Festus (Acts 24:27) in 59. With this calculation other evidence agrees.

When arrested, Paul addressed Felix, who had become procurator of Judea in 52 or 53 (Josephus, *Antiquities* xx,6.3–8.1; *War* ii,12.7-8; Tacitus, *Annals* xii,54), as having been for many years a judge over this nation, i.e., of Judea (Acts 24:10). The four or five years prior to 57 are adequately described as "many," though "many" would seem to exclude a date as early as 55, for Paul's arrest in Jerusalem.

Second, the amply described events of Felix's procuratorship under Nero (*Antiquities* xx,8.4-8; *War* ii,13.2-7) are distributed more or less equally before and after the trouble which was instigated by an Egyptian at Jerusalem some time before Paul's arrest. It is a reasonable assumption that this disturbance occurred not far from the middle of Festus's period in office under Nero. Allowing for the two years of Paul's imprisonment under Felix (Acts 24:27) and a few months between the Egyptian's revolt (Acts 21:38) and Paul's arrest, we would guess that the revolt occurred about the same length of time (i.e., about $2\frac{1}{4}$ to $2\frac{1}{2}$ years) after Nero's accession to the throne (October, 54), namely, in the opening months of 57.

Third, the last coin of procuratorial Judea was issued in the fifth year of Nero's rule (ending in October, 59), due probably to the arrival of a new procurator.[8]

Fourth, as N. P. Workman [9] argued long ago, Acts 27:9 best fits the year of 59 because the Fast of 10 Tishri (Lev. 16:29) fell so late, on October 5. In the other four years worth considering, 57, 58, 60, or 61, the Fast fell on September 27, 16, 24, and 12, respectively. Two weeks later the shipwreck at Malta occurred (Acts 27:18, 27, 33ff.), whence, after a three-month winter sojourn (28:11), a ship to Italy was boarded. Presumably this took place as early in February as it was deemed safe. This would mean that the shipwreck occurred not far from November 1 and that Acts 27:9 describes a situation typical of the middle of October, rather than in September.

Finally, Albinus, the successor of Festus as procurator, was already in office during the Tabernacles of 62 (four years before the beginning of the war, and seven years and five months before the siege of Jerusalem). At this time of great peace and prosperity, Jesus, the son of Ananus, prophesied approaching woes (Josephus, *War* vi,5.3). But, due to the activities of the Sicarii terrorists, Jerusalem had not been at peace when Albinus first arrived in Jerusalem (*Antiquities* xx,9.2-3). Coins, moreover, show that the refounding of Caesarea Philippi as "Neronias" during Albinus's procuratorship took place in 61–62. Though William Ramsay was perhaps too confident in dating Albinus's arrival at Caesarea in late May or June, 61, [10] he does seem justified in finding [11] that Festus came into office not long before the dispatch to Rome of the embassy of ten Jerusalem Jews which, in May, 60, won its case concerning a new temple wall blocking Agrippa's view (*Antiquities* xx,8.11). Since Josephus gave little information about the reign of Festus, who died in office (*Antiquities* xx,8.9-9.1; *War* ii,14.1), his reign is unlikely to have been a long one. At the latest he died in 61.

If Paul reached the imperial capital in March, 60, then some account must be given of the years between 60 and his death. Walter Bauer [12] listed the earliest evidence for the traditions on Paul's martyrdom under Nero by beheading and in association with Peter's death. The most significant reference is 1 Clement 5:1–6:2:

> But to pass from ancient examples, let us come to those who have most recently proved champions. . . . Because of jealousy and envy the greatest and most upright pillars of the church were persecuted and competed unto death . . . Peter . . . bore a martyr's witness and went to the glorious place. . . . Because of jealousy and strife Paul pointed the way

to the reward of endurance; seven times he was imprisoned, he was exiled . . . he was a preacher in both east and west . . . teaching uprightness to the whole world, and reaching the farthest limit of the west, and bearing a martyr's witness before the rulers he passed out of the world. . . . With these men . . . has been gathered a great multitude of God's chosen, who have set a splendid example among us in enduring many humiliations and tortures on account of jealousy. On account of jealousy women have been persecuted . . . and won the true prize.[13]

This great multitude of the elect who suffered from jealousy and received their reward is associated with Peter and Paul. All of these examples, which are given in apparently chronological order, [14] had stemmed from recent times (1 Clement 5:1). The sufferings of the great multitude can readily be understood as referring to Nero's persecution,[15] that is, the one following the fire in July, 64 (Tacitus, *Annals* xv,39 and 44). Because this is the only persecution under Nero about which we have any information and because persecutions almost always touched Christian leaders, the odds favor the martyrdom of Paul at this time. There would then be some four and one-half to five years between the arrival and the death of the apostle in Rome. On the other hand, some improbable chronological assumptions would be necessary for postulating Paul's death at the end of the two whole years ascribed to his evangelizing at his own hired quarters (Acts 28:30-31).

THE ENDING OF ACTS

At the end of the two-year period following Paul's arrival, there was a major change in Paul's status. He no longer remained a teacher living at his own expense and confined to the same dwelling in Rome. The tradition that he went to Spain presupposes that he was not executed at the end of two years, but that he was released (Eusebius, *H.E.*ii,22.2) or exiled. If he died a natural death, all the various traditions about him are inexplicably erroneous. No more likely an outcome would be Paul's acquittal or the dismissal of the charges against him as matters of the Jewish Law. The imperial refusal to judge according to the Torah is stressed in Acts 18:12-15 and 25:18-20, but it is omitted here. Why would such a favorable outcome as acquittal or dismissal not be mentioned by Luke and other apologists? Would not the granting of freedom by Caesar be the final proof of the good relations between Paul and Roman officials (Acts 13:12; 16:37-39; 19:31, 35-36, 37; 22:25-29; 27:3)? Nor would the historical problem be solved by positing that Luke was writing before Nero's persecution and the outcome of Paul's confinement, for he would tell of Paul's manner of dwelling in Rome "until now," or "for the last two years." Lindsey P. Pherigo has shrewdly observed: "Since the author of Acts seems to have known the *duration* of the imprisonment, it certainly seems to follow that he knew also of its termination." [16]

Rather, Luke's silence must be taken as due to discretion arising from a partial embarrassment. The outcome of Paul's case did not suit Luke's purposes of writing. There was some merit in the suggestion of Ramsay, [17] Kirsopp Lake, [18] and Henry Cadbury [19] that the case against Paul lapsed because the prosecution failed to appear and present a *prima facie* case against him within eighteen months or two years. However, F. F. Bruce shows that the document allegedly illustrating the existence of such a Roman statute belongs to the third century and is not altogether relevant. [20] Possibly, a Roman judge may have ruled that the four and one-half years of detention which Paul had already undergone were sufficient for whatever crime Paul may have been guilty. Some hint of the outcome of his case might be found in Acts 28:21 (cf. 25:26), where the Roman Jewish leaders say to Paul: "We have received no letters from Judea about you." Yet it is hard to believe that the virulent Jewish opposition to Paul so died down that accusation papers (25:26-27) lost in the shipwreck were not redrawn and that nothing was done in Rome to prosecute him. Even more remote is the possibility that "Caesar" sentenced the apostle to death at the end of the two-year confinement. Luke would not have stressed that the Roman officials who had previously investigated the case judged him to be unworthy of death (23:29; 24:26-27; 25:10-11, 25; 26:31-32; 28:18) if the final disposition were a sentence of death. His house arrest in Rome did not befit a criminal considered so dangerous as to be worthy of death. Had the imperial court at Rome so condemned Paul at the end of two years, Luke would have owed his reader an explanation of the sudden reversal of prior legal opinions. We might anticipate some reference to Jewish influence in Rome or perhaps to the corruption of Nero.

PAUL'S EXILE

The report in 1 Clement 5:6 that Paul was once banished has not received the attention it merits. [21] Because the apostle did not include exile among his lengthy, if not exhaustive, catalog of misfortunes already experienced (2 Cor. 11:23-28), it would be hazardous to suggest the occurrence of such a fate in his earlier days. However, after two years of indecision had passed at Rome, an exile to Spain would have been the ideal compromise between alternative adjudications. Paul would fulfill his long-postponed desire to preach there (Rom. 15:24, 28), while his Jewish opponents would be happy that he would thereby be effectively removed from his churches and Roman followers. He would be located in a land where there were few Jews and synagogues. [22] His evangelizing work (if, indeed, any were permitted) among them would be hindered by the stigma of exile for being "an agitator among all the Jews throughout the world" (Acts 24:5; cf. 21:27-28; 25:7-8). That the Romans sometimes punished troublesome Christian preachers with exile is illustrated by the case of John at Patmos (Rev. 1:9). If it were the Roman and Jewish intent to get Paul out of the way and to make him as harmless as possible, then Spain would have been an adequate place of exile. In this they apparently succeeded. Paul's work in Spain, if any, was not an overwhelming success, for he is not mentioned in the earliest liturgies of the Spanish church. This fact is better explained from the assumption of an exile (accompanied perhaps by a prohibition of public teaching) than of an acquittal and voluntary journey in freedom to "the limits of the West." Luke, who wished to tell how Paul's gospel reached the imperial capital, perhaps omitted reference to the Spanish journey as a potential anticlimax following the disgrace of banishment. As Lindsey Pherigo explained: "That such a conclusion did not further the purposes of the author of Acts might satisfactorily account for its suppression." [23] But he hints that at the end of two years Paul no longer preached and taught at his residence, and the insistence that Paul committed no crime worthy of death does not exclude a lesser punishment. If Luke does suggest a fate for the apostle, the clue might be found in his teaching the gospel unhindered and with all boldness (Acts 28:31). How might we expect Nero and his officials to react to this dangerous propagation in Rome of an unauthorized foreign cult which was disowned by most Jews? An exile of Paul would be compatible with the words of Theodore of Mopsuestia (*Argumentum in Eph.* 1; ed.Swete,i,117): "... *liberatus, securus abire iussus est,*" and of Pelagius (*Expositio in Philem.* 22; *Texts & Studies* ix,2,539): "*prime vice sit ex Urbe dimissus.*"

Several forms of exile were possible for Paul. *Deportatio* was unlikely, because it was to an island and involved loss of citizenship. But if the tradition that Paul was eventually put to death by a sword (*The Martyrdom of Paul* in his *Acts;* Tertullian, *de praescr. haer.*36.3) be valid, then he apparently retained his Roman citizenship. None of the usual crimes punishable by deportation could have been applicable to Paul. The same may be said of *interdictio:* neither the crimes nor loss of citizenship would be applicable to Paul. However, *relegatio (exilium relegationis),* [24] which involved no deprivation of the rights of a citizen and required no military surveillance, would have been a sufficiently mild punishment for the apostle. Such an exile might be permanent or temporary. In some cases the place of exile was specified; confinement or internment would be to an island or the limits of a province. In other cases the person could choose where to live outside a forbidden area; he was expelled and excluded from specified places. In either case Paul could well have gone to Spain. Certainly the Roman court learned of Paul's plan to go to Spain and was not averse to finding an easy way out of a thorny, long-standing problem.

Relegatio was often applied against members or propagators of foreign sects. As early as 139 B.C. the praetor Hispalus banished from Rome Jewish propagandists who were not citizens (Valerius Maximus, *Epitome* i,3.2-3). [25] Tiberius took more drastic measures [26] in A.D. 19. On account of a scandal caused by a Palestinian proselytizer in Rome and his three partners (Josephus, *Antiquities* xviii,3.5; cf. Dio Cassius, *Roman History* lvii,18.5), the emperor expelled to Sardinia some four thousand Jews for military service (Josephus, *op. cit.;* Tacitus, *Annals* ii,85; Suetonius, *Tiberius* 36) and banished from Rome on pain of slavery all remaining Jews who did not renounce their ceremonial laws. In this same passage Suetonius tells also of the banishment of astrologers from Rome and the abolition of

Egyptian rites. In his life of Claudius (25,4) he wrote the well-known words: "He expelled from Rome the Jews continually making disturbances at the instigation of Chrestus *(Iudaeos impulsore Chresto assidue tumultuantes Roma expulit)."* Acts 18:2 tells that the Hebrew Christian teachers Aquila and Priscilla were among the Jews whom Claudius commanded to depart from Rome. They were already baptized when Paul met them at Corinth (1 Cor. 1:16) and, upon arrival at Ephesus, they had an even more accurate knowledge of the Way than Apollos had (Acts 18:26). Because in *ca.* A.D. 41 the same emperor ordered Roman Jews not to hold meetings (Dio Cassius, *Roman History* lx,6.6), the later expulsions were due apparently to disturbances in synagogues occasioned by Christian evangelists or (from the Roman viewpoint) ringleaders. It would be in keeping with these precedents that Nero banished from Rome the troublesome apostle to the Gentiles. He was converting too many natives to his "superstitious ways."

It is altogether unlikely that the apostle returned to his churches in the East. There would be no guarantee that old conflicts and charges would not be renewed; from Rome's point of view, there would be more peace if he stayed away, whatever his degree of responsibility and guilt in the conflicts involving Paul; the delay itself is proof. Rather than permitting further disturbance in the East, Roman officials would prefer Paul to follow the course of the sun at the end of his Roman imprisonment. Luke does indicate that the apostle did not return to the center of his earlier activity in the Aegean. In his farewell speech to the elders of Ephesus Paul said: "I know that all you among whom I have gone about preaching the kingdom will see my face no more" (Acts 25:25). Hearing these prophetic words, "they all wept and embraced Paul . . . sorrowing most of all because of the word he had spoken, that they should see his face no more" (20:37-38). This was a true farewell. A. H. McNeile remarked: "It is difficult to think that St. Luke would have written his account of this solemn and affecting farewell, and the grief caused by Paul's words, unless he had known for a fact that the apostle had never revisited Ephesus." [27]

Paul's original intent to pass on to Spain after a visit to Rome is clear enough (Rom. 15:20, 24, 28). That he willingly left Rome for Spain is assumed in the quasi-historical Acts of Peter (chaps. 1–3, 6 Vercelli) . "Quartus, a prison officer . . . gave leave *(permisit)* to Paul to leave the city (and go) where he wished." After a three-day fast Paul "saw a vision, the Lord saying to him, 'Paul, arise and be a physician to those who are in Spain.' " No reference is made in the Acts of Peter to Romans 15:24, 28. The brethren in Rome implored him not to stay in Spain longer than a year, but a voice from heaven revealed that "Paul the servant of God is chosen for (this) service for the time of his life; but at the hands of Nero . . . he shall be perfected before your eyes." (chap. 1; trans. Hennecke-Schneemelcher). The apostle was conducted to the harbor by a crowd which included two Roman knights and a senator. Two young believers sailed with him (chap. 3) . Evidently neither an escape nor a judicially fixed place of exile was assumed by our apocryphal writer. Nothing excludes a temporary *relegatio* (of perhaps one year) with the right to choose where to go, but the easiest assumption is that of release and full liberty. Paul supposedly returned to Rome after the martyrdom of Peter (chap. 40) . The Muratorian Canon (lines 38-39) comments that Luke omitted from Acts mention not only of the passion of Peter *(passio Petri),* but Paul's proceeding from the city (or Rome) to Spain *(. . . profectionem Pauli ab urbe ad Spaniam proficiscentis).* This language suggests that Paul was not unwilling to leave Rome for Spain. There is some unknown connection of this wording with the Acts of Peter: *"In eodem erat ut profisceretur ab urbe. Paulus profectus est in Spaniam."* [28] The Acts of Peter and the Muratorian Canon are witnesses of the Roman tradition from Encratitic and Catholic circles, respectively, of the last quarter of the second century.

Their historical worth, however, is overshadowed by that of 1 Clement 5, as quoted above. It would be strange if only about thirty-one or thirty-two years after the death of Paul a leading official of the Roman church, Clement, were altogether misinformed on the final years of the apostle honored as one of the two "greatest and most righteous pillars" of the church (1 Clement 5:2) . The temptation, if any, for Clement would be to leave Paul in Rome rather than to exile him to the Western Mediterranean. J. B. Lightfoot demonstrated from Strabo's *Geography* (ii,1,chap. 67; iii,5.chap. 169) and Velleius Paterculus *(Roman History* i,2) that at this time the Pillars of Hercules in the Straits of Gibraltar and Cadiz constituted the *"terma tes duseos,* limits of the West." [29] Theodoret of Cyrus, in chapter 26 of his *Religious History,* treated the Spaniards, Britons, and Gauls as "inhabitants of the west." Over half of Italy and over 40 percent of the Roman Empire lay to the west of Rome. How could the approximate center be considered to belong to the West, much less the limit of the West, by the Roman who wrote 1 Clement? It was only for Easterners that Rome was in the West. But was the information in 1 Clement deduced from Romans 15:24, 28? Against this subjective hypothesis [30] is the fact that in Clement's letter there is no trace of an allusion to Romans 15. Are we to imagine that the Roman church conjectured on the basis of Romans 15 that Paul was exiled and went to Cadiz?

LOCATION IN SPAIN

Where did Paul labor in Spain? Tarragona (Tarraco) most persistently claims Paul. [31] This was the port and commercial center closest to Rome. It was not a city that Paul would bypass. Fare for transportation from Ostia would have been lowest to this city. For centuries it was of highest importance in Spanish ecclesiastical affairs. In going to Spain it is extremely unlikely that Paul would choose the most difficult land route. After nearly five years in prison, his age and loss of strength would deter him. Jerome has Paul going to Spain by ship: *"ad Hispanias alienigenarum portatus est navibus"* (*Comm. in Isa.*iv,11; Migne, *P.L.* 24,154). In Romans 15:24-25, 28 Paul gives no hint of wishing to visit Gaul on the way. In fact, he indicates that he intends to reach the Peninsula by the end of the sailing season, for he wishes to be sped on his way. "In passing," "for a little," and "by way of you" all point to an intentionally short stay in Rome. Pliny (*Nat. Hist.*19.1) relates that from Ostia Hispania Citerior could be reached in as little as four days and Cadiz in seven (cf. Strabo, *Geogr.*iii,2.5-6). These were the most natural ports of entrance. [32] The southern coastal region was the most thoroughly Romanized section of the country.

After making Tarragona his first headquarters and possibly visiting Tortosa (Dertosa), [33] Paul may have sailed via Cartagena (Cathago Nova) to Cadiz at the limits of the West. Paul's old desire to carry the gospel as far as possible to the West from Jerusalem would have urged him onward. "The wealth and importance of Gades was so great at this period that under Augustus it was the residence of no fewer than 500 *equites,* and was made a *municipium* with the name of 'Augusta Urbs Gaditana,' with citizenship ranking next to that of Rome. . . . And throughout the Roman world its cookery and dancing girls were famous." [34]

ROMAN MARTYRDOM

A mission in Spain does not necessitate the conclusion that Paul died there. The Acts of Peter (chap. 1) tell that he was perfected at the hands of Nero before the eyes of the believers in Rome. Tacitus (*Annals* xv,44) records that Christians were put to death as a public spectacle after they had been convicted by legal process. If Paul were executed with a sword, he must have been convicted and sentenced. In this context may be placed the statement in 1 Clement 5:7 that Paul bore his witness before rulers after he reached the limits of the West and before he departed from the world. That is, he was a martyr in both senses of the word. Most commentators find a reference to Paul in the apocalypse of Mark 13 (vv.9-11), where Jesus promises that the apostles would "stand before governors and kings for my sake, to bear testimony before them. And the gospel must first be preached to all nations. And when they bring you to trial . . . say whatever is given you in that hour. . . ." But one cannot press too hard these verses of the Roman gospel for specific information on Paul's last years. Acts 23:11 may yield more trustworthy data. The Lord revealed to Paul: ". . . as you have testified about me at Jerusalem, so you must bear witness also at Rome." Two days earlier, the apostle had addressed the angry crowd in Jerusalem about the revelation of Christ to him (22:1-23). Did the same thing happen in Rome after the fire of July, 64? Why would Paul have to face a hostile Roman mob before that time? If news of the fire did not bring him back from Spain, news that Christians were being blamed for it certainly did. Having reached the limits of the West and having helped to preach the gospel to all nations, Paul would feel ready to face death in Rome. The martyr's attitude had been growing in him (Acts 20:23; 21:13-14; Phil. 1:23; 2:17-18; cf. 2 Cor. 1:6-10).

GENERAL CONCLUSION

Paul's ministry was divided into a series of two-year periods: 31–33 (34) in Damascus and Arabia, 46–47 in Cyprus and Asia Minor, 51–53 in Corinth, 54–56 at Ephesus, 57–59 in Caesarea, 60–62 in Rome, and 62–64 in Spain. A total of nearly nine years (34 to the winter of 42–43) was spent in Cilicia and environs, and a total of four and one-half years (43, 44–46, 48–49, 53–54) at Antioch. We might assume, on the basis of these figures, that the apostle left his stamp on the churches of Cilicia and Syria more than elsewhere, were it not for the immeasurable influence of his letters on other churches and of other apostles on the Cilician and Syrian churches. The complexity of influences on communities was reflected in the controversy and division which followed Paul's departures from Corinth, Galatia, and Ephesus (Acts 20:29-31; Rom. 16:17ff.). The church of Antioch also experienced a variety of teachers and controversies (Acts 11: 19-28; 13:1; 15:1-2, 30-39). The preservation and propagation of Paulinism were certainly aided by his letters, but his churches treasured other writings from apostolic times as well.

Fortunately, a glimpse into the life and theologies of Paul's churches and co-workers shortly after he left for Rome and Spain is given by the Epistle to the Hebrews. The setting of this letter, like that of Ephesians or of Titus 3:12-15, may shed light on other hypotheses which have already been advanced.

7

The Epistle
to the
Hebrews

Most of the evidence generally cited in behalf of the tradition that Hebrews was addressed to Jewish readers really is sufficient only to demonstrate that the author was a Hebrew and that he was resisting apostasy to an imperfect Jewish Christianity (3:5-14; 6:1-2). It might be further granted that the line of reasoning in the Epistle was most meaningful to Hebrew Christians, and that they were the ones deemed most in need of the author's message. [1] But it does not follow that the readers were exclusively Hebrew Christians who were in danger of relapsing into ceremonial or rabbinic Judaism. For, the Old Testament, from which the author argued, was authoritative for Gentile believers as well. The interpretation of the Septuagint rather than the practice of Judaism was under discussion. The "seed of Abraham" and "the people" of God (e.g., 2:16-17, KJV) meant not the Hebrew race and nation, but all believers (2:12-15; 4:3, 9; chap. 7; 8:10-13; 11:17-18, 24-26; 13:12-15). Christians in general, irrespective of their origin, were being instructed and exhorted. Theological controversies made many Gentiles aware of issues discussed in Hebrews. The readers knew Timothy (13:23), Paul's co-worker among Gentiles as well as Hebrews.

Consequently, there is no need to look for a Palestinian destination of Hebrews. [2] It is unlikely, anyway, that a teacher of the "Diaspora" would aspire to instruct Palestinians in the finer points of the faith. Or if the recipients were Egyptian or Syrian, it would be difficult to explain the dubious tradition of a Pauline authorship in these churches. [3] Such an explicit belief, suggested T. W. Manson, was derived from the letter's attachment to the locally circulating corpus of Paul's epistles. [4] Thus the early third-century Egyptian P[46] manuscript includes it inside the Pauline corpus, between Romans and Corinthians. Moreover, Timothy (Heb. 13:23) has no known connection with Antioch or Alexandria. A stronger case can be made for a Roman destination. [5] But Hebrews 12:4, concerning the shedding of blood (cf. the milder persecution of 10:32-34), would hardly be possible after Nero's ferocious persecution, whereas before then the non-apostolic (2:3) author, whose name was not worthy of being preserved, would not dare to scold the Romans as being "dull of hearing" and as babes in need of "milk" (5: 11-14). For, even Paul in Romans 1:8 commended the Romans for their universally acclaimed faith. That Christianity was already well established in Rome is indicated by Romans 15:23, "I have longed for many years to come to you," i.e., since he met Prisca and Aquila, who told him about the stormy spread of the gospel there (Acts 18:1-3). Moreover, who would write to Rome ca. A.D. 60-64 without mentioning Paul or Peter (Heb. 13:24) while exhorting obedience to their leaders (13:7, 17)? The probable omission of reference to Hebrews by the Muratorian Canonist, Justin and Hermas, indicates that it was not treasured in mid- and late-second century Rome.

Only a few expositors (F. W. Farrar, Vernon Bartlett, M. E. Clarkson, W. F. Howard, and J. B. Legg) [6] have argued for Ephesian readers. But the cumulative evidence is rather compelling. The nautical metaphors of an anchor holding fast (3:6, 14), of drifting away (2:1; cf. 13:9), and the innumerable sands of the seashore (11:12) are employed. The author was known personally to his readers (13:18-19, 23) and was well acquainted with specific facts of their local church's history and current situation (2:3; 5:11-12; 6:9-12; 10:23-25, 32-34; 12:4; 13:7, 17). Such a long-term relationship with the Ephesian community existed in the case of Apollos (Acts 18:24-27; 1 Cor. 16:12), a probable author of Hebrews. [7] Another figure known to the readers was Timothy, who had been released and was expected to see the readers again (Heb. 13:23). His earlier work at Ephesus is manifest from Acts 19:22; and 1 Corinthians 4:17; 16:10. According to the Apostolic Constitutions (7, 46), he became the first bishop of Ephesus. Eusebius (*H.E.* iii, 4.6) seems to be relying on a written source when writing: "Timothy, so it is recorded, was the first to receive the episcopate of Ephesus." About the church addressed in Hebrews we may deduce the following. "Greet all your leaders and all the saints" (Heb. 13:24) points to a large city with a well-developed church. Paul addressed its presbyters or pastors from Ephesus at Miletus (Acts 20:17, 28), and in Romans 16:5, 14, 15, he mentioned the community's three house-groups. The favorable reference to Timothy in Hebrews 13:23 indicates that the readers were in fellowship with the Pauline community. From Hebrews 2:3 it is evident that both the author and the readers had received the gospel not through hearing the Lord himself but from those who had heard him speak and who confirmed his words. Thus the church was outside Palestine and was founded by apostles who had seen the Lord. Ephesus had received at least three such apostles: Paul (1 Cor. 9:1), Andronicus, and Junias, who were "in Christ before" Paul (Rom. 16:7). Hebrews 13:7, "Remember your leaders, those who spoke to you the word of God; consider the outcome of their life," would be a fitting reference to Paul, Timothy (see p. 160), and Aristarchus (Col. 4:10; Acts 19:29; 27:2), who were leaders of the Ephesian community imprisoned *ca.* 59–62. Hebrews 13:3 ("Remember those who are in prison") is a more general reference which includes all who were being ill-treated for their faith (cf. 10:34).

Hebrews 10:32-34 and 12:4 seem to describe the persecution of believers at Ephesus when Paul was there (*ca* 53–56). There were sufferings, public exposure to abuse and affliction, imprisonment, and plundering of property, but *no* shedding of blood in self-defense, according to Hebrews in "the former days" (10:32). In Romans 16:7, which was probably addressed to Ephesus, Paul greets his (former) fellow prisoners and apostles. Prisca and Aquila had risked their lives for Paul (Rom. 16:3-4). In 2 Corinthians 11:23 (written from Ephesus) Paul speaks of "far more imprisonments," although Acts (16:24) mentions but one. In 1 Corinthians 4:9-13, also written from Ephesus, Paul writes: We [apostles] have become a spectacle to the world. . . . We [are held] in disrepute. To the present hour we . . . are . . . buffeted . . . reviled . . . persecuted . . . slandered." "I fought with beasts at Ephesus" (1 Cor. 15:32). "There are

many adversaries" (1 Cor. 16:9). Two months after leaving
Ephesus he wrote of the afflictions which he and Timothy had
experienced in Asia; they were so utterly crushed that they
despaired of life; they were in so deadly a peril that they felt
that they had received a sentence of death (2 Cor. 1:4-10). "We
are afflicted in every way . . . perplexed . . . persecuted . . .
struck down" (4:8-9). In 2 Corinthians 6:4-10 Paul continues
their list of hardships, though not referring specifically to Ephesus. Acts 19:23–20:1 describes "no little stir" and "uproar."
Gaius and Aristarchus were dragged about (19:29). Alexander
did Paul great harm (2 Tim. 4:14; cf. Acts 19:33). The Christians were in danger of being charged with rioting (Acts 19:40).
And, in his farewell speech to the elders of Ephesus, Paul speaks
of serving the Lord there with tears and with trials from the
plots of Jews (20:19-20).

In 2 Timothy 1:15 Paul or the Pastor wrote: "You are aware
that all who are in Asia turned away from me. . . ." Several
passages in Hebrews point to such a decline in fervor. Its readers
are accused of, or warned against, hardness of heart, unbelief
(Heb. 3:7-13; 4:11), dullness of hearing, immaturity, apostasy
(5:11–6:8), willful sin, forsaking assemblies, trampling on the
Son of God (10:24-31), laxness, division, and immorality (12:
12-18). It is not unfitting that the author calls his writing a
"word of exhortation" (paraklesis) (13:22). Such a resemblance
to the degeneration at Corinth and, to a lesser extent, at Galatia makes it quite plausible by analogy that many of the addressees of Hebrews, too, would desert Paul after his departure
from their area.

Letters of Paul were probably first collected at Ephesus. [8]
That Hebrews first circulated with this collection of Romans,
Ephesians, and First Corinthians is indicated by its position
among them. [9] The Egyptian P[46], the earliest Pauline collection,
begins with Romans, Hebrews, Corinthians, and Ephesians. The
great scholar Theodore of Mopsuestia knew the order: Romans,
Corinthians, Hebrews, Ephesians. The Sahidic Pauline corpus
agrees with Theodore's order except that Galatians precedes
Ephesians. The archetype of Codex Vaticanus ran: Romans,
Corinthians, Galatians, Hebrews, Ephesians. It is not surprising
that in second-century Egypt Hebrews was considered to be
Paul's. Is it by accident that the earliest evidence of knowledge

of the sixteen-chapter edition of Romans (including the appended letter to Ephesus, chap. 16) is found in P[46], Clement of Alexandria, and Origen? This indicates that the earliest Alexandrian Pauline corpus containing Hebrews came from Ephesus; this partially accounts, too, for its superior readings. Charles P. Anderson believes that Hebrews "may have gained admittance to the canon through association with a Pauline letter or letters prior to the formation of the corpus as a whole." [10] First Clement's acquaintance with Hebrews was connected with his knowledge of Romans and First Corinthians. [11]

An Ephesian origin would explain the anonymity of the Epistle. Francesco Lo Bue surmises that "the preservation of the letter was chiefly due to its immediate inclusion within Paul's correspondence and that the first Christian generation could find no particular reason to perpetuate the memory either of the writer's name or of the unhappy situation owing to which he had written." [12] In writing Acts, Luke was in a position to have obviated our ignorance, but he tended to glorify Ephesus. [13] Moreover, if letters of Paul were first collected at Ephesus, its church would be in a position to omit the greeting of a letter to their church and to circulate the truncated epistle. Without an endorsement of the churches where the Pauline collections were assembled, the non-apostolic Epistle to the Hebrews was far less likely to have entered the Canon. By including Hebrews at the end of the abbreviated Pauline corpus, the Ephesian editor endowed the anonymous edifying Epistle with a better claim to acceptance. But why did the Ephesian community omit the address of Hebrews? One motive would be the desire to avoid the shame of Hebrews' harsh reproaches to the addressees. But the value of Hebrews was recognized in Asia; Polycarp of Smyrna (Phil. 12:2) called Jesus Christ "the eternal High Priest Himself," [14] and the author of First Peter, who addressed believers in Asia Minor (1 Pet. 1:1) and who may have written there, knew much of the thought and language found in Hebrews. [15] As late an Asian writer as Methodius of Olympus (d. 311) considered the Epistle to be anonymous. [16]

Whence did Hebrews originate? Corinth seems most likely. A number of investigators [17] have perceived its connections with Corinth and judged it to be the destination. Timothy was well known at Corinth (Acts 18:5; Rom. 16:21; 1 Cor. 4:17; 16:10;

2 Cor. 1:19). If Timothy had been imprisoned at Philippi (see p. 160), the news of his release would have reached Corinth somewhat sooner than it would Ephesus, and Timothy might be expected to go by way of Thessalonica and Corinth to Ephesus. A more direct clue is the form of greeting from *hoi àpo tes Italías* (Heb. 13:24). As "Italy is a large area from which to send greetings," [18] we take the term to mean Italians residing abroad in one of the colonies. They either were of Italian origin, came from Italy temporarily, or were Roman colonists. In any case, those of Italy in the company of our author were not then resident in Italy. Why would those emigrants (or travelers?) living outside of Italy send greetings to fellow Christians in Ephesus? Three alternatives may be suggested, each of which points to Corinth, which was the midway point between Italy and Ephesus. "Those . . . from Italy" may have been messengers from Rome, but Hebrews contains no news from Rome and conveys no other greetings from those who were with the author. More likely is the explanation given by Hugh Montefiore:

> It might be that a group of Italians was known both to the recipients of the letter and to our author. For example, Aquila and Prisca were Jews who had left Rome when Jews were banished by Claudius (Acts 18:2). They had gone to Corinth . . . and later went with Paul to Ephesus (Acts 18:19). . . . They are the only people in the New Testament described as "from Italy." [19]

Possibly those Italian Jewish exiles who remained at Corinth were greeting Aquila, Prisca (Rom. 16:3), and others at Ephesus whom they knew (cf. Rom. 16:21-23). A fuller explanation may be found in the fact that Corinth, rebuilt in 47 B.C. by Caesar and settled by 80,000 Romans, remained a center of Roman life in Greece. Its political and priestly organizations, inscriptions, sports, architecture, sculpture, and coins were Roman. Roman names associated with Corinth by the New Testament include Crispus (Acts 18:8; 1 Cor. 1:14), Titius Justus (Acts 18:7), Gaius, Tertius, Quartus (Rom. 16:22-23), and Fortunatus (1 Cor. 16:17). The *populus* of the colony of Roman citizens were divided into *tribus* (e.g., Atia, Calpurnia, Aurelia, Agrippia, Vinicia, Hostilia, Mareia). [20] It would therefore be intelligible that Corinthian believers were designated "those from Italy." These may have also included the messengers telling of Tim-

othy's release from imprisonment at Philippi, i.e., the Roman
"Colonia Iulia Philippensis" (Acts 16:12).

Heinrich Appel, in propounding a Corinthian destination of
Hebrews, rested his case largely on the letter's supposed use of
First and Second Corinthians [21] and its use by the letter of
Clement to Corinth. [22] The resemblances to Romans, [23] a
(circular?) letter written at Corinth (Acts 20:2-3; Rom. 15:25;
16:1), likewise tend to show that our author could have been
influenced by the Pauline letters already read at Corinth. But,
strictly speaking, one is justified in concluding that Hebrews
mirrors the thought and language common to Rome, Corinth,
and Ephesus by virtue of the labors of Paul and Silas (Silvanus)
(Acts 18:5; 2 Cor. 1:19; 1 Pet. 5:12), at least if Hebrews is given
an early date. Corinth's ecclesiastical ties were primarily with
Rome and Ephesus. Yet if Hebrews were addressed toward
the same theological conflict that occasioned so many of Paul's
letters, it would be natural for its author, especially if he were
Apollos, to send a copy to Rome. If its salutation and ending
were omitted for brevity's sake, the Roman church would have
no record of its authorship.

This hypothesis brings us to the question of the Epistle's date.
For several reasons it is advisable to place it after Paul's departure for Jerusalem with the contribution for "the poor."
If Paul were present in either city, it would be unlikely that a
lesser teacher would write from Corinth to Ephesus. Decline
in the ardor of church life had set in (see p. 154), though it is
noteworthy that it didn't take long for vexing problems to arise
among the new converts at Corinth. The thoughts and language
held in common with Romans and First Corinthians had developed. The readers are called upon to remember their afflictions
from persecution in former days (Heb. 10:32-34), i.e., during
Paul's long stay at Ephesus. The readers are also exhorted to
remember those leaders "who spoke to you the word of God:
consider the outcome of their life" (13:7). Implicitly most of
them have left the community being addressed. Either they
are dead, their life has been in danger, or their behavior (ékbasin
tes anastrophes) reveals an underlying faith which is to be imi-
tated. The context supports the latter interpretation, but it may
be their conduct when confronting (the threat of) death which
is held up as an example. The mortal dangers faced with faith

by Paul and Timothy (2 Cor. 1:4-10), Gaius and Aristarchus (Acts 19:29), and Prisca and Aquila (Rom. 16:4) were well known to the Ephesians as edifying models. Still the Ephesians knew no examples of martyrdoms for the faith (Heb. 12:4), and the leaders of churches were generally among the first to be martyred. Finally, if Apollos were the author, then his return to Corinth from Ephesus must be dated after the writing of 1 Corinthians 16:12, at which time he found it still inopportune to go. He was not yet at Corinth when Romans was written there. Moreover, he had returned from his journey via Crete to Rome on Paul's behalf and had no current news of the mission to report (see pp. 119-120).

On the other end of the time scale, the dependence of First Clement on Hebrews is well established. [24] A date prior to 85 may be deduced also from the lack of parallels to the canonical Gospels, the omission of quotations from the Pauline letters, the survival of Timothy (Heb. 13:23), and the still lively expectation of the Parousia (1:2; 3:13-14; 6:11; 8:13; 9:28; 10:25, 37). A date before 70 is suggested by the lack of martyrdoms (12:4) and by the lack of appropriate references to the destruction of the Jerusalem temple and to the cessation of its ritual as carried on by the Levitical priesthood. The present tense is used as though the sacrifices were still going on. George A. Barton, in studying the author's employment of present and past tenses in Hebrews 9:1-25, has observed that his use of tenses is accurate and that there is "no demonstrable use of the 'historical present.'" [25] Barton also points out that the author of Hebrews uses the term "tabernacle" *(skene)* broadly to include not only the wilderness tent, but also the heavenly Holy of Holies into which Christ has entered (9:11) and the Jerusalem temple (13:10-14). We might add that all three were united in principle because "without the shedding of blood there is no forgiveness of sins. Thus it was necessary for the copies of the heavenly things to be purified with these rites . . ." (9:22-23). The common concern was the interpretation of the Old Testament rather than whether or not the Christian should honor the contemporary Jerusalem priestly cultus. The point at issue was whether or not the Levitical sacrifices of the old covenant had been made obsolete in principle by the once for all offering by Christ the High Priest in the heavenly sanctuary. Evidently the opponents, if any, in Hebrews were looking forward to a purified ritual in an eschatological sanctuary by a true priesthood; all would be a heavenly counterpart of the wilderness cultus. Against such a hope, which presupposes the eternal nature of priestly institutions, the author of Hebrews presses every ingenious argument that came to him. But why did he omit the crowning argument: the End is at hand and the old cultus has passed away forever? God has permitted the destruction of the temple and the disruption of the Levitical services and priesthood as a sign of its transitory nature; they do not pertain to the new covenant, even if reformed. As B. F. Westcott observed, "No event . . . could mark more distinctly the close of the old Dispensation than the fall of Jerusalem." [26] The destruction of the Mosaic system marks the further approach of the "time of reformation" (Heb. 9:10). But instead of this potential line of reasoning, our author must be content with: "In speaking of a new covenant he treats the first as obsolete. And what is becoming obsolete and growing old is ready to vanish away" (Heb. 8:13).

A still earlier date is implicit in three further clues. The leaders (hegoumenoi) (13:7, 17, 24; cf. the proistámenoi of Rom. 12:8; 1 Thess. 5:12-13) are not only unspecified, as if their offices (of episkopos and presbuteros, presumably) were not yet distinct, but include those who first spoke the word of God (Heb. 13:7). A continuity of leadership has been provided from the outset, presumably by Prisca and Aquila (Acts 18:18; Rom. 16:3-4; 1 Cor. 16:19; 2 Tim. 4:19; cf. 2 Tim. 1:15-16, where Onesiphorus also is located in Asia). All believers still have the responsibility of exhortation (Heb. 3:13; 10:24), supervision (12:15), and teaching (5:12; cf. 8:11). Secondly, though the converts ought to be teachers, they are still infants with faculties inexperienced in understanding "the first principles of God's word" and in distinguishing good and evil (5:12-14). Since Paul advised the recently converted Galatians (Gal. 6:6) and Colossians (Col. 1:5-9) to teach and admonish each other (Col. 3:16), no great amount of time need have elapsed since the conversion of the recipients of Hebrews. Thirdly, Hebrews 6:10 ("God is not so unjust as to overlook your work and the love which you showed (enedeíxasthe) for his sake in serving the saints"), a reference to a past deed worthy of recollection, is a natural allusion to a generous contribution to "the saints" in Jerusalem (Rom. 15:25-26, 31). The force of such an illustration would dissipate after a few years.

If we are justified in dating Hebrews after 59, but not after 64, the release of Timothy (Heb. 13:23) can provide a more exact clue. When Paul wrote him from Rome (2 Tim. 1:17), Timothy had been absent from Paul long enough for the apostle to write that he remembered him day and night in his petitions, longing to see him (2 Tim. 1:3-4). Timothy did not respond to Paul's plea to come to him soon (2 Tim. 4:9, 21). That his absence may have been enforced by imprisonment is intimated by 2 Timothy 1:8 ("Do not be ashamed then of testifying to our Lord, nor of me his prisoner, but take your share of suffering for the gospel . . .") and by 2:3 ("Take your share of suffering as a good soldier of Christ Jesus"). For the location of his confinement, one can look to Philippians 2:19 and 23, wherein Paul promises to send Timothy soon to Philippi. The same journey, which we have dated in the summer of 59 [27] correlates well with that of 2 Timothy 4:10-21, [28] which was still to take him to the areas of Colossae, Troas, and Ephesus. Paul had barely escaped a Jewish plot against him in Macedonia when on the way to Jerusalem (Acts 20:3). From this date we may conclude that Timothy was imprisoned at Philippi, where he received the instructions of 2 Timothy 4:10-21 and, some time later, the comforting 2 Timothy 1. Hebrews was written subsequently, in 62 or 63, i.e., about the same number of years after Apollos, Prisca, and Aquila established the incipient church at Ephesus (Acts 18:18-19, 24) as the duration (eleven or thirteen years) of a child's education in Greek and Jewish schools (Pirke Aboth 5, 27; cf. Heb. 5:12-14). Moreover, if Paul went to Spain [29] after his release from a two-year Roman imprisonment, Apollos may have had no news of him to report at this time.

CONCLUSION

Such a setting for Hebrews supports the following deductions concerning Paul: (1) he wrote from Rome to the imprisoned Timothy; (2) at the time Hebrews was written, he had not returned to Corinth, Philippi, and Ephesus, nor was he expected to return soon; (3) no news of Paul's status or death was then current among *hoi àpo tes Italías;* (4) after he left Ephesus, church life degenerated; and (5) the inclusion of Hebrews in the first corpus of Pauline letters indicates a comparable esteem for the Epistle and its author.

Appendix—
Pauline Corpus

All of Paul's letters, including Romans 1–16, were received in Asia Minor or in the Aegean area (see Zuntz, *The Text of the Epistles* [London: Oxford University Press, 1953], p. 279, n. 1), and it was here that his personal influence was greatest. Ignatius of Antioch (*ad Eph.* 12:1) and Polycarp of Smyrna (*ad Phil.* 11:3) knew a substantial collection. The corpus of the letters of Ignatius, which was written in Asia Minor, or of John of Patmos may reflect a local collecting tendency. Titus and Timothy, to whom later edited letters were written, were active in this area. Timothy was directed to remain at Ephesus (1 Tim. 1:3) to deal with problems described in the Pastoral Epistles (cf. Titus 1:5). The latter letters preserved Pauline fragments and traditions, and all material was attributed to him because of his memory and apostolic authority in the area. As an alternative to Ephesus as the place of origin of the full Pauline Corpus, Corinth might be suggested. The editorial compilation, Second Corinthians, was late in being released from the Corinthian church archives. "The Latinity of the Pastorals" (Montgomery Hitchcock, *Expository Times,* 39 [1928], 347-353) would be especially intelligible if the editor lived in the Roman colony of Corinth. First and Second Corinthians headed the Corpus. First Timothy 2:13-15 provides the earliest attestation for Second Corinthians 11:1-3 (Anthony T. Hanson, *Studies in the Pastoral Epistles* [London: S.P.C.K., 1968], pp. 71-72). But as the assembling of the Epistles was a cooperative process, it matters little on which side of the Aegean the chief impetus arose.

The original order of the church letters (Cor., Gal., Eph., Phil., Col., Thess., Rom.) perhaps can be reconstructed from a comparison of the following sequences:

Muratorianum (lines 50-60)	Tertullian (de praescr. 36; adv. Marc. iv, 5)	Origen (contra Celsum iii, 20)	P46 (earliest Egyptian)	Alexandrian uncials; Athanasius (Festal Letter 39)
			Rom.	Rom.
			Heb.	
Cor.	Cor.	Cor.	Cor.	Cor.
Eph.	Gal.	Eph.	Eph.	Gal.
Phil.	Phil.		Gal.	Eph.
Col.		Col.	Phil.	Phil.
Gal.	Thess.	Thess.	Col.	Col.
Thess.	Eph.	Phil.	Thess.	Thess.
Rom.	Rom.	Rom.		Heb.

Although elsewhere Amphilocius of Iconium and Theodore of Mopsuestia in the last quarter of the fourth century and possibly the somewhat earlier Synod of Laodicea (Zahn, *Geschichte d. ntl. Kanons*, vol. 2, pp. 201-202, 219, 360, n.2) gave first place to Romans, they lend some support to our original order:

Amphilocius	Theodore	Synod of Laodicea, Canon 59
Rom.	Rom.	Rom.
Cor.	Cor.	Cor.
Gal.	Heb.	Gal.
Eph.	Eph.	Eph.
Phil.	Gal.	Phil.
Col.	Phil.	Col.
Thess.	Col.	Thess.
	Thess.	Heb.

Theodore and P46 differ only in that Hebrews is placed before or after Corinthians. The Sahidic Coptic order differs from Theodore's only in that Galatians precedes, rather than follows, Ephesians. The early widespread existence of the Pauline Corpus in a special sequence is evidence of an original collection. The order is evidently pre-Alexandrian, as the critical text of Alexandria did not have much influence in the second century. Many variants are from a common pre-"Western" and pre-"Alexandrian" source. Widespread ancient variants would be more intelligible if there were more than one "edition" of the Corpus.

Behind the completed Corpus there apparently lay a shorter collection of First Corinthians, Ephesians, and Romans which also arose in either Corinth or Ephesus. In the four earliest lists (Muratorianum, Tertullian, Origen, and P[46]), Ephesians either followed Corinthians or preceded Romans immediately. The originality of this order is suggested by the fact that it was not upset in the various enlarged early lists, whether they be seen as variants of the original order of the whole Corpus, or as products of accidental piecemeal additions to a growing Corpus, or (more probably) as a mixture of both sources. That these three epistles were better and longer known in the early church is suggested by the fact that it was from them that Pauline reminiscences and quotations were largely drawn by the authors of Revelation, First Peter, First Clement, the Gospel and Letters of John, Ignatius, Polycarp, and James. Romans and Ephesians were natural selections as the best summaries of Paul's theology, and First Corinthians as his fullest treatment of problems of church life; such a trio could be read profitably by many churches when the apostle passed from the scene. Perhaps Timothy assembled these three at Ephesus at a very early date.

A basically different type of order remains to be considered:

Marcion (see Zahn, *Gesch. d. ntl. Kan.*, i [1889], 623	Ephraem	Mt. Sinai MS. God. Syr. 10 (Agnes Smith Lewis, *Studia Sinaitica*, London, i [1894]), 11-13
Gal.	Gal.	Gal.
Cor.	Cor.	Cor.
Rom.	Rom.	Rom.
Thess.	Heb.	Heb.
Eph. (Laodiceans)	Eph.	Col.
Col.	Phil.	Eph.
Phil.	Col.	Phil.
	Thess.	Thess.

The identical position of the first three letters is scarcely coincidental. The Mt. Sinai list, which testifies to the Syrian canon of about A.D. 400, differs from Ephraem's earlier one only in locating Colossians. Two sources of Ephraem's order may be suggested: Marcion via Tatian for the first three Pauline letters, and the original Corpus sequence for the last four letters. J. Rendel Harris (*Four Lectures on the Western Text of the New Testament* [London: C. J. Clay, 1894], pp. 18-22) and Josef Kerschensteiner ("Neues zum altsyrischen Paulustext," *Studiorum Paulinorum Congressus Internationalis Catholicus*

1961 [Rome: Pontif. Inst. Bibl., 1963], pp. i, 535-536, 538) have called attention to the Western and Marcionized text used by Ephraem; they suggested that this text had been brought to eastern Syria by Tatian from Rome. Ephraem hardly borrowed a Pauline text directly from the Marcionites whom he strongly opposed. But Tatian's Syriac Gospel harmony, the Diatesseron, was also based on a "Western" text and contains some traces of Marcionite influence (Harnack, *Marcion* [T.U. 45], Leipzig, 1921, p. 255); cf. E. C. Blackman, *Marcion and His Influence* (London: S.P.C.K., 1948), pp. 63, 169-171. Arthur Vööbus has shown that Tatian wrote his Diatesseron in Rome and brought it back to Syria, where it strongly influenced the Syriac text of the gospels. He leans toward the hypothesis that Tatian also translated Acts and Paul's letters (*Early Versions of the New Testament* [Stockholm, 1954], pp. 27-31). Eusebius (*H.E.* iv, 29.6) knew a tradition that Tatian "dared to modify some of the utterances of the apostle, correcting certain expressions of their style." This paraphrasing more probably was a loose Syriac translation or a commentary than a literary polishing according to Attic Greek models. Tatian was acquainted with the major letters of Paul (Barnett, *Paul Becomes a Literary Influence* [Chicago: University of Chicago Press, 1941], pp. 228-231):

Address to the Greeks 4:2	Rom. 1:20
Address to the Greeks 5:1	Col. 1:15–16
Address to the Greeks 11:1	1 Cor. 7:21
Address to the Greeks 11:2	Rom. 6:10; Col. 2:20; Rom. 7:14–15
Address to the Greeks 15:2	1 Cor. 2:14–15; 3:16; 6:19; 2 Cor. 6:16; Eph. 2:21–22
Address to the Greeks 16:2	Eph. 6:11, 13–14, 17 (cf. 2 Cor. 10:4; 1 Thess. 5:8)
Address to the Greeks 20:2	1 Cor. 15:53 (cf. 2 Cor. 5:1)
Address to the Greeks 30:1; Clement, *Strom.* iii, 12.82	Rom. 7:2; Eph. 4:14, 22–24; Col. 3:9–10
Fragment *ap.* Clement, *Strom.* iii, 12.81	1 Cor. 7:5
Fragment *ap.* Jerome, *Comm. in Gal.* 6:8 (Migne, *P.L.* xxvi, 560)	Gal. 6:8
Fragment *ap.* Irenaeus, *Adv. Haer.* iii, 23.8	1 Cor. 15:22

Jerome *(Praef. in Comm. in Tit.)*, probably drawing a false conclusion from the superficial citation of Titus 1:12 in *Address to the Greeks,* 27, related that Tatian accepted Titus while rejecting some other Pauline epistles as did Marcion.

Notes

1. A CHRONOLOGY OF JESUS' MINISTRY

[1] August Strobel, "Das apokalyptische Terminproblem in der sogen. Antrittspredigt Jesu (Luke 4:16-30)," *TLZ*, 92 (1967), 251-254.

[2] Joseph A. Fitzmyer, "Further Light on Melchizedek from Qumran Cave 11," *JBL*, 86 (1967), 29, 33-36.

[3] G. B. Caird, "Chronology of the N.T.," *Interpreter's Dictionary of the Bible* (Nashville: Abingdon Press, 1962), vol. 1, pp. 599-601; Hugh Montefiore, *Josephus and the New Testament* (London: A. R. Mowbray, 1962), pp. 8-16; Jack Finegan, *Handbook of Biblical Chronology* (Princeton: Princeton University Press, 1964), pp. 215-248.

[4] Finegan, *op. cit.*, pp. 259-273. Patterning Luke 3:1-2 on Jer. 1:1-3 in the Septuagint, Luke listed the governor and three tetrarchs and the puzzling joint priesthood (cf. John 18:13). This information more likely came from a secular source than from a priestly Baptist one (cf. Luke 1) using a Jewish calendar with its later dating of Tiberius's years as emperor.

[5] Hans Windisch ("Die Dauer der öffentlichen Wirksamkeit Jesu nach den vier Evangelisten," *ZNTW*, 12 [1911], 161, 165; cf. 149, 157) calculated that Luke allows for a $6\frac{1}{2}$ months' ministry, compared to the $4\frac{1}{2}$ months allotted by Mark. R. Bultmann (*The History of the Synoptic Tradition*, trans. J. Marsh [Oxford: Basil Blackwell, 1963], pp. 362, 360) finds that, while Luke "is interested in an historically continuous and connected presentation," he "knows that the few stories that have been passed on do not completely fit the course of events, but are only examples and illustrations." Hans Conzelmann (*The Theology of St. Luke*, trans. Geoffrey Buswell [London: Faber and Faber, Ltd., 1960], pp. 46-47, 60-64, 72-73) concludes that as the material and chronological clues available to Luke were meager, the journeys he describes are literary devices. Through Paul at least (cf. Gal. 1:17ff.) he learned or calculated the crucifixion date.

[6] B. H. Streeter (*The Four Gospels* [London: Macmillan & Co., Ltd., 1930], p. 424) observed that "Mark presents a detailed and coherent account" of the last journey to Jerusalem and of Passion Week. "The rest of the Gospel is clearly a collection of detached stories—as indeed tradition affirms it to be; and the total number of incidents recorded is so small that the gaps in

the story must be the more considerable part of it." Bultmann (*op. cit.*, p. 243) notes that "the elements of the tradition very seldom contain dates and times." On the editorial connections of traditional material in the Synoptic Gospels, see Bultman, *op. cit.*, pp. 339-342, 350-353, 358-364.

[7] George Ogg, *The Chronology of the Public Ministry of Jesus* (New York: Cambridge University Press, 1940), p. 39.

[8] Sydney Temple, "Geography and Climate in the Fourth Gospel," in *The Joy of Study* (Papers presented to honor F. C. Grant), ed. S. E. Johnson (New York: The Macmillan Company, 1951), pp. 66-68.

[9] J. C. Trever, "Lily," *Interpreter's Dictionary of the Bible*, vol. 3, p. 133.

[10] References in Caird, *art. cit.*, pp. i, 602.

[11] Finegan, *op. cit.*, pp. 144, 150.

[12] Ogg, *op. cit.*, pp. 252-253.

[13] J. D. Frotheringham, "The Evidence of Astronomy and Technical Chronology for the Date of the Crucifixion," *JTS*, 35 (1934), 159-160; Ogg, *op. cit.*, pp. 261-276; Caird, *art. cit.*, i, 603; Finegan, *op. cit.*, pp. 291-298.

[14] "Fig," *Dictionary of the Bible*, ed. James Hastings, revised by F. C. Grant and H. H. Rowley (Edinburgh: T. & T. Clark, 1963, 2d ed.), p. 297.

[15] This passage, then, and Mal. 3:1-5 shaped and corresponded to the Messianic and eschatological views of John and Jesus. The heart of John's preaching was a commentary on Malachi's prophecy: because the Messiah is coming with fire, those who fear judgment should replace their oppression and false witness with mercy (Matt. 3:7-12; Luke 3:7-17). In this context we must understand the words of Jesus, "I came to cast fire upon the earth" (Luke 12:49; cf. 13:27-29; 17:29-30; cf. also Matt. 11:20-24; 13:40-42; 25:40-43; 2 Thess. 1:7-9; 2:8). Also, at the outset of his ministry he sought to fulfill Mal. 3:1-3 ("the Lord whom you seek shall suddenly come to his temple . . .") ; cf. Mark 1:2.

2. PAUL'S VISITS TO JERUSALEM

[1] In his excellent chronological study ("Paul's 'Missionary Journeys' as Reflected in His Letters," *JBL*, 74 [1955], 81), Thomas H. Campbell writes: "Certainly Paul's letters are our primary sources for a reconstruction of his career, whereas Acts is at best a secondary source except at those points where the author is writing as an eyewitness. . . ." Cf. John H. Hurd, Jr., "Pauline Chronology and Pauline Theology," in *Christian History and Interpretation: Studies Presented to John Knox*, ed. W. R. Farmer, C. F. D. Moule, and R. R. Niebuhr (New York: Cambridge University Press, 1967), pp. 233-234; "The Sequence of Paul's Letters," *Canadian Journal of Theology*, 14 (1968), 189-192.

[2] See A. Harnack, "Chronologische Berechnung des 'Tages von Damaskus,'" *Sitzungberichte der preussischen Akademie der Wissenschaft zu Berlin*, 37 (1912), 673-682; Maurice Goguel, *The Life of Jesus*, tr. Olive Wyon (New York: The Macmillan Co., 1933), pp. 229-230. Harnack thought the number eighteen to be pre-Gnostic because it was interpreted mystically like the numbers of twelve or thirty (years) (Irenaeus, *Adv. Haer.* i, 3.1-3). The tradition of resurrection appearances for such a period appears also in the Apocryphon of James (Edgar Hennecke, *New Testament Apocrypha*, ed. Wilhelm Schneemelcher, trans. and ed. R. McL. Wilson [Philadelphia: The Westminster Press, 1963], vol. 1, p. 336) and in Valentinian and Ophite teaching (Irenaeus, *Adv. Haer.* i, 3.2; 30.14).

[3] An early date for Paul's conversion, which occurred shortly after

Stephen's martyrdom, is confirmed by the fact that he was a young man (*neanias*: Acts 7:58) at the time of the stoning, but had become an old man (*presbutes*) when he wrote to Philemon (v. 9). The time required for this translation was at least a generation. A fourth- or fifth-century homily attributed to John Chrysotom related that Paul served God for thirty-five years (see William M. Ramsay, *Pauline and Other Studies* [London: Hodder & Stoughton, Ltd., 1906], pp. 362-363). Such a figure would be appropriate for his conversion in 30 or 31 and a death during Nero's persecution of 64-65. This dating cannot be upset by an appeal to Paul's reference to Aretas, king of the Nabateans (2 Cor. 11:32). There is no evidence that the Romans ceded Damascus to him. The ethnarch was the head of the Nabatean community there, which maintained its own separate customs and religious laws while living under Roman control in an alien environment. The ethnarch apparently was the representative appointed or accepted by Aretas; he was responsible to Aretas for the people's welfare and to Rome for their civil obedience. This required the use of sufficient police power to govern and maintain order. Such a degree of autonomy may have been expedient for a proud nomad people. Cf. George Ogg, *The Chronology of the Life of Paul* (London: Epworth Press, 1968), pp. 18-19; he concedes: "in the spring of A.D. 37 Damascus was in Roman hands" (p. 22).

⁴ Theodor Zahn, *Introduction to the New Testament*, translation directed by M. W. Jacobus (New York: Charles Scribner's Sons, 1917, 2d ed.), pp. ii, 461-463; Philipp Bachmann, *Der zweite Brief des Paulus an die Korinther* (Leipzig & Erlangen, 1922), pp. 391-392; E. B. Allo, *St. Paul: Second Épitre aux Corinthiens* (Paris: Librairie Lecoffre, 1956), p. 307.

⁵ Tarsus seems to have been the center of the apostle's work after the brethren sent him home (Acts 9:28-30) via Caesarea "three years" after his conversion. Barnabas sought him in Tarsus (Acts 11:25-26) in the province of Syria and Cilicia, where Paul said he preached (Gal. 1:21–2:1) before returning to the Holy City. The decrees of the Jerusalem Council were directed to the churches of the province and were delivered to the churches there (Acts 15:23, 41). Thereby Jerusalem exercised authority over Paul's churches (cf. Acts 15:19; 16:4). Some of Paul's misfortunes enumerated in 2 Cor. 11:24-27 belong to this period.

⁶ Concerning Paul's thorn in the flesh and his physical infirmity, see H. A. W. Meyer, *Critical and Exegetical Commentary on II Corinthians* (Edinburgh: T. & T. Clark, 1879), pp. 474-479; E. B. Allo, *Second Épitre aux Corinthiens* (Paris: Librairie Lecoffre, 1956), pp. 313-323; P. E. Hughes, *Paul's Second Epistle to the Corinthians* (New London Comm.) (London and Edinburgh: Marshall, Morgan & Scott, 1962), pp. 442-448. L. Osiander and J. L. von Mosheim understood the thorn to be remorse for persecution. We suggest that it was associated with the control of his digestive tract. Such attacks would be repulsive, emotion-related, and aggravated by seasickness. He was apparently unable to return by boat to Antioch, but pushed on to Galatia (Gal. 4:13) from Perga after John Mark upset him by returning to Jerusalem (Acts 13:13-14; 15:37-39). Satan, distress, and affliction kept the anxiety-filled apostle from returning in person to the Thessalonians (1 Thess. 2:18; 3:1, 7). He wrote to the Galatians (6:11) in large letters after being troubled (6:17). Yet he showed no signs of progressive physical or psychic deterioration.

⁷ For bibliographies of this opinion (first expressed by Calvin), see Robert G. Hoerber, "Galatians 2:10 and the Acts of the Apostles," *Concordia Theological Monthly*, 31 (1960), 483, n. 8; Stanley D. Toussaint, "The

Chronological Problem of Galatians 2:10," *Bibliotheca Sacra,* 120 (1963), 338, n. 10. Also, Emile Osty, *Le Nouveau Testament* (Paris: Editions Siloë, 1949–1950), pp. 403ff.; Campbell, *art. cit., JBL,* 74 (1955), 87; J. N. Sanders, "Peter and Paul in the Acts," *NTS,* 2 (1955–1956), 137; Francois Amiot, *St. Paul: Épître aux Galatiens, Épîtres aux Thessaloniciens* (Paris: Beauchesne, 1956), pp. 27-34; Charles H. Talbert, "Again: Paul's Visits to Jerusalem," *Novum Testamentum,* 9 (1967), 35-40; F. F. Bruce, "Galatian Problems. 1. Autobiographical Data," *BJRL,* 51 (1969), 305-306.

[8] George S. Duncan, *The Epistle of Paul to the Galatians* (Moffatt N.T. Commentary), (New York: Harper & Row, Publishers, 1934), p. 52. See also Bruce, *art. cit., BJRL,* 51 (1969), 305, n. 3. On the other hand, see Ernst Haenchen, *Die Apostelgeschichte* (Meyers Komm.) (Göttingen: Vandenhoeck & Ruprecht, 1961, 13th ed.), p. 321.

[9] Charles H. Talbert, *art. cit., Novum Testamentum,* 9 (1967), 38-39.

[10] Kirsopp Lake, *The Earlier Epistles of St. Paul* (London: Rivingtons, 1911), pp. 287-288; cf. 290.

[11] W. Schmithals, *Paul and James,* trans. Dorothea M. Barton (London: SCM, 1965), pp. 80-83 (65-69), quoting from p. 82.

[12] *Ibid.*

[13] *Ibid.,* p. 89 (73-74); cf. pp. 66-68 (53-55).

[14] *Ibid.,* p. 107 (89-90).

[15] J. Meyshan, "The Coinage of Agrippa the First," *Israel Exploration Society,* 4 (1954), 188, 190, 194, 197.

[16] T. Zahn, *op. cit.,* ii, 456; cf. Ogg, *The Chronology of the Life of Paul,* pp. 41-42. The consulate of C. Passienus Crispus II, during which Claudius returned to Rome, ended on May 4. Festival preparations for faraway Caesarea would take several weeks.

[17] On the disputed meaning of this phrase, see Kirsopp Lake, "Note XXXIV. The Chronology of Acts," in *The Beginnings of Christianity,* ed. F. J. Foakes-Jackson and Kirsopp Lake (London: Macmillan & Co., Ltd., 1933), vol. 5, pp. 454-455; Andres M. Tornos, "La Fecha del Hambre de Jerusalem alududa por Act. 11, 28-30), "*Estudios Eclesiasticos,* 33 (1959), 307-308, 315.

[18] Tornos, *op. cit.,* pp. 311-315.

[19] Stein, "Gotarzes," Pauly-Wissowa, *Real-encyclopädie der classischen Altertumswissenschaft* (Stuttgart, vii, 2, 1912), pp. 1677-1678; Rudolf Hanslick, "Vardanes," Pauly-Wissowa, *op. cit.,* in A1 (1955), pp. 369-370.

[20] See Robert H. McDowell, *Coins from Seleucia on the Tigris* (Ann Arbor: The University of Michigan Press, 1935), pp. 189-190, 225-227; Streck, "Seleukia (am Tigris)," Pauly-Wissowa, *op. cit.,* ii, A1 (1923), pp. 1162, 1179-1180.

[21] R. Helm, "C. Vibius Marsus," Pauly-Wissowa, *op. cit.,* viii, A2 (1958), pp. 1974-1975.

[22] Kenneth S. Gapp, "The Universal Famine Under Claudius," *HTR,* 28 (1935), 258-266.

[23] *Ibid.,* 261-262.

[24] Theodor Zahn, *Forschungen zur Geschichte des neutestamentliche Kanons* (Leipzig: A. Deichert, vi, 1900), p. 265.

[25] *Ibid.,* ii, 459.

[26] See H. Latimer Jackson, *The Problem of the Fourth Gospel* (New York: Cambridge University Press, 1918), pp. 142-148.

[27] Their hopes are expressed in Mark 10:37 and Luke 9:54. Cerinthus's expectation of a millennium were compared to those of the apostle John (Gaius of Rome and Dionysius of Alexandria, *ap.* Eusebius, *H.E.* iii, 28.2;

vii, 25.3; Dionysius bar Salibi, *In Apocalypsim, Actus et Epistulas Canonices,* ed. I. Sedlacek, *CSCO,* Scrip. Syr., Ser. 2, vol. 10 [1910], p. 2) . If Rev. 11:2-13 refers to the sons of Zebedee, as Robert Eisler cogently argued (*The Enigma of the Fourth Gospel* [London: Methuen & Co., Ltd., 1938], pp. 86-89), then they had the gift of prophecy (Rev. 11:3, 6, 7, 10) .

[28] Proponents of this and other positions are named by Talbert, *art. cit.,* *NT,* 9 (1967), 26; Pierson Parker, "Once More, Acts and Galatians," *JBL,* 86 (1967) , 175-182; Ogg, *The Chronology of the Life of Paul,* pp. 43-57, 72-88.

[29] William Sanday, "The Apostolic Decree (Acts xv. 20-29)," in *Theologische Studien. Theodor Zahn zum 10 Oktober 1908 dargebracht* (Leipzig: A. Deickert, 1908) , p. 330.

[30] T. W. Manson, "The Problem of the Epistle to the Galatians," in *Studies in the Gospels and Epistles,* ed. Matthew Black (Manchester: University Press, 1962) , pp. 180-181, 181, n. 1.

[31] The "Western" text presents a basic moral code for Gentiles entering the church. Joseph Klausner (*From Jesus to Paul,* trans. William F. Stinespring [Boston: Beacon Press, 1961], p. 368, n. 18) succinctly noted: "It was natural that Christianity at a later time should *omit* Jewish rules, such as those against eating meat not ritually slaughtered ('strangled') and blood; but it was not natural that it should *add* them later."

[32] See A. R. S. Kennedy, "Food," *Encyclopaedia Biblica,* ed. T. K. Cheyne and J. S. Black (London: A & C Black, Ltd., 1901) , vol. 2, pp. 1545-1546.

[33] D. Plooij, "The Apostolic Decree and Its Problems," *Expositor,* viii, 25 (1923), 88-92.

[34] Marc Philonenko, "Le décret apostolique et les interdits alimentaires du Coran," *Revue d' Histoire et de Philosophie Religieuses,* 47 (1967) , 165-172.

[35] See Benjamin Bacon, "The Apostolic Decree against *Porneia,*" *Expositor,* viii, 7 (Jan., 1914), 40, 61; J. de Zwaan, "Was the Book of Acts a Posthumous Edition?" *HTR,* 17 (1924) , 113-115, 121-122; Lucien Cerfaux, "Le Chapitre XVᵉ du livre des Actes à la lumière de la littérature ancienne," in *Miscellanea Giovanni Mercati* (Studi e Test 121, I), Città de Vaticano, 1946, 114-120. A. F. J. Klijn, "The Pseudo-Clementines and the Apostolic Decree," *NT,* 10 (1968), 306-310. D. Plooij (*art. cit.,* *Expositor,* viii, 25 [1923], 33) observed: "The most striking and outstanding feature of the Law was its tendency to separate the nation of Israel from the nations of the world, to make them avoid every pollution with the Gentiles who did not keep the ritual Law. Here is the conflict: How far does Christian freedom go?"

[36] Schmithals, *op. cit.,* pp. 97-98, 101, n. 24 (81-82, 84-85) . The Noachite rules are contained in the tract, *Sanhedrin* 56b.

[37] For a bibliography, see Heinrich Schlier, *Der Brief an die Galater* (Meyers Kommentar) (Göttingen: Vandenhoeck & Ruprecht, 1951) , 40; D. W. B. Robinson, "The Circumcision of Titus, and Paul's 'Liberty,' " *Australian Biblical Review,* 12 (1964), 28-39.

3. PAUL'S MIDDLE YEARS

[1] Adolf Deissmann, *Paul: A Study in Social and Religious History,* trans. William E. Wilson (London: Hodder & Stoughton, Ltd., 1926) , pp. 261-286; Jack Finegan, *Handbook of Biblical Chronology* (Princeton, N.J.: Princeton University Press, 1964) , pp. 316-318, where a bibliography is given. Proconculs had to leave Rome by April and be in office by July 1 (Dio Cassius, *Roman History* lvii, 14.5; lx, 11.6 and 17.3) . A one-year term was normal,

but a second year was possible (Dio, lx, 25.6). Gallio's term in office apparently was cut short by fever (Seneca, *Epistle* civ. 1; cf. Pliny, *Nat. Hist.* xxxi, 33), which was most likely contracted during the warm, humid weather. If so, he was in office only for a few months in the spring and summer, and left Corinth for a healthier climate before the end of the sailing season. The Delphi inscription reveals that Gallio was proconsul of Achaia in the twelfth year of Claudius (Jan. 25, 52, to Jan. 24, 53) and after the twenty-sixth imperial acclamation (i.e., before Aug. 1, 52). Now, if Gallio were proconsul at some time during the period of January 25 to July 31, 52, and if he entered upon his abbreviated term of office in May, Paul must have appeared before him in May, June, or July, 52.

² See Robert O. Hoerber, "The Decree of Claudius In Acts 18.2," *Concordia Theological Monthly*, 31 (1960), 690-694. William Ramsay (*St. Paul the Traveler and the Roman Citizen* [London: Hodder & Stoughton, Ltd., 1927], pp. 254, 268; W. Ramsey, *Pauline and Other Studies* [London: Hodder & Stoughton, Ltd., 1906], pp. 361-362) thinks that Orosius's dates for Claudius's reign are a year early and that "the ninth year" means 50.

³ On the months marking out this journey from Antioch to Philippi, see William Ramsay, *The Church in the Roman Empire before* A.D. *170* (London: Hodder & Stoughton, Ltd., 1893), pp. 85-85.

⁴ George Ogg, *The Chronology of the Life of Paul* (London: Epworth Press, 1968), pp. 65, 71.

⁵ Ramsay, *St. Paul the Traveler and the Roman Citizen*, pp. 263-265; Ernst Haenchen, *Die Apostelgeschichte* (Meyers Kommentar) (Göttingen: Vandenhoeck & Ruprecht, 1961, 13th ed.), p. 480, n. 5.

⁶ This argument, however, is weakened by the possibility that Gaius was a Macedonian (Acts 19:29) from Doberus, if we follow the Codex Bezae reading of 20:4, *"Doubérios."*

⁷ Ernest Burton, *A Critical and Exegetical Commentary on the Epistle to the Galatians* (ICC) (Edinburgh: T. & T. Clark, 1952 repr.), xxv-xxvii. Paul's references to the churches of Judea (Gal. 1:22; 1 Thess. 2:14; cf. 2 Cor. 1:16) are an exception, as it was not an official province. But it merited distinction from the rest of Syria. See also Donald Guthrie, *Galatians* (Century Bible) (London: Thomas Nelson & Sons, Ltd., 1969), pp. 21-22.

⁸ Alexander Southern, "Galatia," in *Dictionary of the Bible*, ed. James Hastings, revised by F. C. Grant and H. H. Rowley (Edinburgh: T. & T. Clark, 1963), p. 311.

⁹ Ramsay (*A Historical Commentary on St. Paul's Epistle to the Galatians* [London: Hodder & Stoughton Ltd., 1899], pp. 50-51, 129-146) dates the Hellenization in the second century.

¹⁰ *Ibid.*, pp. 117-121; David Magie, *Roman Rule in Asia Minor* (Princeton, N.J.: Princeton University Press, 1950), vol. 1, pp. 459-467.

¹¹ See Ramsay, *St. Paul the Traveler and the Roman Citizen*, pp. 111-112. Antiochenes such as Luke and inhabitants of Lycaonia Antiochiana and travelers entering it may have referred to Galatian Lycaonia as the "Galatic region *(Galatikè chóra).*" We have no knowledge of Paul's founding churches in Lycaonia Antiochiana.

¹² If the Western reading belongs in this setting (cf. B. H. Streeter, "The Primitive Text of Acts," *JTS*, 34 [1933], 237-238) and preserves historical information, it is possible that Paul considered returning to Jerusalem to complain about the Judaizers who were already creating trouble in Galatia. The Epistle witnesses to the significance of the Jerusalem church in the

dispute between Paul and his opponents. Though most commentators assume that Paul learned through a messenger about the upheaval in his Galatian churches, the oral warning of Gal. 1:9 presupposes Paul's recognition of a threat.

[13] Ramsay, *The Church in the Roman Empire before* A.D. *170*, pp. 25-27, 79; William Calder, "The Boundary of Galatic Phrygia," *Proceedings of the Twenty-Second* (International) *Congress of Orientalists* (Istanbul, 1951) (Leiden: E. J. Brill, 1957), pp. 37-38.

[14] Ramsay, *The Church in the Roman Empire before* A.D. *170*, pp. 37-39; Calder, *art. cit.*, p. 39.

[15] Ramsay, *The Church in the Roman Empire before* A.D. *170*, pp. 77-81, 88-89, 93; *St. Paul the Traveler and the Roman Citizen*, pp. 104, 210-212; "Galatia, Region of," *A Dictionary of the Bible*, ed. James Hastings (Edinburgh & New York, 1905), pp. ii, 89-91.

[16] Such was the later opinion of Kirsopp Lake ("Note XVIII. Paul's Route in Asia Minor," in F. J. Foakes-Jackson and K. Lake, *The Beginnings of Christianity* [London: Macmillan & Co., Ltd., 1933], vol. 5, p. 236) : "Phrygia and Galatian country means territory in which sometimes Phrygian and sometimes Gaelic was the language of the villagers." Calder *(art. cit.*, pp. 40-41) , to the contrary, has shown that, as ascertained from Phrygian tombstones of ca. A.D. 250, the boundary between Greek-speaking Phrygians and the Phrygians using both Greek and Phrygian was found in the province of Asia, well back from the border of Galatia.

[17] Calder, *art. cit.*, pp. 40, 41.

[18] Burton, *op. cit.*, xliv; cf. xl.

[19] For a case against an early date, see Maurice Jones, "The Date of the Epistle to the Galatians," *The Expositor*, viii, 6 (1913) , 198-205.

[20] Edward H. Askwith, *The Epistle to the Galatians: An Essay on Its Destination and Date* (London: Macmillan & Co., Ltd., 1899) . pp. 113-118. His arguments for the South Galatian theory (pp. 7-66) are cogent.

[21] Raymond T. Stamm, "Introduction to Galatians," *IB*, 10, 439-441. See also J. B. Lightfoot, *St. Paul's Epistle to the Galatians* (London: Macmillan & Co., Ltd., 1881, 7th edition), pp. 43-56; Charles H. Buck, Jr., "The Date of Galatians," *JBL*, 70 (1951) , 113-117; Jones, *art. cit.*, *The Expositor*, viii, 6 (1913), 207-208; Chalmer E. Faw, "The Anomaly of Galatians," *Biblical Research*, 4 (1960) , 26-38.

[22] John Knox *(Chapters in a Life of Paul* [Nashville: Abingdon Press, 1950], pp. 51, 54-58) rightly bases his epistle order (Gal.–1 Cor.–2 Cor.– Rom.) on references to the collection.

[23] That the Galatians were slow in responding to Paul's appeal was the opinion of J. B. Lightfoot *(St. Paul's Epistle to the Galatians*, pp. 25, 55, 110-111) and J. N. Sanders ("Peter and Paul in the Acts," *NTS*, 2 [1955–1956], 140-141) .

[24] George Barton, "The Exegesis of *eniautous* in Galatians 4:10 and Its Bearing on the Date of the Epistle," *JBL*, 33 (1914), 118-126.

[25] Alfred Plummer, *A Critical and Exegetical Commentary on the Second Epistle of St. Paul to the Corinthians* (Edinburgh: T. & T. Clark, 1915), p. 364.

[26] For lists of proponents of various views of the harsh letter, see Plummer, *op. cit.*, xxviii; E. B. Allo, *Saint Paul, Seconde Épître aux Corinthiens* (Études Bibliques) (Paris: Librairie Lecoffre, 1956, 2d ed.) , LI-LII.

[27] Paul W. Schmiedel, *Die Briefe an die Thessalonicher und an die Kor-*

inther, Freiburg im Br. (Tübingen: J. C. B. Mohr [Paul Siebeck], 1891), pp. 56-62.

[28] James H. Kennedy, *The Second and Third Epistles of St. Paul to the Corinthians* (London: Methuen & Co. Ltd., 1900).

[29] Kirsopp Lake, *The Earlier Epistles of St. Paul* (London: Rivingtons, 1911), pp. 154-164.

[30] The continued existence of a rebellious group is probably alluded to in 2 Cor. 2:6-7, 10, 14; 7:13. See R. H. Strachan, *The Second Epistle of Paul to the Corinthians* (Moffatt N.T. Commentary) (London: Hodder & Stoughton Ltd., 1935), pp. xvii-iii.

[31] This point is made cautiously by A. Robertson ("II Corinthians," *A Dictionary of the Bible*, ed. James Hastings, vol. 1, p. 497); Kennedy (*op. cit.*, pp. 153ff.); and Strachan (*op. cit.*, xxi-xxii), but confidently by Günther Bornkamm ("The History of the Origin of the So-called Second Letter to the Corinthians," *NTS*, 8 [1962], 258-264).

[32] As done by Johannes Weiss, *Der erste Korintherbrief* (Meyers Kommentar) (Göttingen: Vandenhoeck & Ruprecht, 1910), xl-xliii; cf. *The History of Primitive Christianity*, ed. Frederick C. Grant (New York: Wilson-Erickson, 1937), pp. 324-330, 340-341; Alfred Loisy, *Les livres du Nouveau Testament traduits du grec en français* (Paris: Émile Nourry, 1922), pp. 39-41; Paul Louis Couchod, "Reconstitution et classement des lettres de Saint Paul," *Revue de l'Histoire des Religions*, 87 (1923), 18-20; Maurice Goguel, *Introduction au Nouveau Testament, Les Épîtres Pauliniennes* (Paris: Ernest Leroux, 1926), vol. 4, pp. 2, 72-86; Jean Hering, *La Première Épître de St. Paul aux Corinthiens* (Commentaire du N.T.) (Neuchâtel & Paris: Delachaux & Niestlé, 1949), pp. 10-12; Walther Schmithals, *Die Gnosis in Korinth* (Göttingen: Vandenhoeck & Ruprecht, 1965), p. 89; Wolfgang Schenk, "Der 1 Korintherbrief als Briefsammlung," *ZNTW*, 60 (1969), 219ff.

[33] See Alfred Plummer, *op. cit.*, xxiii-xxvi; Hans Windisch, *Der zweite Korintherbrief* (Meyers Handkommentar) (Göttingen: Vandenhoeck & Ruprecht, 1924), pp. 18-20, 211-220; Allo, *op. cit.*, vol. 53, pp. 189-191.

[34] S. M. Gilmour, "First Corinthians," *IDB*, 1, 687.

[35] Joseph A. Fitzmyer, "Qumran and the Interpolated Paragraph in 2 Cor. 6, 14-7, 1," *CBQ*, 23 (1961), 271.

[36] Bibliographies on this view are given by Allo, *op. cit.*, p. 290; Joachim Gnilka, "2 Kor. 6, 14-7, 1 im Lichte der Qumranschriften und der Zwölf-Patriarchen-Testamente," in *Neutestamentliche Aufsätze; Festschrift für Prof. Josef Schmid*, ed. J. Blinzler, O. Kuss, and F. Mussner (Regensburg: Verlag Friedrich Pustet, 1963), p. 86, n. 1; trans. in Jerome Murphy-O'Connor, ed., *Paul and Qumran* (Chicago: The Priory Press, 1968), p. 49, n. 1; other proponents include Jülicher, Dinkler, and W. Grossouw ("Over de echtheid van 2 Cor. 6.14-7, 1," *Studia Catholica*, 26 (1951), 203-206.

[37] For a bibliography see Bertil Gärtner, *The Temple and the Community in Qumran and the New Testament* (New York: Cambridge University Press, 1965), p. 50, n. 2; also Fitzmyer, *art cit.*, *CBQ*, 23 (1961), 271-280; Hans W. Huppenbauer, *Der Mensch zwischen zwei Welten* (Zürich: Zwingli Verlag, 1959), p. 59, n. 222.

[38] Joachim Gnilka, *art. cit.*, in Schmid Festschrift, 98; Murphy-O'Connor, ed., *op. cit.*, p. 66.

[39] Joseph Fitzmyer, *art. cit.*, *CBQ*, 23 (1961) 279-280.

[40] Karl G. Kuhn, "Die Schriftrollen vom Toten Meer, zum heutigen Stand ihrer Veroffentlichung," *Evangelische Theologie*, 11 (1951–1952), 74; "Les rouleaux de cuivre de Qumran," *RB*, 61 (1954), 203, n. 2.

[41] I.e., after memory of the real first letter had faded.

[42] T. W. Manson ("The Corinthian Correspondence (2)," *BJRL*, 26 [1941–1942], 327-328; reprinted in *Studies in the Gospels and Epistles*, edited by Matthew Black [Manchester: University Press, 1962], p. 211) wrote: "I am inclined to think that in making these plans he was looking at least six months ahead and that I Cor. was probably written in the autumn, or at least the early winter, of the previous year."

[43] Ogg, *The Chronology of the Life of Paul*, pp. 136-137.

[44] See James Moffatt, *An Introduction to the Literature of the New Testament* (New York: Charles Scribner's Sons, 1911), pp. 135-137; Rudolf Schumacher, *Die beiden letzten Kapitel des Römerbriefes*, in *Neutestamentliche Abhandlungen*, ed. Max Meinertz, xix-4 (Münster/Westfalen: Verlag Aschendorff, 1929), p. 63; Joseph Huby, *Saint Paul: Épître aux Romains* (Paris: Beauchesne, 1957), p. 491, n. 1; most recently supported by W. Marxsen *(Introduction to the N.T.* [Philadelphia: Fortress Press, 1968], p. 108); H. M. Schenke *(TLZ,* 92 [1967], p. 883); and J. A. Fitzmyer (in *Jerome Biblical Commentary* [1968], pp. 292-293).

[45] E. J. Goodspeed, "Phoebe's Letter of Introduction," *HTR,* 44 (1951), 56; J. H. MacDonald, "Was Romans xvi a Separate Letter?", *NTS,* 16 (1970), 369-372.

[46] Walther Schmithals, "Die Irrlehrer von Rom. 16, 17-20," *Studia Theologica,* 13 (1959), 67-69.

[47] Jacques Dupont, "Pour l'histoire de la doxologie finale de l'Épître aux Romains," *Revue Bénédictine,* 58 (1948), 7-8, n. 6.

[48] See Lake, *The Earlier Epistles of Saint Paul,* pp. 346-348; T. W. Manson, "St. Paul's Letter to the Romans—and Others," *BJRL,* 31 (1948), 226-228 (repr. in *Studies in the Gospels and Epistles,* ed Matthew Black [Manchester: University Press, 1962], pp. 228-229).

[49] For a summary of scholarship on these two chapters, see Schumacher, *op. cit.;* Dupont, *art. cit., Revue Bénédictine,* 58 (1948), 3-22.

[50] Günther Zuntz, *The Text of the Epistles: A Disquisition upon the Corpus Paulinum* (London: Oxford University Press, 1953), pp. 267-279.

[51] Lake, *op. cit.,* pp. 337-339.

[52] *Ibid.,* pp. 335-337; William Sanday and Arthur C. Headlam, *A Critical and Exegetical Commentary on the Epistle to the Romans* (New York: Charles Scribner's Sons, 1896), xc; Schumacher, *op. cit.,* pp. 125-126.

[53] "La finale marcionite de la lettre aux Romains," *Revue Bénédictine,* 28 (1911), 133-135; Bulletin d'ancienne litter. Chretienne (33), no. 110, *Revue Bénédictine,* 42 (1930). The Monza MS actually has only *"-bus"*; the rest has disappeared, but very likely was the same as in the Munich MSS.

[54] *Ibid.*

[55] P. Corssen, "Zur Uberlieferungsgeschichte des Römerbriefes," *ZNTW,* 10 (1909), 1-45, 97-102. For a bibliography of views on this article, see Dupont, *art. cit., Revue Bénédictine,* 58 (1948), 18, n. 2.

[56] This translation is taken from W. H. Ryder, "The Authorship of Romans xv, xvi," *JBL,* 17 (1898), 187. Origen wrote this Commentary (and presumably knew these codices in the library) at Caesarea (Rolf Gögler, *Zur Theologie des Biblischen Wortes bei Origines* [Düsseldorf: Patmos, 1963], pp. 20, 22).

[57] For a bibliography on the hypothesis of Marcionite origin, see Dupont, *art. cit.,* pp. 3-4.

[58] *Ibid.,* pp. 7-8, n. 6. Yet he considers possible the Marcionite origin of the short recension.

[59] Zuntz, *op. cit.*, pp. 241, 236-238.

[60] Schumacher, *op. cit.*, p. 119.

[61] F. J. A. Hort, "The Epistle to the Romans—Its Structure and Destination," in J. B. Lightfoot, *Biblical Essays* (New York: The Macmillan Company, 1893), pp. 324-329; see also Sanday and Headlam, *op. cit.*, pp. 432-436; L.-M. Dewailly, "Mystère et silence dans Rom. xvi, 25," *NTS*, 14 (1967), 111-118.

[62] See pp. 130-138 in this book.

[63] Kirsopp Lake, *op. cit.*, pp. 343-344.

[64] T. W. Manson, *art. cit.*, *BJRL*, 31 (1948), 231; T. W. Manson, *op. cit.*, p. 232.

[65] Sanday and Headlam, *op. cit.*, xci-ii.

[66] See pp. 125-130 in this book.

[67] See pp. 107-110 in this book.

[68] On "Western" Pauline readings, see M. J. Lagrange, *Introduction a l'étude du Nouveau Testament. Critique textuelle. II. La critique rationnelle* (Paris, 1935), pp. 184-185, 481ff. Proponents of the Antiochene origin of the Western text of the Gospels or Acts, at least, include William Sanday (*The Guardian*, May 18 and 25, 1892); F. H. Chase (*The Old Syriac Element in Codex Bezae* [London, 1893], p. 131); James Ropes (*The Beginnings of Christianity*, F. J. Foakes-Jackson and Kirsopp Lake, eds., I-III [1926], ccxlv); and G. Quispel ("Das Hebraerevangelium im gnostistischen Evangelium nach Maria," *Vigiliae Christianæ*, 11 [1957], 141, n. 5).

[69] For bibliographies, see Moffatt, *An Introduction to the Literature of the New Testament*, pp. 172-176; W. Schmithals, "Die Irrlehrer der Philipperbriefes," *ZTK*, 54 (1957), 299-300; Maurice Goguel, *Introduction au Nouveau Testament*, vol. 4, 1 (1925), pp. 404-405; Helmut Koester, "The Purpose of the Polemic of a Pauline Fragment (Philippians III)," *NTS*, 8 (1962), 317, n. 1. For a valid criticism of the three-epistle hypothesis, see B. S. Mackay, "Further Thoughts on Philippians," *NTS*, 7 (1960–1961), 161-162, 165-167.

[70] Kirsopp Lake, "The Critical Problems of the Epistle to the Philippians," *The Expositor*, viii-7 (1914), 485.

[71] J. Hugh Michael, "The Philippian Interpolation—Where Does It End?", *The Expositor*, viii-19 (1920), 49-63.

[72] The term does not mean "definite, concrete, specific," because the oft-repeated warnings of Philippians 3:2a, 18-19 are obscure. Rather, the emphasis is on reliability and security for the welfare of the readers. The intensity and firmness with which Paul spoke underline his basic concern.

[73] Victor P. Furnish, "The Place and Purpose of Philippians III," *NTS*, 10 (1963), 86-88. See p. 87, n. 1 for his comment on Acts 15:27 *(dià lógou apaggéllontas tà autá)*.

[74] Moreover, whenever dealing with troublesome "false teachers," Paul wrote without such hesitation as leaving his warnings to a postscript as an afterthought. Because he already had often warned his readers in person (3:18), there is no basis for assuming that he expected to give them new oral warnings in person or through his assistants. In chapter 3 he gives no hint of planning a further visit. Finally, had he feared the end of contact with his readers, he would have given some clue in the postscript concerning the outcome of his life.

4. PAUL'S CAPTIVITY LETTERS

[1] For bibliographies see B. Brinkmann, "Num Sanctus Paulus Ephesi fuerit captivus," *Verbum Domini*, 19 (1939), 321, n. 5; Werner Schmauch, Beiheft

to Ernest Lohmeyer's *Die Briefe an die Philipper, an die Kolosser and an Philemon* (Meyers Kommentar) (Göttingen: Vandenhoeck & Ruprecht, 1964), pp. 12-13, 44.

[2] See C. H. Dodd, *New Testament Studies* (Manchester: Manchester University Press, 1953) , pp. 109-118.

[3] See pp. 78-79 of this book.

[4] The location or genuineness of this segment is questionable. It does not belong to the time of Nero's persecution; after the fire of July, 64, incarcerated Christians would hardly be permitted frequent refreshing visits, and the visitor himself would be seized if he were a believer. During Paul's two-year imprisonment after arrival in Rome (Acts 28:30-31) , contact with members of the local church was permitted; but 2 Tim. 1:17 relates that Onesiphorus had to search diligently in order to find Paul, as if the local church did not know or care where he was imprisoned. If the fragment be genuine, Onesiphorus, on his return to Ephesus, could have carried it to Timothy. According to the Acts of Paul (Hennecke-Schneemelcher, *New Testament Apocrypha* [Philadelphia: The Westminster Press, 1965], vol. 2, pp. 353, 364) , Onesiphorus and his family met Paul at Iconium. The reference to his *oikia* (1:17; 4:19) may or may not include him. Another consideration which detracts from the originality of 1:16-18 is the tension between 2 Tim. 4:6-7 ("I am already on the point of being sacrificed; the time of my departure has come. . . . I have finished the race *(drómon)"* and 4:17-18, 21 and 4:9 ("I was rescued from the lion's mouth. The Lord will rescue me from every evil. . . . Do your best to come to me [before winter]") . The verses in 4:6-7, like 1:16-18, presuppose Paul's being in Rome. If the former verse is anachronistic, the latter is also apt to be. We believe that other sections of the Pastoral Epistles include slightly edited fragments from Paul's pen (e.g., 1 Tim. 1:12-16; 2 Tim. 1:1-10,15; 2:1, 3, 8-10) and oral traditions of his words (e.g., Titus 3:4-7) as well as later non-Pauline directives.

[5] See chapter 6 of this book.

[6] F. J. A. Hort, *Prolegomena to St. Paul's Epistles to the Romans and Ephesians* (London: Macmillan & Co., Ltd., 1895) , p. 106; Josef Schmid, *Zeit und Ort der Paulinischen Gefangenschaftsbriefe* (Freiburg/Breisgau: Verlag Herder, 1931) , pp. 144-145.

[7] Brinkmann, "Epistolae captivitatis S. Pauli num Ephesi scriptae sunt," *Verbum Domini,* 21 (1941) , 17-21; R. M. Grant, "Caesar's Household," *IDB*, 1, 480-481; Baruch Lifschitz, "Inscriptions latinae de Césarée en Palestine," *Latomus,* 21 (1962) , 149-150; 22 (1963) , 783-784; Jack Finegan, *The Archaeology of the New Testament* (Princeton, N. J.: Princeton University Press, 1969) , p. 77. The newly found inscription mentioning Pilate is in Latin. E. Stauffer (*Die Pilatusinschrift von Caesarea* [Erlanger, 1966], pp. 10-13) studies the terms "praefectus" and "Tiberium."

[8] The unlikelihood of the praetorium's being a place in Rome was acknowledged by J. B. Lightfoot, *St. Paul's Epistle to the Philippians* (New York: The Macmillan Company, 1894) , pp. 99-101.

[9] Lohmeyer, *op. cit.,* 1930 ed., p. 41, n. 5.

[10] For bibliographies see Heinrich A. W. Meyer, *Critical and Exegetical Handbook to the Ephesians* (New York: Funk & Wagnalls, 1884) , pp. 299-300; *Critical and Exegetical Handbook to the Epistles to the Philippians and Colossians and to Philemon* (New York: 1889) , pp. 3, 198, n. 1; James Moffatt, *An Introduction to the Literature of the New Testament* (New York: Charles Scribner's Sons, 1918) , pp. 158-159.

[11] Lohmeyer, *op. cit.*, pp. 3-4, 14-15, 41. George Johnston (*Ephesians, Philippians, Colossians and Philemon* [Century Bible] [London: Thomas Nelson & Sons, Ltd., 1967], p. 1) writes: "Few modern scholars, except Lohmeyer, have acknowledged how strong are the claims of Caesarea."

[12] Concerning the relevant buildings here, see E. LeCamus, "Césarée du bord de la Mer," *Dictionnaire de la Bible* (Paris: Letouzy et Ané, 1899), vol. 2, pp. 460-461; Leo Haefeli, *Caesarea am Meer* (Münster im W., 1923), pp. 19-20. At Caesarea and Sebaste in A.D. 44 were stationed five cohorts and a wing of cavalry (Josephus, *Antiquities* xix, 9.2) : some 3000 men.

[13] Concerning his identity, J. N. Sanders ("Peter and Paul in the Acts," *NTS*, 2 [1955–1956], 141) wrote: "Among the party which came down from James to Antioch were Judas Barsabbas and Silas. (Judas Barsabbas was probably called 'Jesus' and is to be identified with the Jesus called Justus of them of the circumcision (Col. iv. 11). Acts i. 23 records that Barsabbas was called Justus, and the Philoxonian Syriac and Egyptian verses call him Joses, probably a corruption of 'Jesus,' itself corrupted further in the Western text to Joseph, which in turn led to the substitution of Barnabas for Barsabbas in D and a few old Latin and Vulgate MSS)." The case of the brother of the Lord named Joseph (Matt. 13:55) or Joses (Mark 6:3), or the son of Mary named Joses (Mark 15:40, 47) or Joseph (Matt. 27:56), illustrates the interchangeability of the names. Now, if this be a proper identification, what place would be better than Caesarea to look for a Hebrew Christian active in both Antioch and Jerusalem who brought to the former community the Apostolic decree of Acts 15? Agabus was also active at Jerusalem, Antioch, and Caesarea (Acts 11:27-28; 21:10).

[14] F. F. Bruce, "St. Paul in Rome. 3. The Epistle to the Colossians," *BJRL*, 48 (1966), 273, n. 2.

[15] Ernest F. Scott, "Introduction to Philippians," *IB*, 11, 5.

[16] F. F. Bruce, "St. Paul in Rome," *BJRL*, 46 (1964), 339.

[17] On the tradition of Barnabas's work in Rome, see Richard Adalbert Lipsius, *Die Apokryphen Apostelgeschichte und Apostellegenden* (Braunschweig, 1887), II-2, pp. 271-273.

[18] See N. P. Workman, "New Date-Indication in Acts," *Expository Times,* 11 (1899–1900), 316-319.

[19] See p. 114 of this book.

[20] J. M. Gilchrist, "On What Charges Was St. Paul Brought to Rome?", *Expository Times*, 78 (1967), 264-266.

[21] The only *hapax legomena* found in this fragment are *nomikos* and *leipo* (3:13) ; *kala erga* (3:14; cf. 1:16; 2:7, 14; 3:1, 8; 1 Tim. 2:10; 3:1; 5:10, 25; 6:18; 2 Tim. 2:21; 3:17) is also suspicious. The message is spontaneous enough and was not inspired by references in Acts or Pauline writings.

[22] Robert E. Osborne ("St. Paul's Silent Years," *JBL*, 84 [1965], 64) has suggested a different setting for Titus 1:5; 3:12. He rightly opposes John Knox's elimination of "the silent years" (*Chapters in the Life of Paul* [New York: Abingdon-Cokesbury, 1950], 85). Also Osborne commendably emphasizes the apostle's work in Syria and Cilicia (p. 60), seeks clues in 2 Cor. 11:23ff. (pp. 60-61, 65), repudiates suggestions that Paul's Roman imprisonment preceded the writing of genuine fragments of the Pastoral Epistles (p. 62) and his planning to visit Nicopolis (p. 64), and he recognizes the association of Titus 3:12 (Nicopolis) and Rom. 15:19 (Illyricum) (p. 64). He dates Titus's work in Crete after Paul's arrival in Ephesus (Acts 19:1) (p. 63) and notes that "it is implied in Titus 3:13 that Apollos was now an active Christian, which he did not become until . . . Acts 18:26" (p. 63).

However, did not Paul plan to visit Nicopolis at least one winter (Titus 3:12) *after* Apollos became an associate of Paul (1 Cor. 16:12)? This Nicopolis-Illyricum journey could not belong to the early "silent years" and may have nothing to do with the hypothetical shipwrecks on the coasts of Illyricum and Crete (pp. 61, 63-65). His three shipwrecks (2 Cor. 11:25) could have occurred anywhere in the eastern Mediterranean. If Titus 1:5 were genuine and implies Paul's early personal work in Crete, why did he wait more than ten years to confirm converts through Titus?

[23] For a bibliography on interpreting the reference to Illyricum, see Schumacher, *Die beiden letzen* . . . , *in Neutestamentliche Abhandlungen* (Münster/Westfalen: Verlag Aschendorff, 1929), p. 44.

[24] See Pauly-Wissowa, *Real-encyclopädie der classischen Altertumswissenschaft* (Stuttgart, 1937), vol. 17, pp. 51ff.

[25] William Ramsay, "Roads and Travel (in N.T.)," *A Dictionary of the Bible*, ed. James Hastings (New York & Edinburgh, 1906, 6th impr.), pp. 389a-b.

[26] The strongest cases have been set forth by C. Spicq (*L'Épître aux Hebreux* [Paris: J. Gabalda, 1952], vol. 1, pp. 209-219) and Hugh Montefiore (*A Commentary on the Epistle to the Hebrews* [Harper's N.T. Comm.] [New York: Harper & Row, Publishers, 1964], pp. 9-27).

[27] On problems in reasoning from theological development, see John H. Hurd, "The Sequence of Paul's Letters," *Canadian Journal of Theology*, 14 (1968), 190-191, 193-194.

[28] Upholders of such a theory include F. Hitzig, *Zur Kritik paulinischer Briefe* (Leipzig, 1870), pp. 22ff.; H. J. Holtzmann, *Kritik der Epheser- und Kolosserbriefe* (Leipzig, 1872); C. R. Bowen, "The Original Form of Paul's Letter to the Colossians," *JBL*, 43 (1924), 177-206; Charles Masson, *L'Épître de St. Paul aux Colossiens* (Commentaire du N.T.) (Neuchâtel & Paris, 1950), pp. 83ff.; P. N. Harrison, *Paulines and Pastorals* (London: Villiers, 1964), pp. 65ff.; Ed Parish Sanders, "Literary Dependence in Colossians," *JBL*, 85 (1966), 28-45. For bibliography and discussion of the question, see James Moffatt, *op. cit.*, pp. 155-158; Maurice Goguel, *Introduction au N.T.*, IV, 1 (1925), pp. 29-30; IV, 2 (1926), pp. 413-414; Ernst Percy, *Die Probleme der Kolosser- und Epheser-briefe* (Lund: CWK Gleerup Bokförlag, 1946), pp. 3-4, 18-35.

[29] On Philippians 3:1-19, see above, pp. 86-88.

5. EPHESIANS

[1] Henry J. Cadbury, "The Dilemma of Ephesians," *NTS*, 5 (1959), 94.

[2] F. W. Beare, "Introduction to the Epistle to the Ephesians," *IB*, 10, 601. We would suggest that titles were added to Ephesians and Hebrews when the Corinthian church expanded the earlier, small Ephesians corpus (see Appendix). That the latter lacked titles may be deduced from the fact that "to the Ephesians" is incorrect, whereas Romans 16 was not addressed to the Romans.

[3] "If 'in Ephesus' had already at that time stood in 1:1, Tertullian would certainly have discovered the contradiction in which Marcion was entangled [i.e., in calling it, *ad Laodicenos*]. Thus he supposes that Marcion's text did not have the two words, *en Epheso* in 1:1." Paul Feine, Johannes Behm, and Werner Kümmel, *Introduction to the New Testament*, trans. A. J. Mattill (Nashville: Abingdon Press, 1966), p. 254 (249 ET).

⁴ James Strachan, *The Captivity and the Pastoral Epistles* (Westminster N.T.) (New York and London: 1910), p. 14.

⁵ For a discussion of the problem, see Ernst Percy, *Die Probleme der Kolosser- und Epheserbriefe* (Lund: CWK Gleerup Bokförlag, 1946), pp. 450-451, 460-466.

⁶ See *ibid.*, p. 454, n. 25.

⁷ See C. R. Bowen, "The Place of Ephesians Among the Letters of Paul," *Anglican Theological Review*, 15 (1933), 283-286; N. A. Dahl, "Adresse und Pröomium des Epheserbriefes," *Theologische Zeitschrift*, 7 (1951), 244-245.

⁸ Shirley Jackson Case, "To Whom was 'Ephesians' Written?", *Biblical World*, 38 (1911), 318.

⁹ *Ibid.*, p. 318.

¹⁰ See John Rutherford, *St. Paul's Epistles to Colossae and Laodicea* (Edinburgh: T. & T. Clark, 1908), pp. 77-117; James Moffatt, *An Introduction to the Literature of the New Testament* (New York: Charles Scribner's Sons, 1918), pp. 375-381.

¹¹ M. Dibelius, *An die Kolosser, Epheser, An Philemon* (Handbuch zum N.T.) (Tübingen: J. C. B. Mohr [Paul Siebeck], 1927), pp. 63-65; answered by Percy, *op. cit.*, pp. 379ff.

¹² Charles P. Anderson, "Who Wrote the Epistle from Laodicea?", *JBL*, 85 (1966), 437-438.

¹³ On this hypothesis, see J. B. Lightfoot, *St. Paul's Epistles to the Colossians and Philemon* (London: Macmillan & Co., Ltd., 1892), pp. 278-279; Percy, *op. cit.*, p. 457, n. 31.

¹⁴ For bibliographies see Case, *art. cit.*, *Biblical World*, 38 (1911), 315; Percy, *op. cit.*, p. 453, n. 19; also, J. B. Lightfoot, *op. cit.*, pp. 37, 279; Rutherford, *op. cit.*, pp. 31-44; Otto Roller, *Das Formular der paulinischen Briefe* (Stuttgart: Kohlhammer, 1933), p. 524, n. 382; Harold K. Moulton, *Colossians, Philemon and Ephesians* (Preacher's Commentary) (London: Epworth Press, 1963), vol. 1, p. 67; Feine, Behm, Kümmel, *op. cit.*, p. 255 (249 ET).

¹⁵ Charles Anderson, *art. cit.*, *JBL*, 85 (1966), 438. He believes Epaphras to be the writer. But why is Ephesians so impersonal? Epaphras had evangelized the readers (Col. 1:7-8; 4:12).

¹⁶ Tertullian (*Adv. Marc.* v, 11 and 17): *ad Laodicenos;* Muratorian Canon (lines 63-65): *ad Laudicenses;* Epiphanius (*Haer.* 42, 9.4; 42, 12.3): *pròs Laodikeas;* Philaster (*Haer.* 89): *ad Laodicenses;* Latin Marcionite Prologues: *Laodicenses* (see J. Rendel Harris, "Marcion and the Canon," *Expository Times*, xviii-9 [1907], pp. 392-394).

¹⁷ B. W. Bacon reasoned: "It is unlikely that Marcion drew the inference from Col. 4:16, which does not speak of an epistle *to,* but an epistle *from,* Laodicea. Probably a variant tradition was current in his Phrygian home." (*Introduction to the New Testament* [New York: The Macmillan Company, 1900], p. 115); cf. "St. Paul to the Laodiceans," *The Expositor*, viii-17 (1919), 28: "In the regions of Pauline Christianity, whence Marcion came . . . there existed a tradition which named Laodicea as its destination." Bacon also observed that "Marcion had no theological motive for changing the title."

¹⁸ See M. S. Enslin, "Laodiceans, Epistle to," *IDB* 3, 71-72; W. Schneemelcher, "The Epistle to the Laodiceans," in Hennecke-Schneemelcher, *New Testament Apocrypha* (Philadelphia: The Westminster Press, 1965), vol. 2, pp. 128-129.

[19] Edgar J. Goodspeed, "The Place of Ephesians in the First Pauline Collection," *Anglican Theological Review*, 12 (1929–1930), 189, n. 1. For recent bibliographies see Cadbury, *art. cit.*, *NTS*, 5 (1959), 91, 93, n. 2; Raymond Bryan Brown, "Ephesians Among the Letters of Paul," *Review and Expositor*, 60 (1963), 376, n. 7; 377, nn. 9 & 10.

[20] A fair summary of the cases for and against Pauline authorship is given by C. L. Mitton, *The Epistle to the Ephesians: Its Authorship, Origin and Purpose* (Oxford: Clarendon Press, 1951), pp. 7-40. On p. 346 he writes: "It faithfully represents the Pauline message. . . . It has deservedly been called the quintessence of Paulinism." Support for this conclusion is given by Percy, *op. cit.*, pp. 372-419. He minimizes the differences between Ephesians and Colossians.

[21] See Edgar J. Goodspeed, *The Meaning of Ephesians* (Chicago: University of Chicago Press, 1933); *The Key to Ephesians* (Chicago: University of Chicago Press, 1956); C. L. Mitton, *op. cit.* Even Goodspeed felt the need to suggest a personal disciple of Paul to be the author. For a critique of Goodspeed's hypothesis, see Percy, *op. cit.*, pp. 445-446; Charles H. Buck, Jr., "The Early Order of the Pauline Corpus," *JBL*, 68 (1949), (answered by Goodspeed in "Ephesians and the First Edition of Paul," *JBL*, 70 [1951], 285-291).

[22] C. L. Mitton, "Goodspeed's Theory Regarding the Origin of Ephesians," *Expository Times*, 59 (1947–1948), 325.

[23] F. W. Beare, *art. cit.*, *IB*, 10, 603.

[24] J. Murphy-O'Connor, "Who Wrote Ephesians?", *Bible Today*, 18 (April, 1965), 1201-1209. He explains, "This epistle has numerous contacts with the Qumran literature which cannot be explained on the basis of common dependence on the Old Testament." See David Flusser, "The Dead Sea Sect and Pre-Pauline Christianity," in Chaim Rabin and Yigael Yadin, eds., *Scripta Hierosylmitana* (Jerusalem, 1958), vol. 4, p. 263n.; cf. pp. 250, 255, 262n.; Herbert Braun, "Qumrân und das Neue Testament; Ein Bericht über 10 Jahre Forshung (1950–1959)," *Theologische Rundschau*, 29 (1963), 235-245; Karl Georg Kuhn, "Der Epheserbrief im Lichte der Qumrantexte," *NTS*, 7 (1960–1961), 334-346; Franz Mussner, "Beiträge aus Qumrân zum Verständnis des Epheserbriefes," in *Neutestamentliche Aufsätze. Festschrift für Prof. Joseph Schmid*, ed. J. Blinzler, O. Kuss, and F. Mussner (Regensburg: Friedrich Postet, 1963), pp. 185-198. The latter two articles have been translated and appear in Murphy-O'Connor, ed., *Paul and Qumran: Studies in N.T. Exegesis* (Chicago: The Priory Press, 1968), pp. 115-131, 159-178.

[25] Beare, *art. cit.*, *IB*, 10, 601. Kuhn (*art. cit.*, *NTS*, 7 [1960-1961], 334-335; Murphy-O'Connor, *op. cit.*, pp. 116-117) calls attention to the 1960 Heidelberg Dissertation of Klaus Beyer, wherein evidence of Semitic syntax in Ephesians is presented.

[26] James H. Moulton, *From Egyptian Rubbish Heaps* (London: Charles H. Kelly, 1916), p. 59.

[27] G. H. P. Thompson (*The Letters of Paul to the Ephesians, to the Colossians and to Philemon* [Cambridge Bible Commentary] [New York: Cambridge University Press, 1967], pp. 18-19, 96, 161) considers Tychicus the author.

[28] Ralph P. Martin, "An Epistle in Search of a Life-Setting," *Expository Times*, 79-10 (1968), 300-301.

[29] Gordon J. Bahr, "Paul and Letter Writing in the First Century," *CBQ*, 28 (1966), 476-477.

[30] It is assumed that the Pastoral Epistles are a composite of genuine fragments and editorial teachings. Even in the latter case, the editor had traditions about Timothy. Concerning the prizing of recollections of apostolic figures, see Irenaeus's letter to Florinus (ap. Eusebius, H.E. v, 20.4-7).

[31] C. F. D. Moule, "E. J. Goodspeed's Theory Regarding the Origin of Ephesians," *Expository Times*, 60 (1948–1949) , 225.

[32] T. K. Abbott, *A Critical and Exegetical Commentary on the Epistles to the Ephesians and Colossians* (I.C.C.) (New York: Charles Scribner's Sons, 1897) , p. 61.

[33] See Theodor Zahn, *Introduction to the New Testament*, trans. M. W. Jacobus (New York: Charles Scribner's Sons, 1917, 2d ed.) , vol. 1, pp. 492-493, 500-514.

[34] Heinrich Schlier, *Der Brief an die Epheser; ein Kommentar* (Düsseldorf: Patmos-Verlag, 1957) , pp. 192-194; Hans Conzelmann, *Der Brief an die Epheser* in *Die Kleineren Briefe des Apostels Paulus* (Das Neue Testament Deutsch) (Göttingen: Vandenhoeck & Ruprecht, 1962) , pp. 76-77; J. M. Robinson, "Descent into Hades," *IDB* i, 827; J. Cambier, "La Signification Christologique d'Eph. iv. 7-10," *NTS*, 9 (1963) , 262-275.

[35] Percy (*op. cit.,* pp. 335-353) defends the thought in Ephesians as Paul's; Gottfried Schille ("Der Autor des Epheserbriefes," *Theologische Literaturzeitung*, 82 [1957], 327-329) argues that Paul could not have so portrayed himself.

[36] For some illuminating remarks on the use of secretaries in Paul's letters, see, in addition to Bahr (*art. cit., CBQ*, 28 [1966], 465-477) , Stanislaus Lyonnet, "De arte litteras exarandi apud antiquos," *Verbum Domini*, 34 (1956) , 3-11; J. N. D. Kelly, *A Commentary on the Pastoral Epistles, I Timothy, II Timothy, Titus* (Harper's N.T. Commentaries) (New York: Harper & Row, Publishers, 1963) , pp. 25-27. But they are more applicable to Ephesians than to the Pastorals.

[37] J. H. Moulton, *op. cit.,* pp. 59-62.

[38] See Gottfried Schille's 1953 Göttingen dissertation, *Liturgisches Gut in Epheserbrief* and his bibliography in *art. cit., Theologische Literaturzeitung*, 82 (1957) , 325, n. 3; also J. Coutts, "Ephesians 1:3-4 and 1 Peter 1:3-12," *NTS*, 3 (1957) , 115-127. Verse 5:14 seems not only to stem from a baptismal hymn but it also shows evidence of Semitic syntax. So do 4:28-29; 5:5; and 6:8 (Klaus Beyer, *Semitische Syntax im Neuen Testament* [Göttingen: Vandenhoeck & Ruprecht, 1962], p. 315) , which resemble local church sayings. Such would be expected in a letter written at bilingual Caesarea.

6. PAUL IN SPAIN

[1] For a bibliography, see Rudolph Schumacher, *Die beiden letzten Kapitel des Römerbriefes*, in *Neutestamentliche Abhandlungen*, ed. Max Meinertz, xix-4 (Münster/Westfalen: Verlag Aschendorff, 1929) , p. 40; Justo Fernandez Alonso, "Espagne," *Dictionnaire d'Histoire et de Géographie Ecclésiastiques* (Paris: Letouzey et Ané, xv, 1963) , pp. 898-899; C. Spicq, "San Pablo vino a España," *Cultura Biblica*, 23 (1966) , 143, n. 41.

[2] W. Ramsay, "A Second Fixed Point in Pauline Chronology," *Expositor*, vi-2 (August, 1900) , 88-105; *Pauline and Other Studies* (London: Hodder & Stoughton Ltd., 1906) , pp. 353-360.

[3] D. Plooij, *De Chronologie van het Leven van Paulus* (Leiden: E. J. Brill, 1918) , pp. 49-79.

[4] G. B. Caird, "Chronology of the N.T.," *IDB* 2, 604-605.

[5] W. M. Ramsay, "A Fixed Date in the Life of St. Paul," *Expositor*, v-3 (June, 1896), 336-345; Plooij (*op. cit.*, pp. 83-85) concurs.

[6] He arrived at Troas five days later (Tuesday, the 26th) and departed the following Monday (i.e., after "seven days"). On the preceding day, the Lord's Day, the disciples had assembled to break bread and Paul had spoken to them at length, until midnight (C. C. Richardson, "Lord's Day" *IDB* 3, 152-153).

[7] On pilgrim ships at Passover, see Ramsay, *St. Paul the Traveler and the Roman Citizen* (London: Hodder & Stoughton, Ltd., 1927), pp. 264, 287.

[8] A. R. S. Kennedy, "Palestinian Numismatics," *PEQ* (1914), 198, n. 1; Henry J. Cadbury, *The Book of Acts in History* (New York: Harper & Row, Publishers, 1955), pp. 9-10; A. Kindler, "More Dates on the Coins of the Procurators," *Israel Exploration Society*, 6 (1956), 56; Frederic W. Madden, prolog. by M. Avi-Yonah, *History of Jewish Coinage* (New York: Ktav, 1967, reprint), pp. xxxiv, 153.

[9] N. P. Workman, "A New Date-Indication in Acts," *Expository Times*, xi (1899–1900), 316-319; see also Plooij, *op. cit.*, pp. 86-88.

[10] W. Ramsay, *art. cit.*, *Expositor*, vi-2 (August, 1900), 93ff.; Ramsay, *Pauline and Other Studies*, pp. 355-360.

[11] W. Ramsay, *art. cit.*, *Expositor* vi-2 (August, 1900), 95ff.

[12] Walter Bauer, "The Picture of the Apostle in Early Christian Tradition. 1. Accounts," in Hennecke-Schneemelcher, *New Testament Apocrypha*, trans. and ed. by R. McL. Wilson (Philadelphia: The Westminster Press, 1965), vol. 2, p. 73; see also Theodor Zahn, *Introduction to the New Testament*, translation directed by M. W. Jacobus (New York: Charles Scribner's Sons, 1917, 2d ed.), pp. ii, 75, n. 8; Erich Dinkler, "Die Petrus-Rom-Frage," *Theologische Rundschau*, 25 (1959), 209-210; Jack Finegan, *Handbook of Biblical Chronology* (Princeton: Princeton University Press, 1964), pp. 304ff.

[13] Translation from Edgar J. Goodspeed, *The Apostolic Fathers* (New York: Harper & Row, Publishers, 1950), pp. 51-52.

[14] George Ogg, *The Chronology of the Life of Paul* (London: Epworth Press, 1968), pp. 195-196.

[15] See Robert M. Grant in R. M. Grant and Holt H. Graham, *The Apostolic Fathers: A New Translation and Commentary* (New York: Thomas Nelson & Sons Ltd., 1965), p. 27.

[16] Lindsey P. Pherigo, "Paul's Life after the Close of Acts," *JBL*, 70 (1951), 227.

[17] Ramsay, "The Imprisonment and Supposed Trial of St. Paul in Rome: Acts XXVIII," *Expositor*, viii-5 (1913), 264-284.

[18] K. Lake, "What was the End of St. Paul's Trial?", *The Interpreter*, 5 (1908–1909), 147-156.

[19] Henry Cadbury, "Roman Law and the Trial of Paul," in F. J. Foakes-Jackson and K. Lake, eds., *The Beginnings of Christianity* (London: Macmillan & Co., Ltd., 1933), vol. 5, pp. 325-337.

[20] F. F. Bruce, "St. Paul in Rome," *BJRL*, 46 (1963–1964), 343-345. For various objections to the hypothesis, see Ernst Haenchen, *Die Apostelgeschichte* (Göttingen: Vandenhoeck & Ruprecht, 1961), pp. 648-649; Ogg, *The Chronology of the Life of Paul*, pp. 180-181.

[21] Pherigo, *art. cit.*, *JBL*, 70 (1951), 278 is an exception.

[22] The universal spread of the Jews is witnessed to by the second century B.C. Sibylline Oracle 3 (line 271) and Strabo (63 B.C.–A.D. 21+), who was quoted by Josephus (*Antiquities* xiv, 72; cf. *War* ii, 16.4). But archaeological evidence of their presence in Spain by Paul's day has not yet been uncovered.

[23] Pherigo, *art. cit., JBL,* 70 (1951), 278.

[24] See James Leigh Strachan-Davidson, *Problems of Roman Criminal Law* (Oxford: Clarendon Press, 1912), pp. ii, 61-69; Ugo Brasiello, *La repressione penale in diritto Romano* (Napoli, 1937), pp. 277-285, 292-300, 462-463.

[25] "*Iudaeos, qui Sabazi Iovis cultu Romanos inficere mores connati erant, repetere domos suas coegit.*" See Emil Schürer, *A History of the Jewish People in the Time of Jesus Christ,* trans. Sophia Taylor and Peter Christie (New York: Charles Scribner's Sons, 1891), II-II, pp. 233-234.

[26] Zdzislaw Zmigryder-Konopka, "La nature juridique de la relégation du citoyen romain," *Revue Historique de droit français et etranger,* 18 (1939), 327-334.

[27] A. H. McNeile, *St. Paul: His Life, Letters and Christian Doctrine* (New York: Cambridge University Press, 1920), p. 258.

[28] M. R. James (*Apocrypha Anecdota* [Texts and Studies II, iii] [New York: Cambridge University Press, 1893], pp. 49-50) held that Muratorianum depends on the Acts of Peter.

[29] *The Apostolic Fathers, Part I: S. Clement of Rome* (London: Macmillan & Co., Ltd., II-I, 1890), p. 30.

[30] Ernst Dubowy, *Klemens von Rom über die Riese Pauli nach Spanien* (Biblische Studien xix,3), Freiburg im Breisgau (Herder, 1914), pp. 80-90.

[31] Juan Serra Vilaró, "San Pablo en Tarragona," *Cultura Biblica,* 19 (1962), 179-183. He calls attention to the four mentions of Paul in the Visigothic liturgy in the Codex of Verona, which originated at Tarragona, and to the reference to Prospero, bishop of Tarragona, as "successor of St. Paul" in the *Vita Sancti Prosperi.*

[32] See Spicq, *art. cit., Cultura Biblica,* 23 (1966), 139-140.

[33] See Pius B. Gams, *Die Kirchengeschichte von Spanien* (Regensburg: G. J. Manz, 1862), vol. 1, pp. 69-75.

[34] "Cadiz," *Encyclopaedia Britannica,* 1955 ed., vol. 4, p. 513.

7. THE EPISTLE TO THE HEBREWS

[1] F. F. Bruce, *The Epistle to the Hebrews* (Grand Rapids, Mich.: Wm. B. Eerdmans Publishing Co., 1964), pp. xxv-xxxv.

[2] For the numerous cogent arguments against such a hypothesis, see James Moffatt, *An Introduction to the Literature of the New Testament* (New York: Charles Scribner's Sons, 1918), p. 446; C. Spicq, *L' Épître aux Hebreux* (Paris: J. Gabalda, 1952), pp. i, 241-242; Donald Guthrie, *New Testament Introduction: Hebrews to Revelation* (Chicago: Inter-Varsity Press, 1962), p. 38.

[3] T. W. Manson, "The Problem of the Epistle to the Hebrews," *BJRL,* 32 (1949), 2-4 (reprinted in *Studies . . . ,* pp. 243-245); Spicq, *op. cit.,* pp. 170-174.

[4] Spicq, *op. cit.,* pp. i, 17; G. Zuntz, *The Text of the Epistles* (London: Oxford University Press, 1953), pp. 15, 277; Charles P. Anderson, "The Epistle to the Hebrews and the Pauline Corpus," *HTR,* 59 (1966), 429-433.

[5] Spicq, *op. cit.,* pp. i, 232-233; Guthrie, op. cit., pp. 39-40.

[6] References in Spicq, *op. cit.*, pp. i, 235, n. 4. He comments (i, 236): "La plupart de ces arguments sont excellents et constituent une réelle probabilité pour la these éphesienne." Also, W. F. Howard, "The Epistle to the Hebrews," *Interpretation*, 5 (1951), 82; John D. Legg, "Our Brother Timothy: A Suggested Solution to the Problem of the Authorship of the Epistle to the Hebrews," *Evangelical Quarterly*, 40 (1968), 223.

[7] See p. 179, n. 26.

[8] See Appendix.

[9] W. H. P. Hatch, "The Position of Hebrews in the Canon of the New Testament," *HTR*, 29 (1936), 133-136.

[10] Anderson, *art. cit.*, *HTR*, 59 (1966), 438.

[11] *Ibid.*, 434-435; see notes 22 and 24 below.

[12] Francesco Lo Bue, "The Historical Background of the Epistle to the Hebrews," *JBL*, 75 (1956), 57.

[13] Unfavorable references to Paul's overwhelming troubles at Ephesus are omitted except for the plots of the Jews (which are mentioned for most other cities also) and the story of the self-interested craftsmen who made silver shrines of Artemis (Acts 19:24ff.). But here the author opposes idolatry and implies that nothing happened to Paul himself (cf. 2 Tim. 4:14) and that the town clerk handled the rioters so well that they forgot about their troubles with the Christians. There is no hint that all the Asians turned away from Paul (2 Tim. 1:15); rather, it is implied that Paul's work at Ephesus was an outstanding triumph (Acts 19:1-20). Justification for his original bypassing of Asia is given (16:6). Twice Luke explains why the apostle had to leave Ephesus (18:21; 19:21). When he later sails past Ephesus (20:16), it is explained why he did not stop. But his address to the elders is given considerable space (20:18-35), and his loyalty to them is indicated by the farewell (20:36-38). The "upper country" (19:1) is a reference best understood by readers of Asia. The hall of Tyrannus (19:9), the theater (19:29, 31), and the sacred stone that fell from the sky (19:35) are local allusions familiar to the author and readers. There is local pride in the Ephesian judicial system (19:38-40). Interest is shown in local geography (20:13-15).

[14] For other reminiscences, see Spicq, *op. cit.*, pp. i, 170; Committee of Oxford Society of Historical Theology, *The N.T. in the Apostolic Fathers* (Oxford: Clarendon Press, 1905), 99; cf. Ignatius, *ad Philad.* 9.

[15] Moffatt, *op. cit.*, p. 440; F. J. Badcock, *The Pauline Epistles and the Epistle to the Hebrews in Their Historical Setting* (London and New York, 1937), pp. 191-192; Spicq, *op. cit.*, pp. i, 139-143. If the author of First Peter did not know Hebrews as an epistle written to a local church, he knew it as a part of the first Pauline corpus.

[16] *Conv. dec. Virg.* iv, 1; v, 7 (Migne, *P.G.* xviii, 88, 109).

[17] Spicq, *op. cit.*, pp. i, 234, n. 8. Also F. Lo Bue, *art. cit.*, *JBL*, 75 (1956), 54-57.

[18] As F. D. V. Narborough (*The Epistle to the Hebrews* [Clarendon Bible] [Oxford: Clarendon Press, 1930], p. 27) remarked.

[19] Hugh Montefiore, *A Commentary on the Epistle to the Hebrews* (Harper's N.T. Commentary) (New York: Harper & Row, Publishers, 1964), p. 254. He thinks the Epistle to have been written from Ephesus to Corinth (pp. 28, 254).

[20] R. van Cauwelaert, "L 'Intervention de l'Église de Rome a Corinthe vers l'an 96," *Revue de Histoire Ecclésiastique*, 31 (1935), 284-304; the quotation is from p. 302.

[21] Heinrich Appel, *Der Hebräerbrief: Ein Schreiben des Apollos an Juden-christen der korinthischen Gemeinde* (Leipzig, 1918), p. 32. Seven of the eight passages in Hebrews, which he notes, resemble passages in First Corinthians, which was written when Apollos was with him (16:12). Such affinities tend to confirm Apollos's authorship of Hebrews rather than literary dependence. His memory of Paul's Corinthian epistles would be refreshed by a stay at Corinth. Montefiore (*op. cit.,* pp. 22-30) follows the same line of reasoning as did Appel, but argues for the priority of Hebrews.

[22] Montefiore, *op. cit.,* pp. 27-28, 47. He points out that Holtzman discovered 47 such passages in 1 Clement, "over three times as often as all other N.T. letters." Christ is High Priest according 36:1; 61:3; 64.

[23] Moffatt, *op. cit.,* p. 453; Spicq, *op. cit.,* pp. i, 159-161. Resemblances to Paul's letters in general may be found in Hans Windisch, *Der Hebräerbrief* (Handbuch zum N.T.) (Tübingen, 1931), pp. 128-129.

[24] Spicq, *op. cit.,* pp. i, 177-180; Oxford Society of Historical Theology, *op. cit.,* pp. 46-47. However, see Gerd Theissen, *Untersuchungen zum Hebräerbrief,* (Gütersloh: Gerd Mohn, 1969), pp. 34-37.

[25] George A. Barton, "The Date of the Epistle to the Hebrews," *JBL,* 57 (1938), 198-200.

[26] B. F. Westcott, *The Epistle to the Hebrews* (London: Macmillan & Co., Ltd., 1889), p. xliii.

[27] See pp. 107-110 of this book.

[28] A fragment not belonging to the same letter as 2 Tim. 1:15-17 (see p. 177, n. 4).

[29] See pp. 139ff. of this book.

Index

187

INDEX OF AUTHORS

Calder, William, 173
Campbell, Thomas H., 168, 170
Case, Shirley Jackson, 125, 180
Cerfaux, Lucien, 171
Chase, F. H., 176
Clarkson, M. E., 152
Conzelmann, Hans, 167, 182
Corssen, P., 80, 175
Couchod, Paul Louis, 174
Coutts, J., 182

Dahl, N. A., 180
Deissmann, Adolf, 171
Dewailly, L.-M., 176
Dibelius, M., 180
Dodd, C. H., 177
Dubowy, Ernst, 184
Duncan, George S., 31, 170
Dupont, Jacques, 81, 175

Eisler, Robert, 171
Enslin, M. S., 180

Farrar, F. W., 152
Faw, Chalmer E., 173
Feine, Paul; Behm, Johannes; Kummel, Werner, 179, 180
Fernandez Alonso, Justo, 182
Finegan, Jack, 167, 168, 171, 177, 183
Fitzmyer, Joseph A., 76, 167, 174, 175
Flusser, David, 181
Frotheringham, J. D., 168
Furnish, Victor P., 87, 176

Gams, Pius B., 184
Gapp, Kenneth S., 39, 170
Gartner, Bertil, 174
Gilchrist, J. M., 178
Gilmour, S. M., 75, 174
Gnilka, Joachim, 76, 174
Gogler, Rolf, 175
Goguel, Maurice, 168, 174, 176, 179
Goodspeed, Edgar J., 79, 175, 181, 183
Grant, Robert M., 177, 183
Grossouw, W., 174
Guthrie, Donald, 172, 184

Haefeli, Leo, 178
Haenchen, Ernst, 170, 172, 183
Hanslick, Rudolph, 170
Harnack, A., 128, 166, 168
Harris, J. Rendel, 165, 180
Harrison, P. N., 179
Hatch, W. H. P., 185
Helm, R., 170
Hering, Jean, 174

Hitchcock, Montgomery, 163
Hitzig, F., 179
Hoerber, Robert, 169, 172
Holtzmann, H. J., 179, 186
Hort, F. J. A., 83, 176, 177
Howard, W. F., 152, 185
Huby, Joseph, 175
Hughes, P. E., 169
Huppenbauer, Hans W., 174
Hurd, John H., 168, 179

Jackson, H. Latimer, 170
James, M. R., 184
Johnston, George, 178
Jones, Maurice, 173

Kelly, J. N. D., 182
Kennedy, A. R. S., 171, 183
Kennedy, James H., 73, 174
Kerschensteiner, Josef, 165
Kindler, A., 183
Klausner, Joseph, 171
Klijn, A. F. J., 171
Knox, John, 173, 178
Koester, Helmut, 176
Kuhn, Karl G., 76, 174, 181

Lagrange, M. J., 176
Lake, Kirsopp, 33, 73, 83, 86, 143, 170, 173, 174, 175, 176, 183
LeCamus, E., 178
Legg, J., 152, 185
Lifschitz, Baruch, 177
Lightfoot, J. B., 147, 173, 177, 180
Lipsius, Richard Adalbert, 178
Lo Bue, Francesco, 155, 185
Lohmeyer, Ernst, 98, 177, 178
Loisy, Alfred, 174
Lyonnet, Stanislaus, 182

Madden, Frederic W., 183
Magie, David, 172
Manson, T. W., 83, 152, 171, 175, 176, 184
Marsh, J., 167
Martin, Ralph P., 132, 181
Marxsen, W., 175
Masson, Charles, 179
McDowell, Robert H., 170
McNeile, A. H., 146, 184
Meyer, Heinrich A. W., 169, 177
Meyshan, J., 170
Michael, J. Hugh, 86, 176
Mitton, C. L., 130-131, 181
Moffatt, James, 175, 176, 177, 179, 180, 184, 185, 186